SADLIER
VOCA
WOR SHO
COMMON CORE ENRICHED EDITION
MW01622961
NEW!
FOR
LEVELS D–H
2005
90's
80's
70's
60's
Common Core Enriched Edition
Level E
SADLIER
VOCABULARY
WORKSHOP
JEROME SHOSTAK
2012
SADLIER-OXFORD
Vocabulary
Workshop
New Edition
With Online
Audio Program
poignant
ruminate
muse
alacrity
recalcitrant
solace
Jerome Shostak
SADLIER-OXFORD
Vocabulary
Workshop
Level F
vocabulary
Powerful NEW features
enhance a 50-year tradition
of success.
vocabularyworkshop.com

WHAT'S STILL TRUE?

The new *Vocabulary Workshop, Common Core Enriched Edition* for Grades 9–12+ maintains a high level of academic rigor, focusing on vocabulary development for high-achieving, college-bound students.

vocabularyworkshop.com: iWords audio program interactive word games

Definitions

Note the spelling, pronunciation, part(s) of speech, and definition(s) of each of the following words. Then write the word in the blank spaces in the illustrative sentence(s) following. Finally, study the lists of synonyms and antonyms.

1. abridge (ə brij′)
(*v.*) to make shorter
Travel by air ________________ the time needed to reach far-distant places.
SYNONYMS: shorten, condense, abbreviate
ANTONYMS: expand, enlarge, augment

2. adherent (ad hēr′ ənt)
(*n.*) a follower, supporter; (*adj.*) attached, sticking to
The senator's loyal ________________ campaigned long and hard for her reelection.
Before we co
to remove ar
SYNONYM: (*n.*) dis
ANTONYMS: (*n.*) o

Time-proven list of 300 words found on standardized tests—organized in 15 units with 20 words each.

3

Antonyms

Choose the word from this unit that is most nearly opposite in meaning to the ***boldface*** *word or expression in the phrase. Write that word on the line. Use a dictionary if necessary.*

1. a **demonic** expression on the gargoyle's face ________________
2. the social position of a **wealthy person** ________________
3. showed laudable **temperance** at the buffet table ________________
4. **initiated** talks between the warring parties ________________
5. a **novel** approach to a familiar subject ________________

Completing the Sentence

From the words in this unit, choose the one that best completes each of the following sentences. Write the word in the space provided.

1. Bands of ________________ broke through the frontier defenses of the province and began to plunder the rich farmlands of the interior.

Words reviewed in several contexts and exercises lead to mastery.

I've used *Vocabulary Workshop* for years. My college-bound students have great scores on the SAT*!

*SAT is a registered trademark of the College Entrance Examination Board. SAT is not affiliated with the production of, nor endorses, this product.

WHAT'S NEW?

At Sadlier, we're listening to you and your students. We've studied the latest research and the Common Core State Standards. We've considered the latest technology. This valuable information culminated in this enriched edition of the leading vocabulary development program.

Built for Common Core State Standards for Vocabulary

Expands Vocabulary in Context

Deepens Vocabulary Understanding

Blends Print with Powerful Online Components

I can check out vocabulary words on my smartphone—anytime!

NEW!

1 Built for Common Core State Standards for Vocabulary

Word Study, a new five-page section, aligns to Common Core State Standards for Vocabulary Acquisition and Use and expands students' knowledge of vocabulary words with instruction and practice.

Learn and write with Idioms/Proverbs/Adages.

WORD STUDY

Writing with Idioms

Find the meaning of each idiom. (Use an online or print dictionary if necessary.) Then write a sentence for each idiom.

1. get the ball rolling
2. get up on the wrong side of the bed

WORD STUDY

Expressing the Connotation

Read each sentence. Select the word in parentheses that expresses the connotation (positive, negative, or neutral) given at the beginning of the sentence.

negative	1. The secret agent's (**dilemma, situation**) was that his disguise was weak.
positive	2. The woman's (**comely**, **gorgeous**) appearance made for a good stage presence.
positive	3. The winning debater's closing argument was an example of (**eminent, satisfactory**) speech making
neutral	4. The police showed res unreliable suspect.
negative	5. The heavy bag felt (**ful**

Explore Denotations and Connotations.

WORD STUDY

Classical Roots

pos, pon—to put, place

The root *pos* appears in **predispose** (page 16). The literal meaning is "to put away before," but the word has come to mean "to incline" or "to make susceptible." Some other words based on the same root are listed below.

component	**impose**	**composite**	**juxtapose**
depose	**repository**	**disposition**	**transpose**

From the list of words above, choose the one that corresponds to each of the brief definitions below. Write the word in the blank space in the illustrative sentence below the definition. Use an online or print dictionary if necessary.

1. to put or place upon or over something else

Use Classical Roots to build vocabulary.

2 Expands Vocabulary in Context

NEW!

Reading Passages and **Vocabulary in Context** support Common Core State Standards for Reading Literature and Informational Texts.

Common Core Connection

UNIT 1

*Read the following selection, taking note of the **boldface** words and their contexts. These words are among those you will be studying in Unit 1. As you complete the exercises in this unit, it may help to refer to the way the words are used below.*

I'll Wait for the Movie

<Compare-and-Contrast Essay>

Cue scene: Middle-Earth characters Aragorn, Legolas, and Gimli leap off a ship, swords in hand, to **breach** archenemy Sauron's lines in the epic Battle of Pelennor Fields. This is a crucial moment in the movie version of *The Lord of the Rings: Return of the King*. Alas, the haunting showdown with the ghostly **brigands** does not actually occur in author J.R.R. Tolkien's books.

Film fans do not have to speak Elvish to enjoy director Peter Jackson's blockbuster *Lord of the Rings* (LOTR) trilogy. But do the movies do justice to Tolkien's enduring and popular novels? And is it possible for the LOTR purist to watch the films without cringing at every discrepancy? Readers are often disappointed with movie adaptations of their favorite novels. In fact, they might be **predisposed** to dislike any movie version. This is a perennial problem for film directors, scriptwriters, readers, and moviegoers alike.

Filmmakers often **commandeer** the story and make it their own. Their motivation might be this cliché: "a picture paints a thousand words." They eliminate characters or events, or they add new ones. And authors can't complain: When they sell the rights to their work, they usually **relinquish** control. Filmmakers understand that their audience is **opinionated**, as evinced by LOTR fans posting online comments about Jackson's adaptation. Some claim that Jackson made a **muddle** of the books, that his tinkering is **spurious**, or that the films show only **spasmodic** flashes of greatness. Other fans show **unbridled** enthusiasm, saying that Tolkien's **perennial** classics are too long and **diffuse** and that the director's snipping was essential. And some fans are more **circumspect** in their criticism, realizing it is impossible to please everyone.

The **dilemma** facing filmmakers is that reading a book is a more interactive experience than watching a movie. A reader visualizes every scene in the book and decides what the characters look and sound like, what they wear, how their environs appear. For those who read the LOTR books first, the movie's Frodo may not resemble the Frodo they imagined. How can Peter Jackson's vision of Middle-Earth reflect the ones created in the mind's eye of millions of readers?

It is easy to imagine that moviegoers and readers are always **deadlocked** over which medium is better. Those who have read the book may come away from the multiplex disappointed: *The movie left out so much! Why was that memorable scene transposed to the beginning?* On the other hand, those who see the movie first may be awed by the director's imaginative retelling or by the stirring music and special effects. Most movies based on books retain key characters, scenes, and themes. Directors and scriptwriters strive to tell the same story and evoke the same emotions as the author of the original book. Both share an audience yet address one that is exclusively their own.

In the end, directors must rely on fans to accept the limitations of the movie. How is it possible for a two-hour movie (or even a sprawling movie trilogy) to include all of the details woven throughout a long novel? A movie that attempted to do this would end up unwieldy and **cumbersome**—a surefire way to disappoint moviegoers and book lovers alike.

iWords

Snap the code, or go to vocabularyworkshop.com

A poster for the first movie in director Peter Jackson's *Lord of the Rings* trilogy.

J.R.R. Tolkien's epic fantasy is one of the most popular novels of all time.

12 ■ Unit 1

Unit 1 ■ 13

Introduce vocabulary in context of informational text to activate students' prior knowledge.

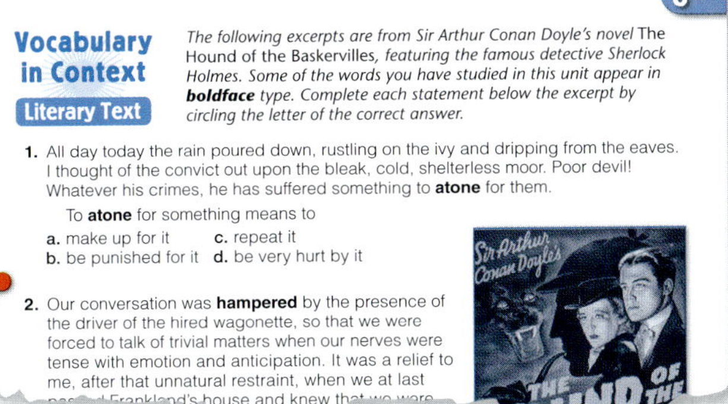

6

Vocabulary in Context
Literary Text

The following excerpts are from Sir Arthur Conan Doyle's novel The Hound of the Baskervilles, *featuring the famous detective Sherlock Holmes. Some of the words you have studied in this unit appear in **boldface** type. Complete each statement below the excerpt by circling the letter of the correct answer.*

1. All day today the rain poured down, rustling on the ivy and dripping from the eaves. I thought of the convict out upon the bleak, cold, shelterless moor. Poor devil! Whatever his crimes, he has suffered something to **atone** for them.

   To **atone** for something means to

   a. make up for it c. repeat it
   b. be punished for it d. be very hurt by it

2. Our conversation was **hampered** by the presence of the driver of the hired wagonette, so that we were forced to talk of trivial matters when our nerves were tense with emotion and anticipation. It was a relief to me, after that unnatural restraint, when we at last

Promote understanding of words with excerpts from canonical literature.

NEW!

3 Deepens Vocabulary Understanding

Writing: Words in Action has students use the vocabulary words in an extended context. Two writing prompts allow students to demonstrate their understanding of new vocabulary.

The first prompt asks students to use the Unit words to respond to a question about the Reading Passage.

Writing: Words in Action

1. Look back at "I'll Wait for the Movie" (pages 12–13). How do the challenges of a filmmaker differ from those of an author? Write a short expository essay in which you explore how some of the major artistic decisions a filmmaker has to make differ from those a novelist has to make. Use at least two details from the passage and three unit words to support your understanding.
2. Do you prefer reading a book to seeing a movie, or do you think that movies tell a story in a more interesting way? In a brief essay, support your opinion with specific examples from your observations, studies, reading (refer to pages 12–13), or personal experience. Write at least three paragraphs, and use three or more words from this unit.

The second prompt is modeled after writing tasks found on standardized tests.

Students continue to deepen their understanding of vocabulary through **Vocabulary in Context** and **Word Study** sections.

With *Words in Action*, my students are writing and using new vocabulary in context just like they do on standardized tests.

NEW!

4 Blends Print with Powerful Online Components

Online Components reinforce print content and make the program more accessible for students. Extend learning beyond the classroom at vocabularyworkshop.com with:

- iWords™ Audio Program
- Audio of Unit Passages
- Interactive quizzes
- Interactive flashcards
- Interactive word games
- Additional practice

QR Codes (or Quick Response) are bar codes at point-of-use on student pages that link to selected online components when snapped with a smartphone.

UNIT 1

Read the following selection, taking note of the ***boldface*** *words and their contexts. These words are among those you will be studying in Unit 1. As you complete the exercises in this unit, it may help to refer to the way the words are used below.*

I'll Wait for the Movie

<Compare-and-Contrast Essay>

Cue scene: Middle-Earth characters Aragorn, Legolas, and Gimli leap off a ship, swords in hand, to **breach** archenemy Sauron's lines in the epic Battle of Pelennor Fields. This is a crucial moment in the movie version of *The Lord of the Rings: Return of the King*. Alas, the haunting showdown with the ghostly **brigands** does not actually occur in author J.R.R. Tolkien's books.

Film fans do not have to speak Elvish to enjoy director Peter Jackson's blockbuster *Lord of the Rings* (LOTR) trilogy. But do the movies do justice to Tolkien's enduring and popular novels? And is it possible for the LOTR purist to watch the films without cringing at every discrepancy? Readers are often disappointed with movie adaptations of their favorite novels. In fact, they might be **predisposed** to dislike any movie version. This is a perennial problem for film directors, scriptwriters, readers, and moviegoers alike.

Filmmakers often **commandeer** the story and make it their own. Their motivation might be this cliché: "a picture paints a thousand words." They eliminate characters or events, or they add new ones. And authors can't complain: When they sell the rights to their work, they usually **relinquish** control. Filmmakers understand that their audience is **opinionated**, as evinced by LOTR fans posting online comments about Jackson's adaptation. Some claim that Jackson made a **muddle** of the books, that his tinkering is **spurious**, or that the films show only **spasmodic** flashes of greatness. Other fans show **unbridled** enthusiasm, saying that Tolkien's **perennial** classics are too long and **diffuse** and that the director's snipping was essential. And some fans are more **circumspect** in their criticism, realizing it is impossible to please everyone.

The **dilemma** facing filmmakers is that reading a book is a more interactive experience than watching a movie. A reader visualizes every scene in the book and decides what the characters look and sound like, what they wear, how their environs appear. For those who read the LOTR books first, the movie's Frodo may not resemble the Frodo they imagined. How can Peter Jackson's vision of Middle-Earth reflect the ones created in the mind's eye of millions of readers?

It is easy to imagine that moviegoers and readers are always **deadlocked** over which medium is better. Those who have read the book may come away from the multiplex disappointed: *The movie left out so much! Why was that memorable scene transposed to the beginning?* On the other hand, those who see the movie first may be awed by the director's imaginative retelling or by the stirring music and special effects. Most movies based on books retain key characters, scenes, and themes. Directors and scriptwriters strive to tell the same story and evoke the same emotions as the author of the original book. Both share an audience yet address one that is exclusively their own.

In the end, directors must rely on fans to accept the limitations of the movie. How is it possible for a two-hour movie (or even a sprawling movie trilogy) to include all of the details woven throughout a long novel? A movie that attempted to do this would end up unwieldy and **cumbersome**—a surefire way to disappoint moviegoers and book lovers alike.

Snap the code, or go to vocabularyworkshop.com

A poster for the first movie in director Peter Jackson's *Lord of the Rings* trilogy.

J.R.R. Tolkien's epic fantasy is one of the most popular novels of all time.

12 • Unit 1

Unit 1 • 13

I can snap QR codes to listen to the *iWords*® and take my quizzes.

iWords™ Audio Program

- Word pronunciations
- Definitions
- Examples

Interactive Quizzes

- Unit Reviews
- Immediate feedback

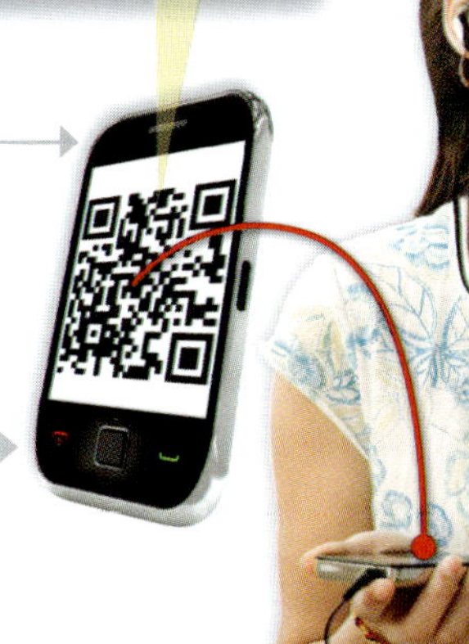

CREATING THE RIGHT BLEND FOR YOU

Vocabulary Workshop, Common Core Enriched Edtion, seamlessly combines print and online resources, personalizing a blended approach for students and teachers.

Student Editon

Online Interactive Student Editon

Online Student Assessment System

Annotated Teacher's Editon

Test Booklet

Test Prep Blackline Masters

Online resources available for students and teachers

Preview now or request a sample at Sadlier.com/previewVWEE

ANNOTATED TEACHER'S EDITION

SADLIER

VOCABULARY WORKSHOP

Common Core Enriched Edition

Level G

Jerome Shostak

Senior Series Consultant

Vicki A. Jacobs, Ed.D.
Associate Director, Teacher Education Program
Lecturer on Education
Harvard Graduate School of Education
Cambridge, Massachusetts

Series Consultants

Louis P. De Angelo, Ed.D.
Associate Superintendent
Diocese of Wilmington
Wilmington, Delaware

John Heath, Ph.D.
Professor of Classics
Santa Clara University
Santa Clara, California

Sarah Ressler Wright, NBCT
English Department Chair
Rutherford B. Hayes High School
Delaware City Schools, Ohio

Carolyn E. Waters, JD, Ed.S.
ELA/Literacy 6–12 Supervisor
Cobb County School District
Marietta, Georgia

Sadlier

Reviewers

The publisher wishes to thank for their comments and suggestions the following teachers and administrators, who read portions of the series prior to publication.

Rivkie Eisen
English Teacher
Ateret Torah High School
Brooklyn, New York

Jennifer Etter
English Dept. Chair
Shorecrest High School
Shoreline, Washington

Eileen Ghastin
English Teacher
John F. Kennedy High School
Bronx, New York

Sheri Goldstein
English Dept. Chair
Ida Crown Jewish Academy
Chicago, Illinois

Claudia Lefkowitz
English Teacher
Central Florida Preparatory
Gotha, Florida

Scott Leventhal
English Teacher, Dept. Chair
Council Rock H. S. South
Holland, Pennsylvania

Jeanne Pellegrino
English Teacher, Dept. Chair
Plantation High School
Plantation, Florida

Jennifer Portilla
English Teacher
Pace Brantley School
Longwood, Florida

Kausam R. Salam, Ph.D.
English Teacher–Dual Credit
Cypress Falls High School
Houston, Texas

Linda Schwartz
English Dept. Chair
Seaford School District
Seaford, New York

Patricia Stack
English Teacher
South Park High School
South Park, Pennsylvania

Barbara Swander Miller
Language Arts Dept. Chair
Cowan Jr/Sr High School
Muncie, Indiana

Stephanie K. Turner
English and French Teacher
St. Ursula Academy
Cincinnati, Ohio

Robert Viarengo
English Dept. Chair
Palma School
Salinas, California

Cover: Concept/Art and Design: MK Advertising and William H. Sadlier, Inc.; Cover pencil: Shutterstock/VikaSuh. **Photo Credits:** Blend/Jose Luis Pelaez Inc: T7 *right*. Corbis/Ian Lishman/Juice Images: T30. iStockphoto/alexsl: T7 *left*; Neustockimages: T1, T8 *center*; shapecharge: T3; sjlocke: T4. Ken Karp: T2, T6. Shutterstock/RTimages: T8 *right background*; vgstudio: T8 *right front*.

Printed in the United States of America.
ISBN: 978-0-8215-8032-5/ 3456789 RRDH 15 14 13

For additional online resources, go to vocabularyworkshop.com and enter the Teacher Access Code: VW12TGPQ52F3

CONTENTS

ENRICHED EDITION: NEW FEATURES

VOCABULARY WORKSHOP has for more than five decades been the leading program for systematic vocabulary development for grades 6–12. It has been proven a highly successful tool in helping students expand their vocabularies, improve their vocabulary skills, and prepare for the vocabulary strands of standardized tests.

This Common Core Enriched Edition of VOCABULARY WORKSHOP preserves and improves key elements of the program that have made it so effective, *and* it introduces important new features that make the series more comprehensive in scope and more current in its approach to vocabulary instruction, especially with respect to standardized testing and the **Common Core State Standards** for English Language Arts.

QR Codes

New QR (Quick Response) codes appear on the **Reading Passage** and **Vocabulary in Context** pages. The code can be read with a smartphone camera. To read the QR code, users may download any free QR code application to a smartphone. Snapping this code links students directly to the relevant VOCABULARY WORKSHOP Web site, where they can listen to iWords or take an interactive vocabulary quiz.

Use a smartphone camera and a QR code application to snap this code to link to the VOCABULARY WORKSHOP home page.

Reading Passages

New Reading Passages open each Unit of VOCABULARY WORKSHOP. At least 15 of the the 20 Unit vocabulary words appear in each Passage. Students read the words in context in informational texts to activate prior knowledge and then apply what they learn throughout the Unit, providing practice in critical-reading skills. Idioms, adages, and proverbs used in Passages provide exposure to figurative language. Passage topics are high-interest and represent a variety of genres, including expository texts, informational essays, historical nonfiction, and biographies. Snap the code or go to the VOCABULARY WORKSHOP home page to listen to iWords, and hear modeled reading of each Unit Passage.

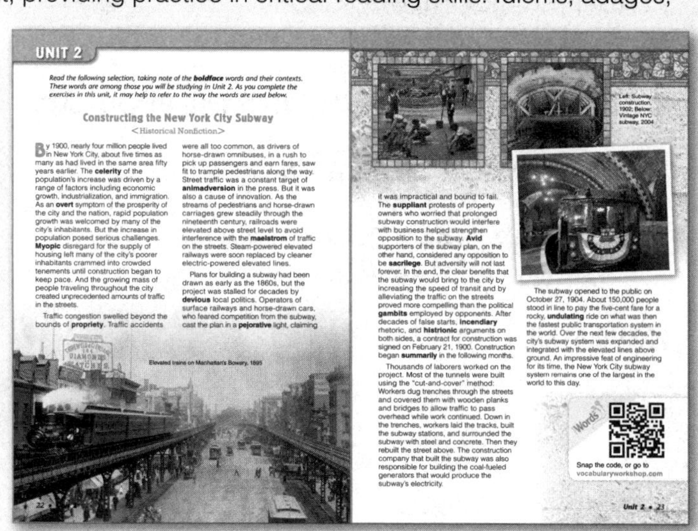

UNIT 2

*Read the following selection, taking note of the **boldface** words and their contexts. These words are among those you will be studying in Unit 2. As you complete the exercises in this unit, it may help to refer to the way the words are used below.*

Constructing the New York City Subway

<Historical Nonfiction>

By 1900, nearly four million people lived in New York City, about five times as many as had lived in the same area fifty years earlier. The **celerity** of the population's increase was driven by a range of factors including economic growth, industrialization, and immigration. As an **overt** symptom of the prosperity of the city and the nation, rapid population growth was welcomed by many of the city's inhabitants. But the increase in population posed serious challenges. **Myopic** disregard for the supply of housing left many of the city's poorer inhabitants crammed into crowded tenements until construction began to keep pace. And the growing mass of people traveling throughout the city created unprecedented amounts of traffic in the streets.

Traffic congestion swelled beyond the bounds of **propriety**. Traffic accidents were all too common, as drivers of horse-drawn omnibuses, in a rush to pick up passengers and earn fares, saw fit to trample pedestrians along the way. Street traffic was a constant target of **animadversion** in the press. But it was also a cause of innovation. As the streams of pedestrians and horse-drawn carriages grew steadily through the nineteenth century, railroads were elevated above street level to avoid interference with the **maelstrom** of traffic on the streets. Steam-powered elevated railways were soon replaced by cleaner electric-powered elevated lines.

Plans for building a subway had been drawn as early as the 1860s, but the project was stalled for decades by **devious** local politics. Operators of surface railways and horse-drawn cars, who feared competition from the subway, cast the plan in a **pejorative** light, claiming it was impractical and bound to fail. The **suppliant** protests of property owners who worried that prolonged subway construction would interfere with business helped strengthen opposition to the subway. **Avid** supporters of the subway plan, on the other hand, considered any opposition to be **sacrilege**. But adversity will not last forever. In the end, the clear benefits that the subway would bring to the city by increasing the speed of transit and by alleviating the traffic on the streets proved more compelling than the political **gambits** employed by opponents. After decades of false starts, **incendiary** rhetoric, and **histrionic** arguments on both sides, a contract for construction was signed on February 21, 1900. Construction began **summarily** in the following months.

Thousands of laborers worked on the project. Most of the tunnels were built using the "cut-and-cover" method: Workers dug trenches through the streets and covered them with wooden planks and bridges to allow traffic to pass overhead while work continued. Down in the trenches, workers laid the tracks, built the subway stations, and surrounded the subway with steel and concrete. Then they rebuilt the street above. The construction company that built the subway was also responsible for building the coal-fueled generators that would produce the subway's electricity.

The subway opened to the public on October 27, 1904. About 150,000 people stood in line to pay the five-cent fare for a rocky, **undulating** ride on what was then the fastest public transportation system in the world. Over the next few decades, the city's subway system was expanded and integrated with the elevated lines above ground. An impressive feat of engineering for its time, the New York City subway system remains one of the largest in the world to this day.

Elevated trains on Manhattan's Bowery, 1895

Left: Subway construction, 1902; Below: Vintage NYC subway, 2004

iWords

Snap the code, or go to vocabularyworkshop.com

22

Unit 2 • 23

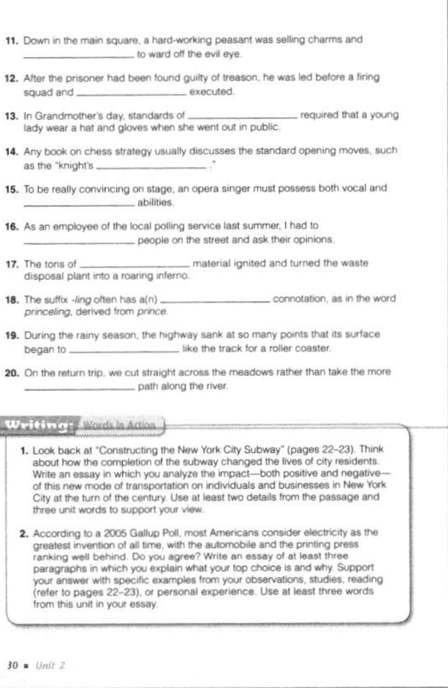
11. Down in the main square, a hard-working peasant was selling charms and ________ to ward off the evil eye.

12. After the prisoner had been found guilty of treason, he was led before a firing squad and ________ executed.

13. In Grandmother's day, standards of ________ required that a young lady wear a hat and gloves when she went out in public.

14. Any book on chess strategy usually discusses the standard opening moves, such as the "knight's ________."

15. To be really convincing on stage, an opera singer must possess both vocal and ________ abilities.

16. As an employee of the local polling service last summer, I had to ________ people on the street and ask their opinions.

17. The tons of ________ material ignited and turned the waste disposal plant into a roaring inferno.

18. The suffix *-ling* often has a(n) ________ connotation, as in the word *princeling*, derived from *prince*.

19. During the rainy season, the highway sank at so many points that its surface began to ________ like the track for a roller coaster.

20. On the return trip, we cut straight across the meadows rather than take the more ________ path along the river.

Writing: Words in Action

1. Look back at "Constructing the New York City Subway" (pages 22–23). Think about how the completion of the subway changed the lives of city residents. Write an essay in which you analyze the impact—both positive and negative—of this new mode of transportation on individuals and businesses in New York City at the turn of the century. Use at least two details from the passage and three unit words to support your view.

2. According to a 2005 Gallup Poll, most Americans consider electricity as the greatest invention of all time, with the automobile and the printing press ranking well behind. Do you agree? Write an essay of at least three paragraphs in which you explain what your top choice is and why. Support your answer with specific examples from your observations, studies, reading (refer to pages 22–23), or personal experience. Use at least three words from this unit in your essay.

30 ■ Unit 2

Writing Prompts

Students practice writing responses to two types of prompts. The first prompt refers to the Passage that introduced the Unit and encourages close reading of the text. The second prompt is modeled on those that appear on standardized tests, such as the SAT® and ACT®.*

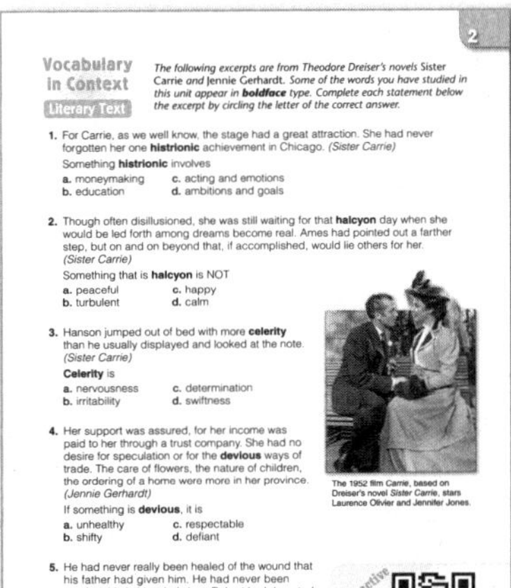
2

Vocabulary in Context
Literary Text

The following excerpts are from Theodore Dreiser's novels Sister Carrie *and* Jennie Gerhardt. *Some of the words you have studied in this unit appear in* ***boldface*** *type. Complete each statement below the excerpt by circling the letter of the correct answer.*

1. For Carrie, as we well know, the stage had a great attraction. She had never forgotten her one **histrionic** achievement in Chicago. *(Sister Carrie)*
   Something **histrionic** involves
   a. moneymaking c. acting and emotions
   b. education d. ambitions and goals

2. Though often disillusioned, she was still waiting for that **halcyon** day when she would be led forth among dreams become real. Ames had pointed out a farther step, but on and on beyond that, if accomplished, would lie others for her. *(Sister Carrie)*
   Something that is **halcyon** is NOT
   a. peaceful c. happy
   b. turbulent d. calm

3. Hanson jumped out of bed with more **celerity** than he usually displayed and looked at the note. *(Sister Carrie)*
   Celerity is
   a. nervousness c. determination
   b. irritability d. swiftness

4. Her support was assured, for her income was paid to her through a trust company. She had no desire for speculation or for the **devious** ways of trade. The care of flowers, the nature of children, the ordering of a home were more in her province. *(Jennie Gerhardt)*
   If something is **devious**, it is
   a. unhealthy c. respectable
   b. shifty d. defiant

The 1952 film Carrie, based on Dreiser's novel *Sister Carrie*, stars Laurence Olivier and Jennifer Jones.

5. He had never really been healed of the wound that his father had given him. He had never been comfortable in his mind since Robert had deserted him so **summarily**. *(Jennie Gerhardt)*
   Something done **summarily** is done
   a. abruptly c. gradually
   b. predictably d. sarcastically

Interactive Quiz

Snap the code, or go to vocabularyworkshop.com

Unit 2 ■ 31

Vocabulary in Context

The **Vocabulary in Context** pages contain excerpts from classic literature. Each excerpt uses one of the vocabulary words from the Unit and provides students with exposure to the vocabulary in the context of authentic literature. Multiple-choice questions give practice in standardized-test format. An interactive quiz using the Unit words is accessible by snapping the QR code on the page or by visiting **vocabularyworkshop.com**.

Word Study

In accordance with the Common Core State Standards, the **Word Study** pages address figurative language with instruction and practice using idioms, adages, and proverbs, as well as provide instruction on determining and applying denotation and connotation. This new section appears every three Units, after the Review.

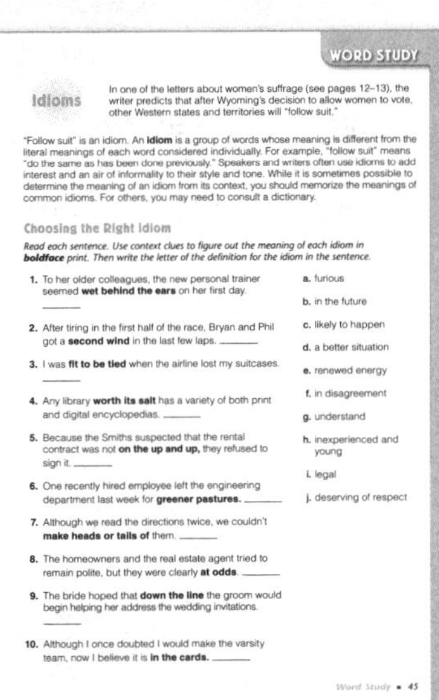
WORD STUDY

Idioms

In one of the letters about women's suffrage (see pages 12–13), the writer predicts that after Wyoming's decision to allow women to vote, other Western states and territories will "follow suit."

"Follow suit" is an idiom. An **idiom** is a group of words whose meaning is different from the literal meanings of each word considered individually. For example, "follow suit" means "do the same as has been done previously." Speakers and writers often use idioms to add interest and an air of informality to their style and tone. While it is sometimes possible to determine the meaning of an idiom from its context, you should memorize the meanings of common idioms. For others, you may need to consult a dictionary.

Choosing the Right Idiom

Read each sentence. Use context clues to figure out the meaning of each idiom in ***boldface*** *print. Then write the letter of the definition for the idiom in the sentence.*

1. To her older colleagues, the new personal trainer seemed **wet behind the ears** on her first day. ________
2. After tiring in the first half of the race, Bryan and Phil got a **second wind** in the last few laps. ________
3. I was **fit to be tied** when the airline lost my suitcases. ________
4. Any library **worth its salt** has a variety of both print and digital encyclopedias. ________
5. Because the Smiths suspected that the rental contract was not **on the up and up,** they refused to sign it. ________
6. One recently hired employee left the engineering department last week for **greener pastures.** ________
7. Although we read the directions twice, we couldn't **make heads or tails of** them. ________
8. The homeowners and the real estate agent tried to remain polite, but they were clearly **at odds**. ________
9. The bride hoped that **down the line** the groom would begin helping her address the wedding invitations. ________
10. Although I once doubted I would make the varsity team, now I believe it is **in the cards.** ________

a. furious
b. in the future
c. likely to happen
d. a better situation
e. renewed energy
f. in disagreement
g. understand
h. inexperienced and young
i. legal
j. deserving of respect

Word Study ■ 45

*SAT is a trademark registered and/or owned by the College Board which was not involved in the production of, and does not endorse, this product. ACT is a registered trademark of ACT, Inc., which was not involved in the production of, and does not endorse, this product.

Vocabulary Workshop and the Common Core State Standards

The Common Core Enriched Edition of **Vocabulary Workshop** is aligned with and supports relevant and applicable standards contained in the Common Core State Standards for English Language Arts. The program is fully aligned with the Vocabulary Acquisition and Use standards and supports them with the kind of instruction, modeling, and practice that promote and cultivate corresponding vocabulary skills. Additionally, the Common Core Enriched Edition of **Vocabulary Workshop** addresses several Common Core Reading and Writing standards—in particular those associated with the role of vocabulary both in determining meaning and nuance within the broader context of reading, and in refining usage and expression in written and oral communication.

In this Teacher's Edition, the Common Core State Standards addressed in the form of instruction and/or practice in any given section of the Student Edition are indicated at the bottom of the corresponding page or pages. The standards are identified in an abbreviated notation. For example, "CCSS Vocabulary 4.c, 4.d" indicates that the vocabulary skill or skills represented on that page support Vocabulary Acquisition and Use standards 4.c and 4.d. Similarly, "CCSS Reading (Informational Text) 4, 6" is shorthand for Reading Standards for Informational Text 4, 6, and "CCSS Writing 2.d, 3.d" stands for Writing Standards 2.d and 3.d.

The full language of the corresponding Vocabulary, Reading (both Informational Text and Literature), and Writing standards for grades 11 and 12 is provided below. Note that in some instances, text is highlighted to show specific correlations between a particular skill and a more general standard. (A full correlation of the **Vocabulary Workshop Common Core Enriched Edition** program to the Common Core State Standards is available at **vocabularyworkshop.com**.)

Common Core State Standards for English Language Arts

Language Standards

(Grades 11–12)

Vocabulary Acquisition and Use

4. Determine or clarify the meaning of unknown and multiple-meaning words and phrases based on *grades 11–12 reading and content*, choosing flexibly from a range of strategies.

- **a.** Use context (e.g., the overall meaning of a sentence, paragraph, or text; a word's position or function in a sentence) as a clue to the meaning of a word or phrase.
- **c.** Consult general and specialized reference materials (e.g., dictionaries, glossaries, thesauruses), both print and digital, to find the pronunciation of a word or determine or clarify its precise meaning, its part of speech, its etymology, or its standard usage.
- **d.** Verify the preliminary determination of the meaning of a word or phrase (e.g., by checking the inferred meaning in context or in a dictionary).

5. Demonstrate understanding of figurative language, word relationships, and nuances in word meanings.
   a. Interpret figures of speech (e.g., hyperbole, paradox) in context and analyze their role in the text.
   b. Analyze nuances in the meaning of words with similar denotations.
6. Acquire and use accurately general academic and domain-specific words and phrases, sufficient for reading, writing, speaking, and listening at the college and career readiness level; demonstrate independence in gathering vocabulary knowledge when considering a word or phrase important to comprehension or expression.

Reading Standards for Literature

(Grades 11–12)

Craft and Structure

4. Determine the meaning of words and phrases as they are used in the text, including figurative and connotative meanings; analyze the impact of specific word choices on meaning and tone, including words with multiple meanings or language that is particularly fresh, engaging, or beautiful. (Include Shakespeare as well as other authors.)

Reading Standards for Informational Text

(Grades 11–12)

Key Ideas and Details

2. Determine two or more central ideas of a text and analyze their development over the course of the text, including how they interact and build on one another to provide a complex analysis; provide an objective summary of the text.

Craft and Structure

4. Determine the meaning of words and phrases as they are used in a text, including figurative, connotative, and technical meanings; analyze how an author uses and refines the meaning of a key term or terms over the course of a text (e.g., how Madison defines *faction* in *Federalist* No. 10).
6. Determine an author's point of view or purpose in a text in which the rhetoric is particularly effective, analyzing how style and content contribute to the power, persuasiveness, or beauty of the text.

Writing Standards

(Grades 11–12)

Text Type and Purposes

2. Write informative/explanatory texts to examine and convey complex ideas, concepts, and information clearly and accurately through the effective selection, organization, and analysis of content.
   d. Use precise language, domain-specific vocabulary, and techniques such as metaphor, simile, and analogy to manage the complexity of the topic.
3. Write narratives to develop real or imagined experiences or events using effective technique, well-chosen details, and well-structured event sequences.
   d. Use precise words and phrases, telling details, and sensory language to convey a vivid picture of the experiences, events, setting, and/or characters.

ENRICHED VOCABULARY APPROACH: Systematic Vocabulary Instruction

The VOCABULARY WORKSHOP program focuses on the words, their meanings, their ranges of application, and their uses in context. The approach is systematic because it begins with and builds upon a word list drawn from vocabulary that students will encounter in their reading. It provides students with the vocabulary skills they will need to achieve higher-level reading proficiency and to succeed at standardized tests.

With the introduction of reading passages and literary text, the Enriched Edition goes further than previous editions in integrating vocabulary instruction in the context of reading. (For a discussion of the importance of vocabulary in reading comprehension, see pages T31–T32. For more on how VOCABULARY WORKSHOP can be used to complement a literature program, see pages T33–T35.)

A cornerstone of the VOCABULARY WORKSHOP approach is intensive practice through varied and abundant "hands-on" exercises. This method provides both exposure to different meanings of the key words studied and coverage of the range of each key word through its appearance in many different contexts. The aim of the pattern of intensive practice is to embed the words in the students' active, daily-use vocabulary.

Grade-Level Placements

The chart below shows suggested grade placement for each Level of VOCABULARY WORKSHOP. In determining proper placement of a particular Level, consider the following:

- Grade placements are based on teacher experience and recommendations.
- Differences in grade are reflected in the difficulty of the words presented, the maturity of the sentences, and other contexts in which those words are used.
- Grade levels should not be taken too literally. Experimentation and the use of the program's online diagnostic materials will establish the correct placement of a particular Level in a given situation.
- The use of Level H with above-average students is designed to enhance preparation for the SAT and other college entrance examinations.

Grade Placements

Average Students		Above-Average Students	
Level	**Grade**	**Level**	**Grade**
D	9	D	8
E	10	E	9
F	11	F	10
G	12	G	11
		H	12

Word Lists

Each Student Level presents 300 vocabulary words organized into 15 Units. Mastering these words will help students understand academic texts and increase their everyday language abilities.

For a discussion by Vicki A. Jacobs of the importance of academic vocabulary to reading comprehension, see pages T31–T32.

Criteria for Selection: The selection of VOCABULARY WORKSHOP words is based on four criteria: currency in and usefulness for present-day American oral or written communication; frequency on recognized high-utility and academic vocabulary lists; applicability to standardized tests; current grade-placement research.

General Sources: The lists of key words were developed from many sources: traditional, classic, and contemporary literature, including novels, short stories, essays, newspaper and magazine articles, plays, and films. Spelling and vocabulary lists recognized as valid bases for teaching language skills at the middle and secondary levels are used, as well as current subject-area textbooks, glossaries, and ancillary materials (especially for general, nontechnical terms).

Dictionary and Reference Sources: The following were the primary dictionary resources used for word (and definition) selection:

- *Webster's Third International Dictionary of the English Language* (unabridged)
- *Merriam-Webster's Collegiate Dictionary* (Ninth, Tenth, and online editions)
- *The American Heritage Dictionary of the English Language* (editions 1–4)
- *The Random House Dictionary of the English Language* (unabridged editions)
- *The Compact Edition of the Oxford English Dictionary*

Standard Word-Frequency Sources: Standard word-frequency studies were conducted to evaluate and revise the word list.

- *Primary* Dale-O'Rourke: *The Living Word Vocabulary*, Carroll-Davies-Richman: *The American Heritage Word Frequency Book*
- *Supplementary* Harris-Jacobsen: *Basic Reading Vocabularies*, Thorndike-Lorge: *The Teacher's Word Book of 30,000 Words*, Zeno-Ivens-Millard-Duvvuri: *The Educator's Word Frequency Guide*

"Sliding-Scale" Placement

Each word list works on a sliding scale based on the following principles: Any word that according to Dale-O'Rourke is known in a given grade is not presented in that grade. It is presented two or three grades earlier. Each grade level contains mostly words not known (according to Dale-O'Rourke) two or three grades later, with an admixture (in decreasing numbers) of words not known four or more grades later. The higher the grade, the larger the percentage of more difficult words contained in the word list. This ambitious approach accommodates as many "SAT-type" words as possible in the key word lists for Grades 10–12.

Professional development papers discussing the research supporting the instructional approach of VOCABULARY WORKSHOP may be found in the Teacher Center of **vocabularyworkshop.com**.

PRINT COMPONENTS

This Enriched Edition of Vocabulary Workshop, Levels D–H, consists of an integrated array of print and digital components. Print materials for each Level include:

- Student Texts
- Teacher's Annotated Editions
- Test Booklets with Combined Answer Keys (Forms A and B)
- SAT-Type TEST PREP Blackline Masters (answers included)

Student Texts/Teacher's Annotated Editions

Each of the five Student Texts (Levels D–H) presents 300 key words and is organized in the same way: 15 Units of 20 words each and 5 Reviews following Units 3, 6, 9, 12, and 15. Preceding the first Unit is a section on types of questions students will find throughout the program. Concluding each Student Text is a Final Mastery Test.

In the Teacher's Annotated Editions, answers are shown for each student page. Correlations to Common Core State Standards are also noted on page.

Reading Passages

New nonfiction Reading Passages open each Unit of Vocabulary Workshop. At least 15 of the Unit vocabulary words, as well as examples of figurative language such as idioms, adages, or proverbs, are used in each Passage. Students read the words in context to activate prior knowledge, and then they apply what they learn throughout the Unit and the Review.

Definitions

DEFINITIONS The definitions provided are clear, useful, and informal. The intent is to give students a reasonably good core idea of what each word means without extensive detail or secondary connotations. Generally, only a single meaning of maximum usefulness is given.

PART OF SPEECH Simple abbreviations give the part of speech with each definition. When a word functions as several parts of speech, the appropriate abbreviation appears before the corresponding definition.

PRONUNCIATION A simple set of diacritical marks presented at the beginning of every Student Text (inside front cover) indicates the pronunciation. Only one pronunciation is given for each word, except when a word changes its pronunciation in accordance with its use as different parts of speech (*ob′ ject* and *ob ject′*).

Students may utilize the **Online** iWords **Audio Program** for each Unit. Available at **vocabularyworkshop.com**, this program provides nearly four hours of spoken material per Student Text, including pronunciation and examples of usage.

ILLUSTRATIVE SENTENCE Concluding each key entry is an illustrative sentence. These sentences provide a context that clarifies the meaning of each word. By writing the word in such contextual settings, students begin to see how the word can be used effectively in their own writing.

SYNONYMS AND ANTONYMS Each word has a list of synonyms and/or antonyms if there is one or more of either for the word. By studying the given synonyms and antonyms, students will better understand the denotational family of words of which each key word is part; and by comparing specific usages of key words and their synonyms, students can better appreciate appropriate contexts for these words. Note that the lists of synonyms and antonyms are not exhaustive.

Choosing the Right Word

In this activity, students choose one of a pair of words that most satisfactorily completes the sentence. Completing this activity requires a thorough understanding of a range of a word's definitions.

Synonyms and Antonyms

In this section, students read phrases that include synonyms or antonyms for the Unit words. Students must choose the Unit word that matches the given synonym or antonym. Besides reinforcing meanings, this exercise provides students with further examples of usage and context.

Completing the Sentence

This activity provides a simple completion exercise in which students choose and write the word that logically and meaningfully fits into a blank in a given sentence.

When using this activity in the classroom, the teacher should bear in mind the following considerations:

- The sentences in this activity call for the literal or direct (as opposed to the metaphorical or extended) meaning of the words involved.
- The sentences are designed so that only one of the words fits in the given blank. Context clues have been placed in each sentence.
- The words are to be used as the part of speech given in Definitions. The only exceptions are: Nouns given in the singular in Definitions may be plural in the sentences; verbs given in the base form in Definitions may be used in any tense or form (including participial) required by the sentence.

Writing: Words in Action

New prompts provide practice with writing responses to two modes of writing. The first prompt is a text-dependent question that asks students to respond to the Reading Passage at the beginning of the Unit. The second prompt is modeled on those that appear on standardized tests. Students write their responses on a separate sheet of paper. Teachers should grade the responses using a rubric of their choice.

Vocabulary in Context/Literary Text

This activity provides Unit vocabulary words used in classic literature, which:

- gives examples of usage for the selected words,
- offers an opportunity to derive meaning from context, and
- provides practice in the sort of vocabulary exercises found on standardized tests.

Refer students to Student Text page 7 for an introduction to the strategies involved in studying vocabulary in context.

Review

A Review follows every three Units.

- Vocabulary for Comprehension: This section is designed to help students prepare for the critical-reading sections of standardized tests. Students read a Passage and then answer vocabulary-in-context and comprehension questions related to the texts.
- Two-Word Completions: Students practice with word-omission (cloze) exercises that appear on typical standardized tests, including the SAT.

Word Study

A Word Study section follows every Review. Exercises include instruction and practice with figurative language and relationships in meaning:

- Choosing the Right Idiom/Adage/Proverb
- Writing with Idioms/Adages/Proverbs
- Denotation and Connotation/Shades of Meaning
- Building with Classical Roots

The Final Mastery Test

The Final Mastery Test in the Student Text is a practice test of 70 items that gives students and teachers fair insight into how much progress has been made during the year and what kind of additional work is in order.

The purpose of the Final Mastery Test is threefold.

- It can serve as a dry run in preparation for the more formal (and secure) tests available as optional components of this program.
- It can serve as an informal evaluation of achievement to date.
- It can serve as a reinforcement activity.

Test Booklets (Optional)

Two Test Booklets (Form A and Form B) may be used to reduce the risk of answers being passed on. Though the formats of the Test Booklets are the same, the items tested in any given section are completely different. The contents are: a list of the 300 tested vocabulary words; a Warm-Up Test; 15 Unit Tests, each consisting of 25 items focusing on pronunciations, parts of speech, spelling, definitions, synonyms, antonyms, and sentence completions; and 5 Cumulative Tests of 52–110 items each.

TEST PREP Blackline Masters (Optional)

The TEST PREP component provides practice with SAT-type test questions and formats and also with review tests covering the corresponding Student Text. Prep Tests approximate the word-omission sections of the SAT and provide practice in the vocabulary-in-context strand with brief reading passages as well. Answer sheets in SAT-type test format develop student ease and familiarity with standardized testing materials. Mastery Tests are used when students have completed the corresponding group of three Units in the Student Text. Each test covers basic meanings, synonyms, antonyms, and sentence completions. Answer keys, including selected answer rationales, are provided for all tests.

DIGITAL COMPONENTS

Digital resources for each Level are available at **vocabularyworkshop.com** and include:

- iWords Audio Program
- Audio of Unit Passages
- Online Interactive Games
- Vocabulary in Context: Informational Text
- Diagnostic Tests and Cumulative Reviews
- Professional Development Videos
- Interactive Quizzes

The components have been designed for use in an integrated year-long vocabulary program, as suggested in the chart on pages T24–T26.

PDFs of the following materials may be found online for each level:

- Correlations to the Common Core State Standards
- Vocabulary in Context: Informational Text
- SAT and ACT Practice Worksheets
- Additional Practice and Quiz pages for each lesson
- Greek and Latin Roots Reference Guide
- Diagnostic Tests and Cumulative Reviews
- Pacing Guides

iWords Audio Program

The VOCABULARY WORKSHOP iWords Audio Program provides students with pronunciations, definitions, and examples of usage for all program vocabulary words and word meanings. Students can visit **vocabularyworkshop.com** to listen to each word or download MP3 files of the words.

- The audio program is ideal for English Language Learners (ELL) and ELL classrooms.
- Students hear the recommended pronunciation of each word at least six times and are given two opportunities to pronounce each word themselves.
- Pronunciations are followed by brief definitions and examples of the word used in complete sentences.
- For recommendations on when to use iWords, see pages T24–T30.

Online Interactive Vocabulary Games

For each Level, students are provided interactive word games using the vocabulary presented in the Units. These activities include flashcards, crossword puzzles, word searches, "hangman," and Test Your Vocabulary questions. Additional Practice and Quiz pages including Interactive Quizzes provide more possibilities for academic assessment.

Vocabulary in Context: Informational Text

A Reading Passage that uses key Unit words provides another opportunity to read vocabulary in context. Each Passage is followed by multiple-choice questions for extra practice with nonfiction texts, the Unit vocabulary words, and question types found on standardized tests.

Diagnostic Test and Cumulative Reviews

- A **Beginning-of-Year Diagnostic Test** contains a sampling of words from the program to assess students' prior knowledge.
- After Units 3, 6, 9, 12, and 15, students can complete **Cumulative Review Tests**. Questions on Choosing the Right Meaning and Two-Word Completions provide practice on SAT-style questions. Activities on analogies and vocabulary enrichment are also included.

SAT and ACT Practice Worksheets

For teachers who wish to offer their students extra practice for the SAT or ACT, 45 standardized-test worksheets are available online for each Level. These practice worksheets are accessible only to teachers.

For each Level, there are 15 worksheets in standardized-test format for each of the following:

- comprehension and vocabulary skills assessed on the SAT and ACT,
- multiple-choice grammar and usage items included in the Writing section of the SAT and in the ACT, and
- step-by-step guidance in crafting a timed essay of the kind that is required on the SAT (and is optional on the ACT).

Teacher Resources

Available in PDF format:

- Correlations to the Common Core State Standards
- Pacing Guides
- Greek and Latin Roots Reference Guide
- Graphic Organizers

Online Student Assessment System (Optional)

The Web-based VOCABULARY WORKSHOP Online Student Assessment System allows teachers to quickly and easily create secure, interactive Unit practice and assessment pages that are automatically scored and provide students with immediate, prescriptive feedback. With a database of nearly 4,000 test items per Level, teachers have the option to individualize tests.

The Online Student Assessment System provides:

- the ability to create and edit question sets and tests,
- the ability to scramble answer choices and/or questions so that multiple versions of the same test can be administered securely,
- a wide assortment of question types: pronunciation, part of speech, spelling, definitions, synonyms, antonyms, sentence completions, sentence framing,
- formatted Unit tests, ready for immediate use,
- a secure portal to assign practice/test pages, with the option to print these pages,
- immediate feedback on each question,
- a detailed end-of-assignment report to help you know exactly how students are progressing,
- the ability to track student progress through a comprehensive reporting system,
- a way to create detailed reports on class and individual student results, and
- the option to send practice/test pages and student results to learning management systems.

The VOCABULARY WORKSHOP Online Student Assessment System is a convenient and secure source of assessment and/or extra practice. The Online Student Assessment System is easy to use, either as needed or more systematically, as an integral part of the VOCABULARY WORKSHOP series. See pages T24–26 for recommendations on how it may be used in conjunction with the Student Text and other components.

IMPLEMENTING THE PROGRAM

VOCABULARY WORKSHOP not only provides vocabulary instruction but also teaches students a variety of other essential Language Arts skills. Teachers have many options for pacing VOCABULARY WORKSHOP'S activities to best meet the needs of their students and classes.

Overview of Weekly Vocabulary Instruction

The charts on pages 24–26 offer multiple ways to provide consistent vocabulary instruction to high-school students. Both the weekly schedule charts and the daily activity charts offer specific methods to integrate VOCABULARY WORKSHOP into the Language Arts classroom. Schedules among districts vary greatly, however, so the program methods suggested provide ideas that each teacher can tailor to ensure success within his or her own classroom.

Weekly Schedule

Week	Student Text	Suggestions for Implementing the Program
1	**Beginning-of-Year Diagnostic Test**	When reviewing the Beginning-of-Year Diagnostic Test, available at vocabularyworkshop.com, encourage students to use the words in their writing and speaking, not just to recognize meaning.
2	**Unit 1**	Start by reviewing the Unit 1 words through the Reading Passage. Implement a focused study of four words each day with students (see "Suggestion for Studying Four Words a Day" on page 27). Complete VOCABULARY WORKSHOP activities in the book and online (see the "How to Use VOCABULARY WORKSHOP Exercises" charts on the following pages). Examine Best Practices on pages 28–30 for further vocabulary activities. Testing Options: Assign Unit 1 Test from Test Booklets or from the Online Student Assessment System.
3	**Unit 2**	Follow procedure for Unit 2 as shown in Unit 1. Testing Options: Assign Unit 2 Test from Test Booklets or from the Online Student Assessment System, and review Unit 1 Test to encourage deeper recall of all words.
4	**Unit 3**	Follow procedure for Unit 3 as shown in Unit 1. Testing Options: Assign Unit 3 Test from Test Booklets or from the Online Student Assessment System, and review Units 1–2 Tests to encourage deeper recall of all words.
5	**Review Units 1–3**	Complete Review Units 1–3 activities, and ensure knowledge of all 60 vocabulary words as well as the mastery of other essential English skills. Mastery Test Units 1–3 available as Test Prep Blackline Masters.

Continue with the above pattern for weeks 2–5 for the rest of the year, having students complete the Final Mastery Test for Units 1–15 at the end of the year.

For Each Unit

How to use VOCABULARY WORKSHOP Exercises & Online Activities with Three Sessions/Periods

Assignment	Day 1	Day 2	Day 3
Class work	**1.** Review previous Unit's test results. **2.** Review word meaning and usage in context in the Unit's Reading Passage. **3.** Present any words not used in the Reading Passage.	**1.** Review Choosing the Right Word, Synonyms, and Antonyms. **2.** Assign Writing: Words in Action Prompt 1 and/ or 2. **3.** Assign SAT/ACT Practice Worksheets at **vocabularyworkshop.com**.	**1.** Review Vocabulary in Context: Literary Text. **2.** Assign the Unit Test (Test Booklet or Online Student Assessment System).
Homework	**1.** Have students download and listen to iWords. **2.** Assign Choosing the Right Word, Synonyms, and Antonyms. **3.** Have students play online Unit games.	**1.** Assign Vocabulary in Context: Literary Text. **2.** Have students play online Unit games. **3.** Assign Interactive Quiz.	Have students read the next Unit's Reading Passage.

How to use VOCABULARY WORKSHOP Exercises & Online Activities with Five Sessions/Periods

Assignment	Day 1	Day 2	Day 3	Day 4	Day 5
Class work	**1.** Review previous Unit's test results. **2.** Review word meaning and usage in context in the Unit's Reading Passage. **3.** Present any words not used in the Reading Passage.	**1.** Review Choosing the Right Word. **2.** Assign online SAT/ ACT Practice Worksheets.	**1.** Review Synonyms and Antonyms and also Completing the Sentence. **2.** Assign the first prompt for Writing: Words in Action.	**1.** Share excerpts (with vocabulary usage) from Writing: Words in Action. **2.** Assign Vocabulary in Context: Literary Text.	Assign Unit Test (Test Booklet or Online Student Assessment System).
Homework	**1.** Download and listen to iWords. **2.** Assign Choosing the Right Word.	**1.** Assign Synonyms and Antonyms, and also Completing the Sentence. **2.** Have students play online Unit games.	**1.** Assign the second prompt of Writing: Words in Action.	Assign online interactive quiz.	Have students read the next Unit's Reading Passage.

For Review Units

How to use VOCABULARY WORKSHOP Review Exercises & Online Activities with 3 Sessions/Periods

Assignment	Day 1	Day 2	Day 3
Class work	**1.** Review previous Unit's test results. **2.** Complete Vocabulary for Comprehension. **3.** Present Word Study Idioms/Adages/Proverbs.	**1.** Review Two-Word Completions and Word Study Idioms/Adages/ Proverbs. **2.** Present Word Study Denotation/Connotation.	**1.** Assign Mastery Test (Test Prep Blackline Masters). **2.** Review Word Study Denotation/Connotation. **3.** Present Building with Classical Roots.
Homework	**1.** Assign Two-Word Completions. **2.** Assign Word Study Idioms/Adages/Proverbs.	**1.** Have students finish Word Study Denotation/ Connotation. **2.** Have students play online Unit games.	Have students read the next Unit's Reading Passage.

How to use VOCABULARY WORKSHOP Review Exercises & Online Activities with 5 Sessions/Periods

Assignment	Day 1	Day 2	Day 3	Day 4	Day 5
Class work	**1.** Review previous Unit's test results. **2.** Assign Vocabulary for Compre-hension.	**1.** Review SAT/ACT Worksheets and Two-Word Completions. **2.** Present Idioms/ Adages/ Proverbs.	**1.** Review Idioms/ Adages/ Proverbs. **2.** Present Denotation/ Connotation.	**1.** Review Denotation/ Connotation. **2.** Present Building with Classical Roots.	Assign Mastery Test (Test Prep Blackline Masters).
Homework	**1.** Assign online SAT/ ACT Practice Worksheets. **2.** Assign Two-Word Completions.	**1.** Assign Idioms/ Adages/ Proverbs. **2.** Play online Unit games.	**1.** Assign Denotation/ Connotation. **2.** Have students play online Unit games.	Review Building with Classical Roots.	Assign the next Unit's Reading Passage.

Implementing the Weekly and Daily Schedules

The following may prove helpful when adapting the foregoing schedules to specific situations.

- Students need to recognize the value of learning vocabulary and completing the vocabulary exercises. Simply assigning words and the exercises for class work or homework does not provide intrinsic value for those who are learning new vocabulary. Teachers should model vocabulary usage and encourage students to learn the words to improve their speaking, writing, reading comprehension, and test scores (see "Best Practices" T28–T30 for suggestions).

- The teacher may adapt the models shown to the situation at hand.
- Activity order and timings are to some extent hypothetical. Teachers may switch items around and adjust timings as needed. Similarly, items may be modified or deleted.
- VOCABULARY WORKSHOP Units may also be adapted so that only 10 words are studied each week. The Online Student Assessment System allows teachers to easily create quizzes for the first or second 10 words of a Unit, if desired. Students completing the exercises in VOCABULARY WORKSHOP can either wait until the second week to work on the activities, or they can identify the words they know and complete only those blanks that relate to the week's words being studied.

Suggestion for Studying Four Words a Day

Each day, teachers may project or write the four vocabulary words of the day in contextual sentences. Students should identify each word's meaning and part of speech through context clues; students can then create their own flashcards or charts that can be used as a study aid. By focusing each day's study on specific words, students can break down their learning into manageable chunks of information.

Student Study Guides

When students employ a review system for their vocabularies, they tend to learn the words and their meanings more thoroughly. However, review systems and study methods may vary among learning styles.

For Basic Vocabulary Learners: A popular and effective method of learning vocabulary words is to use them in context. While VOCABULARY WORKSHOP contains many activities in which students see the words in context, it is important for students to use these words on their own in order to better recall a word's meaning. Teachers should encourage students to use the vocabulary words in other classes or at home. Students can take note of the sentence in which they used a word and to share it so that other students can hear words used in a context they may not have considered.

For Kinesthetic Learners: Students who are kinesthetic learners understand information better when there is activity involved. Teachers may assign kinesthetic learners to be the record keepers during the vocabulary lesson and take notes on the board. Students may retain the lesson better if they are involved in the activity rather than sedentary for a long period of time. Teachers should suggest that students think of a movement or facial expression that they associate with the definition of a vocabulary word to aid in recall of the word's definition.

For Visual/Artistic Learners: Visual learners remember information by how it is organized on a page. Therefore, it would be helpful for them to think of different ways the words relate to one another and make charts based on the categories they come up with. These categories could be based on definition, word origin, connotation, or part of speech.

For Auditory Learners: Auditory learners recall what they hear better than what they see or do. Therefore, it is important to encourage these students to say the vocabulary words out loud often. In class, it may help if two students work together and engage in a dialogue in which they must use a minimum number of vocabulary words. To improve their productivity outside of class, students should review iWords on a daily basis.

BEST PRACTICES FOR USING VOCABULARY WORKSHOP IN THE CLASSROOM

Classroom experience and research have shown that repeated exposure to and application of vocabulary words embed meaning in students' minds. The more teachers and students utilize vocabulary in the Language Arts class period, the more likely students are to understand and use new vocabulary themselves.

Classroom Environment

Depending on the reading proficiencies of their students, teachers may differentiate and/or scaffold instruction to accommodate varying learning styles and backgrounds—for example, by reading aloud or having students read aloud the passages that introduce the Units.

To encourage students' use of vocabulary, teachers may post vocabulary words in the classroom—on bulletin boards, walls, or chalkboards/whiteboards.

Students and teachers may bring in examples of vocabulary from print sources to be displayed in the classroom. Additionally, students may create visual representations or drawings of vocabulary words that can be posted in the classroom.

Recognition of Vocabulary Discovery and Usage

Students may share experiences in which they hear or use vocabulary outside of the classroom. Whether it is another teacher who said a vocabulary word, a television show or movie that incorporated vocabulary, or the student him- or herself who embedded a word in an assignment, it is important to recognize the use of academic vocabulary.

For students who repeatedly find or use vocabulary outside of the classroom, recognize their achievements with points toward a class competition goal or other acknowledgment of their efforts.

Daily Discussion and Review

Teachers may model vocabulary usage by including vocabulary words in their instructions or conversations with students. The more frequently the teacher uses a word, the easier it becomes for students to understand the word's meaning and how to use it properly.

Teachers can have "Words of the Day" that students must incorporate into classroom activities. Whoever correctly uses the words the most might receive a reward.

During debates, discussions, or other times when students are conversing, teachers should require them to use the learned vocabulary words. A set minimum number of words can be established, and students who go above the minimum should be recognized for their efforts.

When there is extra time, the class may review vocabulary words. This activity can be teacher-directed or student-led. If student-directed, begin with one student saying a vocabulary word, then select another student to define it. Once he or she defines the word, that student can then select a new word that another student defines, and so on.

Categorizing Vocabulary

When reviewing vocabulary words, students may categorize words as they relate to current events. By creating meaningful associations with each word, students more easily recall word meaning.

Students can also learn vocabulary by creating more general categories. These categories can be as simple as "praise" or "insult" or as elaborate as students want (travel words, food words, etc.). When students learn new words, they can place them in the categories they have created.

Writing with Vocabulary

Students should incorporate at least one or two vocabulary words into their daily writing prompts, reading journals, or other forms of informal communication.

Whenever students write formally for class (essays, stories, etc.), teachers may require a set minimum number of vocabulary words to be used, check to make sure that the usage is appropriate, and provide feedback.

Teachers may also:

- Have students create puns that incorporate vocabulary. Example: "I have no fear," Tom said **impassively**.
- Ask students to write poems for individual words. Example: "There once was a word called ____."
- Suggest that students write an acrostic poem that defines a word from the Unit.
- Ask students to write a "Where I'm From" poem that explains both a word's origins and use, and that also traces its genealogy to related words.
- Have students write myths about the origins of individual words or groups of words.

Vocabulary Projects

Students may create advertisements for a word to "sell" its uses. Example: "Race to your local dictionary and pick up the word _____. Whether frustrated with your social life or unhappy with a school assignment, this word can be used in a variety of ways...." Alternatively, teachers may have students sell a product, but have them use as many vocabulary words as possible to describe the item's attributes.

Students often learn words best when setting them to music. Students may write lyrics incorporating all (or most) of a Unit's vocabulary words/definitions and then perform or record their finished products.

Vocabulary Games

Groups of students can act in skits or pantomimes that demonstrate a word's meaning; the rest of the class must guess the word being enacted.

Student groups may tell stories using vocabulary words. Groups should be created according to the ability and level of students.

Alternative Assessment

The following types of assessment may be used in addition to or in lieu of the objective-scoring materials provided in VOCABULARY WORKSHOP, Levels D–H.

- Teachers may have students write a story or essay incorporating vocabulary words (word list provided by the teacher).
- Teachers can write a series of true/false statements, each concerning a vocabulary word, and then have students decide whether the statements are true or false based on their understanding of the words.
- Students can use vocabulary words in conversations throughout the week. Students may either write down their statements or collect signatures from peers or adults who heard the student using each word. Students turn in their sheets at the end of the week for an assessment grade.
- Teachers should consider using a suggestion from "Writing with Vocabulary" or "Vocabulary Projects" as a final assessment.

ACADEMIC VOCABULARY AND READING COMPREHENSION

by Vicki A. Jacobs
Senior Series Consultant

As students advance into the high-school grades and reading becomes more and more a matter of comprehending the concepts that represent relationships among facts and information, learning the academic vocabulary that represents those concepts becomes more critical to comprehension.

For example, to understand the vocabulary of literature—plot, characterization, imagery, theme—students must read to understand more than a narrative's simple sequence of events. They need to apply their understanding of the concepts that such vocabulary words represent. They need to know how to inquire about why an author chooses particular events and how an author uses characterization, imagery, and plot to develop a thematic statement.

Similarly, comprehension of content-area text requires more than the location of specific information; it also requires an understanding of the concepts that represent relationships among facts. Successful readers make conceptual connections among facts by activating and organizing relevant background knowledge and experience that they have gained from real-word experience and previous reading (the "given") and then use this foundation as the context for the "new" information and concepts that the text offers.

Comprehension then becomes a complex matter of confirming the relationship between the "given" and "new" and of resolving the differences. Successful readers skillfully identify the relationships among facts and information, analyze and synthesize often conflicting facts and points of view, and test the validity of what they have comprehended and thus learned.

To comprehend increasingly sophisticated content-specific texts, high-school students need to be able to draw upon their knowledge of three kinds of vocabulary.

The first is the language of their everyday experience, often called the "given" of what students bring to a text. The second is the academic language that content areas share (e.g., argument, persuasion, analysis, synthesis, comparison, and contrast). The third kind of vocabulary includes the specialized meanings that content areas assign to more general academic language (e.g., *conflict* and *resolution* represent different concepts in the study of literature and in the study of history), and it also includes discipline-specific concepts (e.g., *allegory, mitosis, sine, colonialism*).

Vocabulary also plays an integral role in the cognitive processes that are characteristic of inquiry-based learning and reading comprehension. Such processes involve three instructional stages: preparation, strategic guidance, and consolidation of learning, as described on the following page.

Stage I:

Preparation for Learning/Reading

Teachers:

- provide the means by which students can activate, extend, and organize their background knowledge and experiences that will be relevant to learning new concepts and the vocabulary that represents those concepts; and
- explain how students' background knowledge and experience will be relevant to understanding a lesson or a text's central concepts and vocabulary.

Stage II:

Strategic Guidance of Learning/Reading

Teachers facilitate students' inquiry/comprehension by providing the means by which students can:

- investigate, enrich, deepen, and revise their understanding of a reading's central concepts and key vocabulary; and
- practice new skills, including vocabulary.

Stage III:

Consolidation of Learning/Reading

Teachers provide students with the means to consolidate their learning and comprehension by:

- providing the means by which they can test the validity of their understanding (comprehension) of new concepts and vocabulary; and
- preparing students to demonstrate their understanding (comprehension) through the application of new concepts and vocabulary to novel contexts.

Above all, the comprehension and vocabulary strategies teachers use must explicitly support their teaching goals, which can span from memorization of facts and information to deep understanding and skilled application of abstract concepts. Strategies for memorizing vocabulary or reading-for-facts are different from strategies designed to support students' deep comprehension and understanding.

Further, students need to understand how to use various strategies as ways to achieve particular learning goals—as well as *why* such strategies are important. One of the biggest differences between successful and struggling adolescent readers is their different approaches to learning. Skilled students monitor their progress in their attempts to achieve learning goals, recognize when learning or comprehension has broken down, and choose the most expedient strategy to correct their course. To become skilled in this way, students need not only instruction in reading strategies but also in direct instruction about how to employ those strategies as well as why and when those strategies are most useful. In other words, students need to be taught explicitly how to learn independently if they are to become ongoing students of an academic discipline and to graduate from high school—or, to adopt the language of the Common Core State Standards, to be "college and career ready."

CLASSIC LITERATURE TO USE WITH THE PROGRAM

Levels D and E

Louisa May Alcott *Little Women*

Maya Angelou *I Know Why the Caged Bird Sings*

Ray Bradbury *Fahrenheit 451*

Charlotte Brontë *Jane Eyre*

Emily Brontë *Wuthering Heights*

Pearl S. Buck *The Good Earth*

Lewis Carroll *Alice's Adventures in Wonderland*

Willa Cather *My Antonia*

Sandra Cisneros *The House on Mango Street*

Daniel Defoe *Robinson Crusoe*

Charles Dickens *A Tale of Two Cities*

Sir Arthur Conan Doyle *The Hound of the Baskervilles*

George Eliot *Silas Marner*

William Golding *Lord of the Flies*

Frank Herbert *Dune*

Harper Lee *To Kill a Mockingbird*

Carson McCullers *Member of the Wedding*

Nicholasa Mohr *El Bronx Remembered*

Walter Dean Myers *Fallen Angels*

George Orwell *Animal Farm*

Alan Paton *Cry, the Beloved Country*

John Steinbeck *The Pearl*

Level F

Sherwood Anderson *Winesburg, Ohio*

James Baldwin *Go Tell It on the Mountain*

Stephen Crane *The Red Badge of Courage*

Kate Chopin *The Awakening*

Ralph Ellison *Invisible Man*

Louise Erdrich *Love Medicine*

Jack Finney *Time and Again*

F. Scott Fitzgerald *The Great Gatsby*

Nathaniel Hawthorne *The Scarlet Letter*

Joseph Heller *Catch-22*

Ernest Hemingway *A Farewell to Arms*

Zora Neale Hurston *Their Eyes Were Watching God*

Henry James *Washington Square*

Maxine Hong Kingston *Woman Warrior*

N. Scott Momaday *The Way to Rainy Mountain*

Toni Morrison *Beloved*

John Steinbeck *The Grapes of Wrath*

Amy Tan *The Joy Luck Club*

Mark Twain *The Adventures of Huckleberry Finn*

Kurt Vonnegut, Jr. *Slaughterhouse Five*

Alice Walker *The Color Purple*

Edith Wharton *The House of Mirth* and *The Age of Innocence*

Richard Wright *Black Boy*

Levels G and H

Chinua Achebe *Things Fall Apart*

Margaret Atwood *The Handmaid's Tale*

Jane Austen *Pride and Prejudice*

Joseph Conrad *Lord Jim* and *Heart of Darkness*

Charles Dickens *David Copperfield*

Isak Dinesen *Out of Africa*

George Eliot *The Mill on the Floss*

Thomas Hardy *The Return of the Native*

Aldous Huxley *Brave New World*

James Joyce *A Portrait of the Artist as a Young Man*

Gabriel García Márquez *One Hundred Years of Solitude*

Mark Mathabane *Kaffir Boy*

V.S. Naipaul *A House for Mr. Biswas*

Mary Wollstonecraft Shelley *Frankenstein*

Muriel Spark *The Prime of Miss Jean Brodie*

Jonathan Swift *Gulliver's Travels*

Virginia Woolf *A Room of One's Own* and *To the Lighthouse*

To coordinate reading and vocabulary study, the following may prove helpful:

- Students may devote a notebook to vocabulary. As they encounter key words in their reading, they should head a page of the notebook with the word; copy the title of the work; and then indicate (a) the definition used in that sentence, (b) its part of speech, and (c) whether it is used in a literal or figurative sense.
- Students may then be instructed to check *Bartlett's Familiar Quotations* for other famous examples of the use of the key word in question. These quotations may be copied into the notebook and shared with others in the class.

Vocabulary in Context

VOCABULARY WORKSHOP uses excerpts from classic literature to show how a Unit's vocabulary words are used in context.

Level F Vocabulary in Context Literary Selections

Unit 1	Charles Dickens	*David Copperfield*
Unit 2	Herman Melville	*Moby-Dick*
Unit 3	Thomas Jefferson	*The Writings of Thomas Jefferson* and *Memoirs, Correspondence, and Miscellanies*
Unit 4	Nathaniel Hawthorne	*The Scarlet Letter*
Unit 5	James Fenimore Cooper	*The Spy*
Unit 6	Edgar Allan Poe	*The Works of Edgar Allan Poe, Vol. II*
Unit 7	Sinclair Lewis	*Main Street*
Unit 8	Henry James	*The Wings of the Dove*
Unit 9	Edith Wharton	*The House of Mirth*
Unit 10	Mark Twain	*Innocents Abroad*
Unit 11	F. Scott Fitzgerald	*The Beautiful and Damned*
Unit 12	Nathaniel Hawthorne	*The Marble Faun*
Unit 13	Margaret Fuller Ossoli	*The Memoirs of Margaret Fuller Ossoli, Volume I*
Unit 14	Charles Dickens	*Bleak House* and *Our Mutual Friend*
Unit 15	Washington Irving	*Tales of a Traveller*

Level G Vocabulary in Context Literary Selections

Unit 1	Charlotte Brontë	*The Professor* and *Shirley*
Unit 2	Theodore Dreiser	*Sister Carrie* and *Jennie Gerhardt*
Unit 3	Herman Melville	*Moby-Dick*
Unit 4	Thomas Hardy	*Jude the Obscure* and *Tess of the d'Urbervilles*
Unit 5	Charles Dickens	*David Copperfield*
Unit 6	Joseph Conrad	*Victory* and *Nostromo*
Unit 7	Henry James	*The Bostonians* and *Roderick Hudson*
Unit 8	William Makepeace Thackeray	*Vanity Fair* and *The History of Henry Esmond*

Unit 9	George Eliot	*The Mill on the Floss* and *Romola*
Unit 10	E.M. Forster	*Howards End* and *A Room with a View*
Unit 11	Anthony Trollope	*The Eustace Diamonds* and *Barchester Towers*
Unit 12	James Fenimore Cooper	*The Last of the Mohicans* and *The Pioneers*
Unit 13	Jane Austen	*Emma, Sense and Sensibility* and *Pride and Prejudice*
Unit 14	F. Scott Fitzgerald	*The Beautiful and Damned*
Unit 15	Edith Wharton	*The Custom of the Country* and *The House of Mirth*

Level H Vocabulary in Context Literary Selections

Unit 1	Charlotte Brontë	*Villette, Shirley* and *Jane Eyre*
Unit 2	Edgar Allan Poe	*Narrative of Arthur Gordon Pym*, "Landor's Cottage," "King Pest," "MS. Found in a Bottle" and "The Spectacles"
Unit 3	Charles Dickens	*Life and Adventures of Martin Chuzzlewit, Oliver Twist, Nicholas Nickleby* and *The Mystery of Edwin Drood*
Unit 4	Henry Fielding	*The History of Tom Jones, Amelia* and *Joseph Andrews*
Unit 5	George Meredith	*The Egoist, Diana of the Crossways, The Amazing Marriage* and *The Ordeal of Richard Feverel*
Unit 6	Henry David Thoreau	*Walden* and *A Week on the Concord and Merrimack Rivers*
Unit 7	Somerset Maugham	*Of Human Bondage, The Explorer* and *The Moon and Sixpence*
Unit 8	Sir Arthur Conan Doyle	*The Return of Sherlock Holmes, The Lost World, The Adventures of Sherlock Holmes* and *The Valley of Fear*
Unit 9	Wilkie Collins	*The Woman in White, Man and Wife, Heart and Science, The Moonstone* and *Basil*
Unit 10	H.L. Mencken	*The American Language, In Defense of Women* and *A Book of Prefaces*
Unit 11	Mark Twain	*The Adventures of Tom Sawyer, The Gilded Age* and *Life on the Mississippi*
Unit 12	Mary W. Shelley	*Frankenstein* and *The Last Man*
Unit 13	Nathaniel Hawthorne	*The Scarlet Letter* and *The House of the Seven Gables*
Unit 14	Jonathan Swift	*Gulliver's Travels* and "The Battle of the Books"
Unit 15	Anthony Trollope	*The American Senator, Miss Mackenzie* and *Sir Harry Hotspur of Humblethwaite*

VOCABULARY STRATEGY: Word Structure

One important way students build vocabulary is to learn the meaning of word parts that make up many English words. These word parts consist of **prefixes**, **suffixes**, and **roots**, or **bases**. A useful strategy for determining the meaning of an unknown word is to "take apart" the word and think about the parts.

Following is a list of common prefixes. Knowing the meaning of a prefix can help students determine the meaning of a word in which the prefix appears.

Prefix	Meaning	Sample Words
bi-	two	bicycle
com-, con-	together, with	compatriot, contact
de-, dis-	lower, opposite	devalue, disloyal
fore-, pre-	before, ahead of time	forewarn, preplan
il-, im-, in-, ir, non-, un-	not	illegal, impossible, inactive, irregular, nonsense, unable
in-, im-	in, into	inhale, import
mid-	middle	midway
mis-	wrongly, badly	mistake, misbehave
re-	again, back	redo, repay
sub-	under, less than	submarine, subzero
super-	above, greater than	superimpose, superstar
tri-	three	triangle

Following is a list of common suffixes. Knowing the meaning and grammatical function of a suffix can help students determine the meaning of a word.

Noun Suffix	Meaning	Sample Nouns
-acy, -ance, -ence, -hood, -ity, -ment, -ness, -ship	state, quality, or condition of, act or process of	adequacy, attendance, persistence, neighborhood, activity, judgment, brightness, friendship
-ant, -eer, -ent, -er, -ian, -ier, -ist, -or	one who does or makes something	contestant, auctioneer, resident, banker, comedian, financier, dentist, doctor
-ation, -ition, -ion	act or result of	organization, imposition, election

Verb Suffix	Meaning	Sample Verbs
-ate	to become, produce, or treat	validate, salivate, chlorinate
-en	to make, cause to be	weaken
-fy, -ify, -ize	to cause, make	liquefy, glorify, legalize

Adjective Suffix	Meaning	Sample Adjectives
-able, -ible	able, capable of	believable, incredible
-al, -ic,	relating to, characteristic of	natural, romantic
-ful, -ive, -ous	full of, given to, marked by	beautiful, protective, poisonous
-ish, -like	like, resembling	foolish, childlike
-less	lacking, without	careless

A base or root is the main part of a word to which prefixes and suffixes may be added. Many roots come to English from Latin. Knowing Greek and Latin roots can help students determine the meaning of a word.

In the Building with Classical Roots sections of this book students will learn more about some of these Latin and Greek roots and about the English words that derive from them.

Greek Root	Meaning	Sample Words
-astr-, -aster-, -astro-	star	astral, asteroid, astronaut
-auto-	self	autograph
-bio-	life	biography
-chron-, chrono-	time	chronic, chronological
-cosm-, -cosmo-	universe, order	microcosm, cosmopolitan
-cryph-, -crypt-	hidden, secret	apocryphal, cryptographer
-dem-, -demo-	people	epidemic, democracy
-dia-	through, across, between	diameter
-dog-, -dox-	opinion, teaching	dogmatic, orthodox
-gen-	race, kind, origin, birth	generation
-gnos-	know	diagnostic
-graph-, -graphy-, -gram-	write	graphite, autobiography, telegram
-log-, -logue-	speech, word, reasoning	logic, dialogue
-lys-	break down	analysis
-metr-, -meter-	measure	metric, kilometer
-micro-	small	microchip
-morph-	form, shape	amorphous
-naut-	sailor	nautical
-phon-, -phone-, -phono-	sound, voice	phonics, telephone, phonograph

-pol-, -polis-	city, state	police, metropolis
-scop-, -scope-	watch, look at	microscopic, telescope
-tele-	far off, distant	television
-the-	put or place	parentheses

Latin Root	**Meaning**	**Sample Words**
-cap-, -capt-, -cept-, -cip-	take	capitulate, captive, concept, recipient
-cede-, -ceed-, -ceas-, -cess-	happen, yield, go	precede, proceed, decease, cessation
-cred-	believe	incredible
-dic-, -dict-	speak, say, tell	indicate, diction
-duc-, -duct-, -duit-	lead, conduct, draw	educate, conduct, conduit
-fac-, -fact-, -fect-, -fic-, -fy-	make	faculty, artifact, defect, beneficial, clarify
-ject-	throw	eject
-mis-, -miss-, -mit-, -mitt-	send	promise, missile, transmit, intermittent
-note-, -not-	know, recognize	denote, notion
-pel-, -puls-	drive	expel, compulsive
-pend-, -pens-	hang, weight, set aside	pendulum, pension
-pon-, -pos-	put, place	component, position
-port-	carry	portable
-rupt-	break	bankrupt
-scrib-, -scribe-, -script-	write	scribble, describe, inscription
-spec-, -spic-	look, see	spectator, conspicuous
-tac-, -tag-, -tang-, -teg-	touch	contact, contagious, tangible, integral
-tain-, -ten-, -tin-	hold, keep	contain, tenure, retinue
-temp-	time	tempo
-ven-, -vent-	come	intervene, convention
-vers-, -vert-	turn	reverse, invert
-voc-, -vok-	call	vocal, invoke

DENOTATION, CONNOTATION, AND SHADES OF MEANING

The ***denotation*** of a word is its specific dictionary meaning. Here are a few examples:

Word	**Denotation**
winsome	charming
ostentatious	overly showy, pretentious
precept	rule

The ***connotation*** of a word is its **tone**—that is, the emotions or associations it normally arouses in people using, hearing, or reading it. Depending on what these feelings are, the connotation of a word may be *favorable* (*positive*) or *unfavorable* (*negative, pejorative*). A word that does not normally arouse strong feelings of any kind has a *neutral* connotation. Here are some examples of words with different connotations:

Word	**Connotation**
winsome	favorable
ostentatious	unfavorable
precept	neutral

Every Word Study section of VOCABULARY WORKSHOP has two pages of instruction on and practice with the denotation and connotation of words. The exercises in this section will prepare students to meet the Craft and Structure requirements of the Common Core State Standards.

FIGURATIVE LANGUAGE

After every three Units of VOCABULARY WORKSHOP, there is a Review and a Word Study section, for a total of five Word Study sections per book. Each Word Study section contains a two-page lesson on idioms, proverbs, or adages. These three types of figurative language, especially problematic for ELL students, are important in light of the Common Core State Standards, which require students in grades 9–12 to demonstrate an understanding of figurative language by interpreting figures of speech in context and analyzing their role in the text. The Common Core directive that students read texts (both literary and informational) of increasing complexity means that students are more likely to encounter figurative expressions in their reading. Furthermore, these three types of figurative language frequently appear in standardized test items.

- An **idiom** is an informal expression whose literal meaning does not help the reader or listener figure out what the expression means. English is particularly rich in idioms and idiomatic expressions, such as "raining cats and dogs," "the apple of my eye," or "a dark horse."
- An **adage** expresses a common experience, often in the form of a sentence, such as "Time flies when you're having fun."
- A **proverb** is a statement that provides a lesson or a moral, such as "A stitch in time saves nine" and "A rolling stone gathers no moss."

Teachers may note with students that every language has its own idioms, proverbs, and adages. Students may find or think of examples from other cultures, especially if another language is spoken at home. Understanding the meaning of common English idioms, adages, and proverbs will improve reading ability and enrich students' writing.

How to Use the Word Study Lessons

The first page of each lesson refers to one of the introductory Reading Passages in the three preceding Units. An idiom, adage, or proverb is embedded in the Passage, where it is used in context. Students next encounter the idiom (or adage or proverb) on the first page of the Word Study section. Following instruction and examples of these figures of speech, students are given ten sentences containing different idioms (or adages or proverbs) in context and are asked to match each with its definition. The second page is a **writing exercise** in which students are required to write original sentences using ten additional idioms (or adages or proverbs).

Enriching the Word Study Lessons

Teachers may suggest that students draw a cartoon that uses a proverb or an adage as a caption, or they might write brief narratives or fables with a proverb or adage as the moral. Standardized tests, such as the SAT, might use a proverb as a writing prompt; students are then asked to discuss the proverb, drawing from their personal experiences, observations, and reading. Students will practice writing such essays in the **Writing: Words in Action** activities during the course of the school year.

SADLIER

VOCABULARY WORKSHOP

Common Core Enriched Edition

Level G

Jerome Shostak

Senior Series Consultant

Vicki A. Jacobs, Ed.D.
Associate Director, Teacher Education Program
Lecturer on Education
Harvard Graduate School of Education
Cambridge, Massachusetts

Series Consultants

Louis P. De Angelo, Ed.D.
Associate Superintendent
Diocese of Wilmington
Wilmington, Delaware

John Heath, Ph.D.
Professor of Classics
Santa Clara University
Santa Clara, California

Sarah Ressler Wright, NBCT
English Department Chair
Rutherford B. Hayes High School
Delaware City Schools, Ohio

Carolyn E. Waters, JD, Ed.S.
ELA/Literacy 6–12 Supervisor
Cobb County School District
Marietta, Georgia

Sadlier

Reviewers

The publisher wishes to thank for their comments and suggestions the following teachers and administrators, who read portions of the series prior to publication.

Rivkie Eisen
English Teacher
Ateret Torah High School
Brooklyn, New York

Jennifer Etter
English Dept. Chair
Shorecrest High School
Shoreline, Washington

Eileen Ghastin
English Teacher
John F. Kennedy High School
Bronx, New York

Sheri Goldstein
English Dept. Chair
Ida Crown Jewish Academy
Chicago, Illinois

Claudia Lefkowitz
English Teacher
Central Florida Preparatory
Gotha, Florida

Scott Leventhal
English Teacher, Dept. Chair
Council Rock H. S. South
Holland, Pennsylvania

Jeanne Pellegrino
English Teacher, Dept. Chair
Plantation High School
Plantation, Florida

Jennifer Portilla
English Teacher
Pace Brantley School
Longwood, Florida

Kausam R. Salam, Ph.D.
English Teacher-Dual Credit
Cypress Falls High School
Houston, Texas

Linda Schwartz
English Dept. Chair
Seaford School District
Seaford, New York

Patricia Stack
English Teacher
South Park High School
South Park, Pennsylvania

Barbara Swander Miller
Language Arts Dept. Chair
Cowan Jr/Sr High School
Muncie, Indiana

Stephanie K. Turner
English and French Teacher
St. Ursula Academy
Cincinnati, Ohio

Robert Viarengo
English Dept. Chair
Palma School
Salinas, California

Cover: Concept/Art and Design: MK Advertising and William H. Sadlier, Inc.; Cover pencil: Shutterstock/VikaSuh.
Photo Credits: Interior: akg-images: 65, 21; IAM/World History Archive: 126 *bottom*; National Maritime Museum: 126 *bottom right*, 127. Alamy/Amoret Tanner: 55; Classic Image: 184 *top*; Corbis: 108 *inset*; Courtesy: CSU Archives/Everett Collection: 113; Danita Delimont/Claudia Adams: 146 *bottom right*; David Levenson: 169; Dmitry Rukhlenko-Travel Photos: 147 *bottom right*; Felix Stensson: 75; Judith Collins: 131; Karen Debler: 41; Keystone Pictures USA: 89 *top right*; Lebrecht Music and Arts Photo Library: 145; North Wind Picture Archives: 189; Pictorial Press Ltd: 89 *top left*, 193; The Print Collector: 117. AP Images/Louis Lanzano: 71. Art Resource, NY/2009 Museum Associates/LACMA: 147 *bottom left*; DeA Picture Library: 146 *bottom left*; The Art Archive/Society of the Friends of Music Vienna/Collection Dagli Orti: 37; The Kobal Collection/Working Title: 173; The Metropolitan Museum of Art: 61; Werner Forman: 27. Blend/LatinStock Collection: 108 *bottom left*. Corbis: 33 *top center*, 99 *bottom center*; Ali Hashisho/X01161/Reuters: 51 *inset*; Bettmann: 141; Classic Stock/H. Armstrong Roberts: 151; David J. & Janice L. Frent Collection: 32, 33 *top left*; J.S. Johnston: 22; Jack Kurtz/ZUMA Press: 70; Michael Ochs Archives: 88; Mike Segar/Reuters: 23 *top right*; Richard Berenholtz: 50 *background*; Science Faction/Michael Rosenfeld: 174 *bottom left*; Sheng Hong/Xinhua Press: 50 *inset*; Underwood & Underwood: 164; Xinhua Press/Xinhua/Yuri Gripas: 98 *bottom left*. Digitalvision: 108 *background*. Estate of Roy Lichtenstein/Private Collection: 60. Everett Collection: 31, 59, 69; Almi Pictures: 97; Cinecom International: 135; Focus features: 107. Georgia Institute of Technology, College of Computing: 175 *bottom left*. Getty Images/AFP/Don Emmert: 175 *top left*; Fotosearch/Stringer: 33; New York Daily News/Joe Petrella: 165 *bottom left*; Time & Life Pictures: 79, 137 *bottom*; Topical Press Agency/Stringer: 103. The Granger Collection, NYC: 13 *center*, 155, 183. Lebrecht Authors: 93. Library of Congress Prints & Photographs Division, Washington, DC: 184 *bottom*. Mary Evans Picture Library: 13. NASA: 137 *top*. National Portrait Gallery/Smithsonian Institution: 99 *bottom left*. National Portrait Gallery, London: 185 *top*. Photo Researchers, Inc./Science Source: 179. The New York Public Library, Astor, Lenox and Tilden Foundations Picture Collection: 23 *top insets*. Photodisc: 98, 99 *frame*, 126 *bottom right*, 127; Punchstock: 98. Shutterstock: Angelina Dimitrova: 88 *background*; ARENA Creative: 60 *background*; argus: 174; boumen&japet: 13 *frame*; Daboost: 108 *center*; Johann Helgason: 33 *top border*; Michaela Stejskalova: 12 *background*; Myotis: 50 *frame*, 51 *frame*; Neo Edmund: 146; Taiga: 70; Thomas Bethge: 164; VikaSuh: 1. US Patent Office: 165 *bottom right*. WHS: 23 *top*. Wikipedia Commons: 17.

Illustration Credits: Tim Haggerty: 46, 84, 122, 160, 198.

Address inquiries to Permissions Department,
William H. Sadlier, Inc.,
9 Pine Street, New York, New York 10005-4700.

 is a registered trademark of William H. Sadlier, Inc.

Printed in the United States of America
ISBN: 978-0-8215-8012-7
3456789 RRDH 15 14 13

For additional online resources, go to vocabularyworkshop.com and enter the Student Access Code: VW12SGCA47NP

ENRICHED EDITION: New Features

For more than five decades, VOCABULARY WORKSHOP has proven to be a highly successful tool for guiding systematic vocabulary growth and developing vocabulary skills. It has also been shown to help students prepare for standardized tests.

New in this edition are the **Reading Passages, Writing, Vocabulary in Context,** and **Word Study** activities. Nonfiction, high-interest passages use 15 or more of the Unit vocabulary words in context. Two writing prompts require a response to the reading and provide practice in writing for standardized tests. New Vocabulary in Context activities present words from the Unit as they are used in classic works of literature. After every three units, Word Study activities, developed in conjunction with Common Core State Standards requirements, provide practice with idioms, adages, and proverbs, as well as denotation and connotation and classical roots.

Look for the new **QR** (Quick Response) codes on the **Reading Passage** and **Vocabulary in Context** pages. The code can be read with a smartphone camera. To read the QR code, download any free QR code application to a smartphone. Snap the code with a smartphone camera to go directly to iWords for the Unit or an interactive quiz. With iWords you can listen to one word at a time or download all of the words in a Unit to listen to them at your convenience.

The new structure of VOCABULARY WORKSHOP is made up of 15 Units. Each Unit consists of the following sections: a **Reading Passage, Definitions, Choosing the Right Word, Synonyms and Antonyms, Completing the Sentence, Writing,** and **Vocabulary in Context**. Together, these exercises provide multiple and varied exposures to the taught words—an approach consistent with and supportive of research-based findings in vocabulary instruction.

Five **Reviews** cover Vocabulary for Comprehension and Two-Word Completions. Vocabulary for Comprehension is modeled on the reading sections of standardized tests, and as in those tests, it presents reading comprehension questions, including specific vocabulary-related ones, that are based on a reading passage.

A **Final Mastery Test** assesses a selection of words from the year with activities on Synonyms, Antonyms, Analogies, Two-Word Completions, Supplying Words in Context, Word Associations, and Choosing the Right Meaning.

In each level of VOCABULARY WORKSHOP, 300 key words are taught. The words have been selected according to the following criteria: currency and general usefulness; frequency of appearance on recognized vocabulary lists; applicability to, and appearance on, standardized tests; and current grade-level research.

ONLINE COMPONENTS

vocabularyworkshop.com

At **vocabularyworkshop.com** you will find iWords, an audio program that provides pronunciations, definitions, and examples of usage for all of the key words presented in this level of VOCABULARY WORKSHOP. You can listen to one word at a time or, if you wish, download to an MP3 player all of the words of any given Unit. You will then be able to listen to the audio program for that Unit at your convenience.

At **vocabularyworkshop.com** you will also find **interactive vocabulary quizzes, flashcards, games and puzzles** that will help reinforce and enrich your understanding of the key words in this level of VOCABULARY WORKSHOP.

CONTENTS

VOCABULARY STRATEGY: Using Context

The **context** of a word is the printed text of which that word is part. By studying the word's context, we may find **clues** to its meaning. We might find a clue in the immediate or adjoining sentence or phrase in which the word appears; in the topic or subject matter of the passage; or in the physical features—such as photographs, illustrations, charts, graphs, captions and headings—of a page itself.

The **Vocabulary in Context**, **Vocabulary for Comprehension**, and **Choosing the Right Meaning** exercises that appear in the Units, the Reviews, and Final Mastery Test provide practice in using context to decode unfamiliar words.

Three types of context clues appear in the exercises in this book.

A ***restatement clue*** consists of a *synonym* for or a *definition* of the missing word. For example:

I peered through the gloomy hall and made out an equally ______________ room at the end of it.

a. fragrant **b.** murky **c.** aesthetic **d.** comfortable

In this sentence, *gloomy* is a synonym of the missing word, *murky*, and acts as a restatement clue for it.

A ***contrast clue*** consists of an *antonym* for or a phrase that means the opposite of the missing word. For example:

While Joanie populates her novels with cheerful people, Seamus's stories center on (**saturnine, defunct**) characters.

In this sentence, *cheerful* is an antonym of the missing word, *saturnine*. This fact is confirmed by the presence of the word *While*, which indicates that the answer must be the opposite of *cheerful*.

An ***inference clue*** implies but does not directly state the meaning of the missing word or words. For example:

Because Lucius's work was always ______________ and never had errors, the teacher gave his essays only a ______________ glance before moving onto more time-consuming papers handed in by his classmates.

a. impeccable . . . perfunctory
b. picayune . . . lackadaisical
c. pusillanimous . . . sylvan
d. vituperative . . . sumptuous

There are a few inference clues in this sentence. The phrase *never had errors* indicates that Lucius's work was flawless, or *impeccable*. The word *glance* suggests that the attention the teacher gave the paper was *perfunctory*. These words are inference clues because they suggest or imply, but do not directly state, the missing words.

VOCABULARY STRATEGY: Word Structure

Prefixes, **suffixes**, and **roots**, or **bases**, are word parts. One strategy for determining an unknown word's meaning is to "take apart" the word and think about the parts. Study the prefixes and suffixes below to help you find out the meanings of words in which they appear

Prefix	Meaning	Sample Words
com-, con-	together, with	compatriot, contact
de-, dis-	lower, opposite	devalue, disloyal
il-, im-, in-, ir, non-, un-	not	illegal, impossible, inactive, irregular, nonsense, unable
super-	above, greater than	superimpose, superstar

Noun Suffix	Meaning	Sample Nouns
-acy, -ance, -ence, -hood, -ity, -ment, -ness, -ship	state, quality, or condition of, act or process of	adequacy, attendance, persistence, neighborhood, activity, judgment, brightness, friendship
-ant, -eer, -ent, -er, -ian, -ier, -ist, -or	one who does or makes something	contestant, auctioneer, resident, banker, comedian, financier, dentist, doctor
-ation, -ition, -ion	act or result of	organization, imposition, election

Verb Suffix	Meaning	Sample Verbs
-ate	to become, produce, or treat	validate, salivate, chlorinate
-fy, -ify, -ize	to cause, make	liquefy, glorify, legalize

Adjective Suffix	Meaning	Sample Adjectives
-al, -ic,	relating to, characteristic of	natural, romantic
-ful, -ive, -ous	full of, given to, marked by	beautiful, protective, poisonous

A **base** or **root** is the main part of a word to which prefixes and suffixes may be added. On the Classical Roots page of the Word Study section, you will learn more about Latin and Greek roots and the English words that derive from them. The following lists may help you figure out the meaning of new or unfamiliar words.

Greek Root	Meaning	Sample Words
-cryph-, -crypt-	hidden, secret	apocryphal, cryptographer
-dem-, -demo-	people	epidemic, democracy
-gen-	race, kind, origin, birth	generation
-gnos-	know	diagnostic
-lys-	break down	analysis

Latin Root	Meaning	Sample Words
-cap-, -capt-, -cept-, -cip-	take	capitulate, captive, concept, recipient
-cede-, -ceed-, -ceas- -cess-	happen, yield, go	precede, proceed, decease, cessation
-fac-, -fact-, -fect-, -fic-, -fy-	make	faculty, artifact, defect, beneficial, clarify
-tac-, -tag-, -tang-, -teg-	touch	contact, contagious, tangible, integral
-tain-, -ten-, -tin-	hold, keep	contain, tenure, retinue

For more prefixes, suffixes, and roots, visit vocabularyworkshop.com.

VOCABULARY AND READING

Word knowledge is essential to reading comprehension. Your knowledge of word meanings and ability to think carefully about what you read will help you succeed in school and on standardized tests, including the SAT, the ACT, and the PSAT.

New **Reading Passages** provide extra practice with vocabulary words. Vocabulary words are boldfaced to draw students' attention to their uses and contexts. Context clues embedded in the passages encourage students to figure out the meanings of words before they read the definitions provided on the pages directly following the passages.

Students read excerpts from classic literature in the **Vocabulary in Context** exercises. Each excerpt includes one of the Unit vocabulary words as it is used in the original work. Students can use what they learn about the word from its use in context to answer questions on the definition.

The **Vocabulary for Comprehension** exercises in each review consist of a nonfiction reading passage followed by comprehension questions. The passages and questions are similar to those that you are likely to find on standardized tests.

Kinds of Questions

Main Idea Questions generally ask what the passage as a whole is about. Often, but not always, the main idea is stated in the first paragraph of the passage. You may also be asked the main idea of a specific paragraph. Questions about the main idea may begin like this:

- The primary or main purpose of the passage is. . .
- The passage is best described as. . .
- The title that best describes the content of the passage is. . .

Detail Questions focus on important information that is explicitly stated in the passage. Often, however, the correct answer choices do not use the exact language of the passage. They are instead restatements, or paraphrases, of the text.

Vocabulary-in-Context Questions check your ability to use context to identify a word's meaning. Use line references to see how and in what context the word is used. For example:

- **Badinage** (line 3) is best defined as. . .
- The meaning of **luminous** (line 15) is. . .

Use context to check your answer choices, particularly when the vocabulary word has more than one meaning. Among the choices may be two (or more) correct meanings of the word in question. Choose the meaning that best fits the context.

Inference Questions ask you to make inferences or draw conclusions from the passage. These questions often begin like this:

- It can be inferred from the passage that. . .
- The author implies that. . .
- Evidently the author feels that. . .

The inferences you make and the conclusions you draw must be based on the information in the passage. Your own knowledge and reasoning come into play in understanding what is implied and in reaching conclusions that are logical.

Questions About Tone show your understanding of the author's attitude toward the subject of the passage. Words that describe tone, or attitude, are "feeling" words, such as *indifferent*, *ambivalent*, *scornful*, *astonished*, *respectful*. These are typical questions:

- The author's attitude toward . . . is best described as. . .
- Which word best describes the author's tone?

To determine the tone, pay attention to the author's word choice. The author's attitude may be positive (respectful), negative (scornful), or neutral (ambivalent).

Questions About Author's Technique focus on the way a text is organized and the language the author uses. These questions ask you to think about structure and function. For example:

- The final paragraph serves to. . .
- The author cites . . . in order to . . . .

To answer the questions, you must demonstrate an understanding of the way the author presents information and develops ideas.

Strategies

Here are some general strategies to help you as you read each passage and answer the questions.

- Read the introduction first. The introduction will provide a focus for the selection.

- Be an active reader. As you read, ask yourself questions about the passage—for example: What is this paragraph about? What does the writer mean here? Why does the writer include this information?

- Refer to the passage when you answer the questions. In general, the order of the questions mirrors the organization of the passage, and many of the questions include paragraph or line references. It is often helpful to go back and reread before choosing an answer.

- Read carefully, and be sure to base your answer choices on the passage. There are answer choices that make sense but are not based on the information in the passage. These are true statements, but they are incorrect answers. The correct answers are either restatements of ideas in the text or inferences that can be drawn from the text.

- Consider each exercise a learning experience. Keep in mind that your ability to answer the questions correctly shows as much about your understanding of the questions as about your understanding of the passage.

WORKING WITH ANALOGIES

A verbal analogy expresses a relationship or comparison between sets of words. Normally, an analogy contains two pairs of words linked by a word or symbol that stands for an equal (=) sign. A complete analogy compares the two pairs of words and makes a statement about them. It asserts that the relationship between the first—or key—pair of words is the same as the relationship between the second pair.

In the **Analogies** exercises in the Final Mastery Test, you will be asked to complete analogies—that is, to choose the pair of words that best matches or parallels the relationship of the key, or given, pair of words. Here are two examples:

1. maple is to **tree** as
- **a.** acorn is to oak
- **b.** hen is to rooster
- **c.** rose is to flower
- **d.** shrub is to lilac

2. joyful is to **gloomy** as
- **a.** cheerful is to happy
- **b.** strong is to weak
- **c.** quick is to famous
- **d.** hungry is to starving

In order to find the correct answer to exercise 1, you must first determine the relationship between the two key words, **maple** and **tree**. In this case, that relationship might be expressed as "a maple is a kind (or type) of tree." The next step is to select from choices a, b, c, and d the pair of words that best reflects the same relationship. The correct answer is (c); it is the only pair whose relationship parallels the one in the key words: A rose is a kind (or type) of flower, just as a maple is a kind (or type) of tree. The other choices do not express the same relationship.

In exercise 2, the relationship between the key words can be expressed as "joyful means the opposite of gloomy." Which of the choices best represents the same relationship? The answer is (b): "strong means the opposite of weak."

Here are examples of some other common analogy relationships:

Analogy	Key Relationship
big is to **large** as **little** is to **small**	**Big** means the same thing as **large**, just as **little** means the same thing as **small**.
brave is to **favorable** as **cowardly** is to **unfavorable**	The tone of **brave** is **favorable**, just as the tone of **cowardly** is **unfavorable**.
busybody is to **nosy** as **klutz** is to **clumsy**	A **busybody** is by definition someone who is **nosy**, just as a **klutz** is by definition someone who is **clumsy**.
cowardly is to **courage** as **awkward** is to **grace**	Someone who is **cowardly** lacks **courage**, just as someone who is **awkward** lacks **grace**.
visible is to **see** as **audible** is to **hear**	If something is **visible**, you can by definition **see** it, just as if something is **audible**, you can by definition **hear** it.
liar is to **truthful** as **bigot** is to **fair-minded**	A **liar** is by definition not likely to be **truthful**, just as a **bigot** is by definition not likely to be **fair-minded**.
eyes are to **see** as **ears** are to **hear**	You use your **eyes** to **see** with, just as you use your **ears** to **hear** with.

There are many different kinds of relationships represented in the analogy questions you will find in the Final Mastery Test, but the key to solving any analogy is to find and express the relationship between the two key words.

UNIT 1

Note that not all of the 20 unit words are used in this passage. *Acquisitive*, *arrogate*, *congeal*, and *reconnaissance* are not included in the passage.

Read the following selection, taking note of the ***boldface*** *words and their contexts. These words are among those you will be studying in Unit 1. As you complete the exercises in this unit, it may help to refer to the way the words are used below.*

CCSS Vocabulary: 4; Reading (Informational Text): 4, 6. (See pp. T14–15.)

Across the Pond

<Letters>

January 27, 1891

My Dear Cora,

Accept my congratulations on the establishment of the National American Women's Suffrage Association. Am I too bold to presume this new unity in the American suffrage movement marks the end of the **invidious** divisions in your ranks? English appetite for American news is **insatiable** of late, with much talk of means by which we might **emulate** your recent achievements. Just yesterday, at a small gathering of friends of our League, I heard Mrs. Pankhurst break off into a rousing **encomium** on the entry of the state of Wyoming into your union. The opinion here is that with one state now granting universal suffrage, it's only a matter of time before the dam breaks.

In England we persuade ourselves to **eschew** hope for such grand achievements till the times make them more **tenable**. There's plenty of work to be done to prepare for the event. The Pankhursts have inspired many of us to push for the women's vote in local elections. This would be no small thing in itself, and should help our effort to reform the conservative spirit of our country. I fear the climate in America is more favorable to the endeavor, while opposition here remains **intransigent**. At tea not long ago, I heard one Mr. Evans produce the most **banal** argument against the women's vote you could imagine. I won't trouble you with details of his **carping** rhetoric, but note that he took pains to demonstrate that women are "unfit for the public duties of citizenship," and greatly feared the prospect that women's votes might "swamp the votes of men." Imagine my delight when, pressed by objections from several present, the good Mr. Evans grew suddenly **taciturn**, and at a loss for any other means of **temporizing**, complimented his hostess and bid us good day!

Charles and I often recall your kindness during our last visit, and look forward to seeing you again this summer.

Affectionately,

Millicent

March 20, 1891

Dearest Millie,

We have many like your Mr. Evans here, which puts our own work ahead of us. I can, however, **substantiate** your optimism where Wyoming is concerned. Other Western states and territories will surely follow suit, with energy already in the project in Idaho, Colorado, and elsewhere. Women's suffrage has firmer roots in the West, and we expect more progress there.

Germane to the topic, I had the privilege of meeting Jane Addams in Chicago, where she has founded the Hull House, devoted to the education of local women of the working class. Miss Addams is a remarkable woman, and strikes me as the very type to carry our movement forward. Initial renovations of the Hull Mansion were funded primarily through her own **largesse**, and she has become an advocate for local suffrage in Chicago and for other progressive causes.

Our new Association might show the extent to which the old arguments that divided us have passed into history, but new excuses for dissent emerge as old ones fade. The new tendency to portray women as "domestic" spirits, superior in moral virtue to men, strikes some of us as misguided. I'll not **belabor** the point here, hoping instead to present a **coherent** argument for you in person when you arrive in New York.

Until then, I keep you in my thoughts.
Your friend always,

Cora

American women fought for the right to vote in each state, until the Nineteenth Amendment was passed in 1920.

Definitions

Note the spelling, pronunciation, part(s) of speech, and definition(s) of each of the following words. Then write the word in the blank spaces in the illustrative sentence(s) following. Finally, study the lists of synonyms and antonyms.

1. acquisitive
(ə kwiz′ ə tiv)

(*adj.*) able to get and retain ideas or information; concerned with acquiring wealth or property

In an **acquisitive** society, there is a great deal of emphasis on buying and selling.

SYNONYMS: greedy, avaricious, retentive
ANTONYM: altruistic

2. arrogate
(a′ rə gāt)

(*v.*) to claim or take without right

The ambitious noblemen will put the young king under house arrest and **arrogate** royal privileges to themselves.

SYNONYMS: expropriate, commandeer
ANTONYMS: renounce, abdicate, abandon

3. banal
(bə nal′)

(*adj.*) hackneyed, trite, commonplace

The new play's **banal** dialogue made it seem more like a soap opera than a serious drama.

SYNONYMS: stale, insipid
ANTONYMS: fresh, original, new

4. belabor
(bi lā′ bər)

(*v.*) to work on excessively; to thrash soundly

His tendency to **belabor** the small points often made him miss the big picture.

SYNONYM: overwork

5. carping
(kär′ piŋ)

(*adj.*) tending to find fault, especially in a petty, nasty, or hairsplitting way; (*n.*) petty, nagging criticism

The trainee resigned after a week rather than put up with the **carping** complaints of the sales manager.

Most artists choose to ignore the **carping** of critics and simply go on with their work.

SYNONYMS: (*adj.*) nit-picking, caviling
ANTONYMS: (*adj.*) approving, uncritical

6. coherent
(kō hēr′ ənt)

(*adj.*) holding or sticking together; making a logical whole; comprehensible, meaningful

The physics teacher gave a surprisingly **coherent** description of quantum mechanics.

SYNONYMS: connected, unified, consistent, cohesive
ANTONYMS: muddled, chaotic, disjointed

CCSS Vocabulary: 4.c., 4.d. (See pp. T14–15.)

7. congeal (kən jēl′)

(*v.*) to change from liquid to solid, thicken; to make inflexible or rigid

If you do not wash your dishes right away, the food on them will ___**congeal**___.

SYNONYMS: harden, jell, solidify
ANTONYM: liquefy

8. emulate (em′ yə lāt)

(*v.*) to imitate with the intent of equaling or surpassing the model

Most beginning writers try to ___**emulate**___ a great writer and later develop their own individual styles.

SYNONYMS: copy, mimic, rival, match, measure up to

9. encomium (en kō′ mē əm)

(*n.*) a formal expression of praise, a lavish tribute

On Veterans Day, the President delivered a heartfelt ___**encomium**___ to those who died for their country.

SYNONYMS: panegyric, eulogy
ANTONYMS: condemnation, castigation, criticism

10. eschew (es chü′)

(*v.*) to avoid, shun, keep away from

The young athletes promised the coach that they would train vigorously and ___**eschew**___ bad habits.

SYNONYMS: abstain from, steer clear of, forgo
ANTONYMS: embrace, adopt

11. germane (jər mān′)

(*adj.*) relevant, appropriate, apropos, fitting

Bringing up examples from the past is not ___**germane**___ to the present discussion.

SYNONYM: pertinent
ANTONYMS: irrelevant, extraneous, inappropriate

12. insatiable (in sā′ shə bəl)

(*adj.*) so great or demanding as not to be satisfied

People with an ___**insatiable**___ appetite for gossip often do not have compelling stories of their own.

SYNONYMS: unquenchable, ravenous

13. intransigent (in tran′ sə jənt)

(*adj.*) refusing to compromise, irreconcilable

Little will get accomplished if the legislators of both parties maintain their ___**intransigent**___ attitudes.

SYNONYMS: uncompromising, unyielding, obdurate
ANTONYMS: lukewarm, halfhearted, yielding

14. invidious
(in vid′ ē əs)

(*adj.*) offensive, hateful; tending to cause bitterness and resentment

Bosses should avoid making **invidious** comparisons between their employees.

SYNONYMS: malicious, spiteful, prejudicial, pejorative
ANTONYMS: flattering, ameliorative

15. largesse
(lär jes′)

(*n.*) generosity in giving; lavish or bountiful contributions

The university was the fortunate beneficiary of the **largesse** of many of its graduates.

SYNONYMS: liberality, bounty
ANTONYMS: stinginess, miserliness, niggardliness

16. reconnaissance
(ri kän′ ə səns)

(*n.*) a survey made for military purposes; any kind of preliminary inspection or examination

The field officer required a thorough **reconnaissance** before ordering any troop movements.

SYNONYM: exploration

17. substantiate
(səb stan′ shē āt)

(*v.*) to establish by evidence, prove; to give concrete or substantial form to

The prospector was unable to **substantiate** his claim to the land where the gold was found.

SYNONYMS: confirm, validate, authenticate
ANTONYMS: refute, disprove, invalidate

18. taciturn
(tas′ ə tərn)

(*adj.*) habitually silent or quiet, inclined to talk very little

Woodrow Wilson has the reputation of having a dour and **taciturn** personality.

SYNONYMS: tight-lipped, uncommunicative, laconic
ANTONYMS: garrulous, loquacious, prolix, verbose

19. temporize
(tem′ pə rīz)

(*v.*) to stall or act evasively in order to gain time, avoid a confrontation, or postpone a decision; to compromise

For most of Shakespeare's great tragedy, the protagonist Hamlet chooses to **temporize** rather than act.

SYNONYMS: dillydally, procrastinate

20. tenable
(ten′ ə bəl)

(*adj.*) capable of being held or defended

The researchers put forth a **tenable** theory, but their conclusions would be reviewed carefully by others.

SYNONYMS: defensible, justifiable, maintainable
ANTONYMS: indefensible, unjustifiable

CCSS Vocabulary: 4.c. (See pp. T14–15.)

Choosing the Right Word

*Select the **boldface** word that better completes each sentence. You might refer to the selection on pages 12–13 to see how most of these words are used in context.*

1. Famous for his monosyllabic replies to questions and a somber and (**taciturn, germane**) nature, President Coolidge had the nickname "Silent Cal."

2. In that moment of grief, the conventional expressions of sympathy I had always considered (**tenable, banal**) were surprisingly comforting.

3. I am proud to have it said of me that I am stubborn and (**invidious, intransigent**) when genuine moral issues are involved.

4. Ethelred the Unready was so reluctant to face the Vikings who invaded his kingdom that in effect he (**arrogated, temporized**) himself off the throne.

5. What evidence can you offer to (**substantiate, eschew**) the assertion that capital punishment does not deter potential murderers?

Stamp issued in 1938 to honor Calvin Coolidge, the thirtieth President of the United States.

6. Suddenly a band of ruffians set upon us and began to (**congeal, belabor**) us with blows and curses.

7. Even a very imperfect human being may sometimes have virtues of mind or character that are worthy of (**carping, emulation**).

8. Aristotle had such a(n) (**tenable, acquisitive**) mind that his writings are a veritable gold mine of odd and interesting information.

9. The mood of easy cordiality with which we began the meeting soon (**congealed, temporized**) into icy politeness.

10. The poor woman was in such a state of shock after the accident that she couldn't give a (**coherent, taciturn**) account of what had happened.

11. The new batting champion in our softball league is a(n) (**insatiable, taciturn**) young man who prefers to let his bat do his talking for him.

12. The speech was so filled with (**encomiums, reconnaissance**) that I found it hard to believe that the subject of all this acclaim was plain old me.

13. "That word has such (**invidious, germane**) connotations in modern American parlance," I said, "that I would hesitate to use it, even in jest."

14. His figure bears witness to his (**acquisitive, insatiable**) appetite for the pleasures of the table.

15. In our attempt to improve the quality of life in America, we should not be too quick to (**eschew, cohere**) old ideas simply because they are old.

CCSS Vocabulary: 4.d. (See pp. T14–15.)

16. When the evidence of his misconduct became irrefutable, he saw that his position was not (**banal, tenable**) and resigned.

17. After the editor read the story, he returned it to the author with only a few (**carping, coherent**) criticisms of minor faults penciled in the margin.

18. The Constitution is uniquely designed to provide protection against those who might seek to (**substantiate, arrogate**) undue power to themselves.

19. Aerial (**reconnaissance, encomium**) of the enemy's positions provided the general with the information he needed to plan his attack.

20. After I mowed the lawn for an hour, he gave me a whole dollar with the air of a feudal lord bestowing (**largesse, intransigence**) on a grateful serf.

21. Your critical comments about my "lack of social background" may be true, but they are not (**coherent, germane**) to my qualifications for office.

22. Because this committee has (**belabored, emulated**) the issue of zoning laws for months, we will not invite public comments on it again in tonight's meeting.

23. The historian needed to scrutinize additional handwriting samples before he could (**eschew, substantiate**) the signature on the document.

24. Instead of opening voters' minds to new ideas, the debate actually (**arrogated, congealed**) their previous objections to the proposed legislation.

25. The (**carping, largesse**) of grateful patients made the clinic's expansion possible.

Synonyms

Choose the word from this unit that is the same or most nearly the same in meaning as the ***boldface*** *word or expression in the phrase. Write that word on the line. Use a dictionary if necessary.*

1. **harp on** the same point again and again ______ belabor
2. the **grasping** real estate developer ______ acquisitive
3. tried to **usurp** control of the finances ______ arrogate
4. tends to **hedge** when confronted by direct questions ______ temporize
5. the puppy's **voracious** hunger ______ insatiable
6. led the **scouting expedition** into the jungle ______ reconnaissance
7. was thanked for her **munificence** ______ largesse
8. could not **verify** the alibi ______ substantiate
9. received a well-deserved **commendation** ______ encomium
10. blood that does not **coagulate** ______ congeal

CCSS Vocabulary: 5. (See pp. T14–15.)

Antonyms

Choose the word from this unit that is most nearly opposite in meaning to the ***boldface*** *word or expression in the phrase. Write that word on the line. Use a dictionary if necessary.*

1. made a very **magnanimous** remark ______ invidious ______
2. an **unretentive** mind that cannot remember details ______ acquisitive ______
3. the **inspired** lyrics to that song ______ banal ______
4. mayor who tries to **relinquish** power ______ arrogate ______
5. butter that does not **soften** ______ congeal ______

Completing the Sentence

From the words in this unit, choose the one that best completes each of the following sentences. Write the word in the space provided.

1. Some of the episodes in the series were wonderfully fresh and original; others were just plain ______ banal ______.
2. I don't object to the inclusion of anecdotes in a serious lecture, but they should at the very least be ______ germane ______ to the subject.
3. There is nothing wrong with ______ emulating ______ the great singers of the past as long as you eventually develop a style that is all your own.
4. When the temperature outside dropped suddenly, the muddy water in the ditch ______ congealed ______ into a mass of icy sludge.
5. The purpose of military ______ reconnaissance ______ remains the same whether cavalry or helicopters are used: to learn as much as possible about the enemy.
6. In any crisis, the longer a person ______ temporizes ______, the greater the danger is likely to become.
7. In spite of his size, he was so ______ taciturn ______ that we tended to forget that he was even in the room.
8. The novel contains an interesting study of a miser's ______ insatiable ______ lust for gold and its evil effects on those around him.
9. By whose authority did you ______ arrogate ______ to yourself the right to decide how the club's money would be spent?
10. She received housing vouchers and food stamps as a result of the government's ______ largesse ______.

11. Students who seek high grades must learn to ___**eschew**___ the joys of that one-eyed monster, the television.

12. "There is no need for you to ___**belabor**___ the point," I replied, "when I already understand clearly what your criticism is."

13. As a result of recent research, earlier theories about the origin of the universe are no longer ___**tenable**___.

14. I doubt very much that he can ___**substantiate**___ his assertion that he won two gold medals in the 1956 Olympics.

15. In my opinion, there is absolutely no justification for making such ___**invidious**___ distinctions between the two types of product.

16. Your essay would be a great deal tighter and more ___**coherent**___ if you removed all the extraneous information it now contains.

17. How can we "meet them halfway" when they are so ___**intransigent**___ in their opposition to what we propose to do?

18. Even the most severe critics showered ___**encomiums**___ on the young writer for the remarkable narrative power of her first novel.

19. Never having any money in one's pockets can be a real trial for someone born with the ___**acquisitive**___ instincts of a pack rat.

20. Despite the ___**carping**___ and nit-picking of a few petty minds, I feel we have substantially improved our local school system of late.

Writing: Words in Action

Answers to both prompts will vary.

1. Look back at "Across the Pond" (pages 12–13). Suppose you are Cora's friend and a fellow member of the National American Women's Suffrage Association. You want to persuade men in the Western states that women should have the right to vote. Write a persuasive essay, using at least two details from the passage and three unit words to support your argument.

2. *"A long habit of not thinking a thing wrong gives it a superficial appearance of being right." —Thomas Paine*

Do you agree with Paine's statement? In a brief essay, explain your opinion with specific examples from your studies, reading (refer to pages 12–13), personal observations and experience, or current events. Write at least three paragraphs, and use three or more words from this unit.

Writing prompt #2 is modeled on that of standardized tests.

CCSS Vocabulary: 6; Writing: 2.d., 3.d. (See pp. T14–15.)

Vocabulary in Context: Informational Text for Unit 1 is available online at **vocabularyworkshop.com**.

The following excerpts are from Charlotte Brontë's novels The Professor *and* Shirley. *Some of the words you have studied in this unit appear in* **boldface** *type. Complete each statement below the excerpt by circling the letter of the correct answer.*

1. I had the conviction that he could only regard me as a poor-spirited slave, wherefore I now went about to shun his presence and **eschew** his conversation. *(The Professor)*

To **eschew** is to

a. repudiate **c.** ridicule
b. clarify **d.** avoid

2. In the course of my next lesson, I made a report of the other devoirs, dealing out praise and blame in very small retail parcels, according to my custom, for there was no use in blaming severely, and high **encomiums** were rarely merited. *(The Professor)*

Encomiums are

a. expectations **c.** successes
b. tributes **d.** condemnations

3. For a day or two Mr. Sympson continued as bland as oil, but also he seemed to sit on pins, and his gait, when he walked, **emulated** that of a hen treading a hot girdle. *(Shirley)*

Something that is **emulated** is

a. foreshadowed **c.** spurned
b. fabricated **d.** imitated

Charlotte Brontë published several novels under the male pen name Currer Bell.

4. "The faults of my manner are, I think, only negative. I am not proud. What has a man in my position to be proud of? I am only **taciturn,** phlegmatic, and joyless." *(Shirley)*

Someone who is **taciturn** is NOT

a. loquacious **c.** serious
b. quiet **d.** ironic

5. But what has been said in the last page or two is not **germane** to Caroline Helstone's feelings, or to the state of things between her and Robert Moore. *(Shirley)*

If something is **germane**, it is

a. sympathetic **c.** worthwhile
b. relevant **d.** reassuring

Snap the code, or go to **vocabularyworkshop.com**

UNIT 2

Note that not all of the 20 unit words are used in this passage. *Accost*, *brackish*, *halcyon*, and *talisman* are not included in the passage.

Read the following selection, taking note of the ***boldface*** *words and their contexts. These words are among those you will be studying in Unit 2. As you complete the exercises in this unit, it may help to refer to the way the words are used below.*

CCSS Vocabulary: 4; Reading (Informational Text): 4, 6. (See pp. T14–15.)

Constructing the New York City Subway

<Historical Nonfiction>

By 1900, nearly four million people lived in New York City, about five times as many as had lived in the same area fifty years earlier. The **celerity** of the population's increase was driven by a range of factors including economic growth, industrialization, and immigration. As an **overt** symptom of the prosperity of the city and the nation, rapid population growth was welcomed by many of the city's inhabitants. But the increase in population posed serious challenges. **Myopic** disregard for the supply of housing left many of the city's poorer inhabitants crammed into crowded tenements until construction began to keep pace. And the growing mass of people traveling throughout the city created unprecedented amounts of traffic in the streets.

Traffic congestion swelled beyond the bounds of **propriety**. Traffic accidents were all too common, as drivers of horse-drawn omnibuses, in a rush to pick up passengers and earn fares, saw fit to trample pedestrians along the way. Street traffic was a constant target of **animadversion** in the press. But it was also a cause of innovation. As the streams of pedestrians and horse-drawn carriages grew steadily through the nineteenth century, railroads were elevated above street level to avoid interference with the **maelstrom** of traffic on the streets. Steam-powered elevated railways were soon replaced by cleaner electric-powered elevated lines.

Plans for building a subway had been drawn as early as the 1860s, but the project was stalled for decades by **devious** local politics. Operators of surface railways and horse-drawn cars, who feared competition from the subway, cast the plan in a **pejorative** light, claiming

Elevated trains on Manhattan's Bowery, 1895

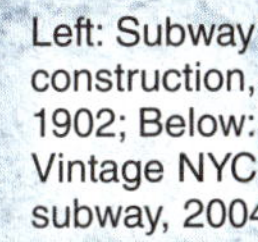

Left: Subway construction, 1902; Below: Vintage NYC subway, 2004

it was impractical and bound to fail. The **suppliant** protests of property owners who worried that prolonged subway construction would interfere with business helped strengthen opposition to the subway. **Avid** supporters of the subway plan, on the other hand, considered any opposition to be **sacrilege**. But adversity will not last forever. In the end, the clear benefits that the subway would bring to the city by increasing the speed of transit and by alleviating the traffic on the streets proved more compelling than the political **gambits** employed by opponents. After decades of false starts, **incendiary** rhetoric, and **histrionic** arguments on both sides, a contract for construction was signed on February 21, 1900. Construction began **summarily** in the following months.

Thousands of laborers worked on the project. Most of the tunnels were built using the "cut-and-cover" method: Workers dug trenches through the streets and covered them with wooden planks and bridges to allow traffic to pass overhead while work continued. Down in the trenches, workers laid the tracks, built the subway stations, and surrounded the subway with steel and concrete. Then they rebuilt the street above. The construction company that built the subway was also responsible for building the coal-fueled generators that would produce the subway's electricity.

The subway opened to the public on October 27, 1904. About 150,000 people stood in line to pay the five-cent fare for a rocky, **undulating** ride on what was then the fastest public transportation system in the world. Over the next few decades, the city's subway system was expanded and integrated with the elevated lines above ground. An impressive feat of engineering for its time, the New York City subway system remains one of the largest in the world to this day.

Snap the code, or go to **vocabularyworkshop.com**

Definitions

Note the spelling, pronunciation, part(s) of speech, and definition(s) of each of the following words. Then write the word in the blank spaces in the illustrative sentence(s) following. Finally, study the lists of synonyms and antonyms.

1. accost (ə käst′)
(*v.*) to approach and speak to first; to confront in a challenging or aggressive way

The nobleman was **accosted** by beggars on his way to the castle.

SYNONYMS: buttonhole, approach
ANTONYMS: avoid, shun

2. animadversion (an ə mad vər′ zhən)
(*n.*) a comment indicating strong criticism or disapproval

The inexperienced filmmaker was disheartened by the **animadversion** of the film critic.

SYNONYMS: rebuke, reproof
ANTONYMS: praise, compliment

3. avid (av′ id)
(*adj.*) desirous of something to the point of greed; intensely eager

Most writers are also **avid** readers who have loved books since childhood.

SYNONYMS: keen, enthusiastic, grasping
ANTONYMS: reluctant, indifferent, unenthusiastic

4. brackish (brak′ ish)
(*adj.*) having a salty taste and unpleasant to drink

The shipwrecked passengers adrift on the lifeboat became ill after drinking **brackish** water.

SYNONYM: saline
ANTONYMS: clear, sweet

5. celerity (sə ler′ ə tē)
(*n.*) swiftness, rapidity of motion or action

Although the heavy snowfall was not expected, the highway department responded with surprising **celerity**.

SYNONYMS: promptness, speed
ANTONYMS: slowness, sluggishness, dilatoriness

6. devious (dē′ vē əs)
(*adj.*) straying or wandering from a straight or direct course; done or acting in a shifty or underhanded way

The interrogator used **devious** methods to try to get the suspect to incriminate himself.

SYNONYMS: roundabout, indirect, tricky, sly, artful
ANTONYMS: direct, straightforward, open, aboveboard

CCSS Vocabulary: 4.c., 4.d. (See pp. T14–15.)

7. gambit (gam′ bit)

(*n.*) in chess, an opening move that involves risk or sacrifice of a minor piece in order to gain a later advantage; any opening move of this type

Asking an interesting stranger about his or her job is a popular party ______gambit______.

SYNONYMS: ploy, ruse, maneuver

8. halcyon (hal′ sē ən)

(*n.*) a legendary bird identified with the kingfisher; (*adj.*) of or relating to the halcyon; calm, peaceful; happy, golden; prosperous, affluent

The teacher read the legend of the ______halcyon______, a mythic bird that nested in a calm sea.

The woman often spoke of the ______halcyon______ days of her childhood.

SYNONYMS: (*adj.*) tranquil, placid, palmy
ANTONYMS: (*adj.*) turbulent, tumultuous

9. histrionic (his trē än′ ik)

(*adj.*) pertaining to actors and their techniques; theatrical, artificial; melodramatic

Upon receiving his award, the young actor gave a ______histrionic______ speech.

SYNONYMS: affected, stagy
ANTONYMS: muted, untheatrical, subdued

10. incendiary (in sen′ dē er ē)

(*adj.*) deliberately setting or causing fires; designed to start fires; tending to stir up strife or rebellion; (*n.*) one who deliberately sets fires, arsonist; one who causes strife

The arsonist planted an ______incendiary______ device in the basement of the store.

The radical ______incendiary______ was sentenced to life imprisonment.

SYNONYMS: (*adj.*) inflammatory, provocative; (*n.*) firebrand
ANTONYMS: (*adj.*) soothing, quieting; (*n.*) peacemaker

11. maelstrom (māl′ strəm)

(*n.*) a whirlpool of great size and violence; a situation resembling a whirlpool in violence and destruction

Many innocent people caught in the ______maelstrom______ of the revolution lost their lives and property.

SYNONYMS: chaos, turbulence, tumult

12. myopic (mī äp′ ik)

(*adj.*) nearsighted; lacking a broad, realistic view of a situation; lacking foresight or discernment

The ______myopic______ foreign policy of the last administration has led to serious problems with our allies.

SYNONYM: shortsighted
ANTONYM: farsighted

CCSS Vocabulary: 4.c. (See pp. T14–15.)

13. overt (ō vert′)

(*adj.*) open, not hidden, expressed or revealed in a way that is easily recognized

In order for Congress to declare war, the President must demonstrate an **overt** threat.

SYNONYMS: clear, obvious, manifest, patent
ANTONYMS: clandestine, covert, concealed

14. pejorative (pə jôr′ ə tiv)

(*adj.*) tending to make worse; expressing disapproval or disparagement, derogatory, deprecatory, belittling

The lawyer was accused of making a **pejorative** remark when referring to the defendant's background.

ANTONYMS: complimentary, ameliorative

15. propriety (prə prī′ ə tē)

(*n.*) the state of being proper, appropriateness; (*pl.*) standards of what is proper or socially acceptable

The social worker questioned the **propriety** of the police's request to see confidential records.

SYNONYMS: fitness, correctness
ANTONYMS: unseemliness, inappropriateness

16. sacrilege (sak′ rə lij)

(*n.*) improper or disrespectful treatment of something held sacred

The anthropologist was accused of committing a **sacrilege** when she disturbed a burial ground.

SYNONYMS: desecration, profanation, defilement

17. summarily (sə mer′ ə lē)

(*adv.*) without delay or formality; briefly, concisely

As soon as there was evidence of criminal wrongdoing, the official was **summarily** ousted from his post.

SYNONYMS: promptly, peremptorily

18. suppliant (səp′ lē ənt)

(*adj.*) asking humbly and earnestly; (*n.*) one who makes a request humbly and earnestly, a petitioner, suitor

He made a **suppliant** address to the parole board.

Stranded in the deserted city of Moscow, Napoleon had to turn to the Czar not as a conqueror but as a **suppliant**.

19. talisman (tal′ iz mən)

(*n.*) an object that serves as a charm or is believed to confer magical powers, an amulet, fetish

Most people do not believe that rabbit's feet and other **talismans** actually bring good luck.

20. undulate (ən′ dyə lāt)

(*v.*) to move in waves or with a wavelike motion; to have a wavelike appearance or form

The baseball fans began to **undulate** as they cheered, so that they appeared to move in a wave.

SYNONYMS: fluctuate, rise and fall

CCSS Vocabulary: 4.c. (See pp. T14–15.)

Choosing the Right Word

*Select the **boldface** word that better completes each sentence. You might refer to the selection on pages 22–23 to see how most of these words are used in context.*

1. In ancient Egypt, (**talismans, sacrileges**) with the image of a scarab beetle were considered sacred and believed to have healing and protective powers.

The scarab beetle on this gold bracelet symbolized rebirth to ancient Egyptians.

2. The infatuated schoolboy, in one of his more restrained expressions, described himself as "a (**sacrilege, suppliant**) at the altar of love."

3. "I realize that this kind of financial (**gambit, sacrilege**) has its risks," she said, "but I expect it to pay off handsomely in the end."

4. "His acts of defiance have been so (**myopic, overt**) and premeditated that I have no choice but to fire him," she said sadly.

5. John Masefield's poem "Sea Fever" has an (**avid, undulating**) rhythm that actually gives one the feeling of being on a rolling ship.

6. Walt tends to react slowly, but when he feels that his own interests are at stake he can move with striking (**celerity, myopia**).

7. Although all politicians must have some ability to dramatize themselves, it is very easy to overdo the (**proprieties, histrionics**).

8. The adoring fan regarded my negative comments about his favorite singer as tantamount to (**maelstrom, sacrilege**).

9. Without even considering the new evidence that I was prepared to present, they (**deviously, summarily**) denied my appeal to reopen the case.

10. She was buffeted about in a veritable (**gambit, maelstrom**) of emotions, caused mainly by her own dissatisfaction with herself.

11. He regarded his Phi Beta Kappa key as a(n) (**talisman, animadversion**) that would open all doors and win him universal acceptance.

12. He is the kind of person who is concerned not with real moral values but simply with appearances and (**propriety, celerity**).

13. Nary a ripple disturbed the (**halcyon, brackish**) calm of the sea on that glorious summer's afternoon.

14. Instead of imbibing the (**brackish, suppliant**) waters of superstition, let us refresh ourselves with long drafts of pure, clean common sense.

15. Because the word *appeasement* is associated with disastrous concessions to Adolf Hitler, it has acquired a(n) (**pejorative, overt**) connotation.

CCSS Vocabulary: 4.d. (See pp. T14–15.)

16. His reckless words had an (**incendiary, overt**) effect on the already excited crowd, and large-scale rioting resulted.

17. As the defendant left the courtroom, he was (**gambited, accosted**) by a group of reporters seeking his reaction to the verdict.

18. I certainly do not claim that my performance in office was beyond criticism, but I deeply resent (**animadversions, maelstroms**) on my honesty.

19. After years of failure to sell a single story, the young writer described himself bitterly as "a(n) (**pejorative, avid**) collector of rejection slips."

20. In an age when the United States has truly global responsibilities, we can ill afford leaders with (**myopic, pejorative**) points of view.

21. His methods were so complicated and his purposes so (**avid, devious**) that we were not sure if he was spying on the enemy or on us.

22. As reported in several online news sites, the (**incendiary, gambit**) accused in the destructive forest fires has admitted his guilt.

23. To the delight of the impatient graduates, the university president offered her comments at the commencement ceremony (**summarily, brackishly**).

24. After the young actor's audition, the casting directors delivered a harsh evaluation of his overly (**histrionic, undulating**) monologue.

25. My (**myopic, suppliant**) request for a later curfew proved successful.

Choose the word from this unit that is the same or most nearly the same in meaning as the ***boldface*** *word or expression in the phrase. Write that word on the line. Use a dictionary if necessary.*

1. a lucky **amulet** — talisman
2. the **vortex** of public opinion — maelstrom
3. **ripple** in the current — undulate
4. was taken in by her **stratagem** — gambit
5. swam in the **briny** water — brackish
6. **abruptly** resigned from the Cabinet — summarily
7. behaved with her usual **decorum** — propriety
8. memories of our **serene** beginnings — halcyon
9. **confronted** the thief at the door — accosted
10. completed the job with **alacrity** — celerity

CCSS Vocabulary: 5. (See pp. T14–15.)

The synonyms and antonyms here do not appear on the Definitions page.

Antonyms

*Choose the word from this unit that is most nearly opposite in meaning to the **boldface** word or expression in the phrase. Write that word on the line. Use a dictionary if necessary.*

1. a pool of **fresh** water — brackish
2. made a very **low-keyed** plea for mercy — histrionic
3. **evade** the nosy neighbor — accost
4. described the **chaotic** surroundings — halcyon
5. took **secret** action to avoid a crisis — overt

Completing the Sentence

From the words in this unit, choose the one that best completes each of the following sentences. Write the word in the space provided.

1. Many a rich southern planter saw all his financial resources swallowed up in the maelstrom of the Civil War.
2. Saying that "people who live in glass houses shouldn't throw stones" is not an effective response to their animadversions on your conduct.
3. My brother is such a(n) avid collector of toy soldiers that I sometimes think our house has been invaded by a pint-sized army.
4. The celerity with which he accepted our invitation to dinner suggested that he was badly in need of a good meal.
5. We looked back on those halcyon years before the war broke out as a kind of "golden age" in our history.
6. The Japanese attack on Pearl Harbor was a(n) overt act of war.
7. His pale face, hunched shoulders, and myopic stare showed that he had spent his life poring over old books and documents.
8. To our dismay, we discovered that the water we had worked so hard to bring to the surface was too brackish for human consumption.
9. I stand before you an abject suppliant, hoping against hope for a sign of your forgiveness.
10. In the eyes of most Americans, people who burn or spit on our flag are guilty of a kind of sacrilege.

CCSS Vocabulary: 4.a. (See pp. T14–15.)

11. Down in the main square, a hard-working peasant was selling charms and **talismans** to ward off the evil eye.

12. After the prisoner had been found guilty of treason, he was led before a firing squad and **summarily** executed.

13. In Grandmother's day, standards of **propriety** required that a young lady wear a hat and gloves when she went out in public.

14. Any book on chess strategy usually discusses the standard opening moves, such as the "knight's **gambit**."

15. To be really convincing on stage, an opera singer must possess both vocal and **histrionic** abilities.

16. As an employee of the local polling service last summer, I had to **accost** people on the street and ask their opinions.

17. The tons of **incendiary** material ignited and turned the waste disposal plant into a roaring inferno.

18. The suffix *-ling* often has a(n) **pejorative** connotation, as in the word *princeling*, derived from *prince*.

19. During the rainy season, the highway sank at so many points that its surface began to **undulate** like the track for a roller coaster.

20. On the return trip, we cut straight across the meadows rather than take the more **devious** path along the river.

Writing: Words in Action

Answers to both prompts will vary.

1. Look back at "Constructing the New York City Subway" (pages 22–23). Think about how the completion of the subway changed the lives of city residents. Write an essay in which you analyze the impact—both positive and negative—of this new mode of transportation on individuals and businesses in New York City at the turn of the century. Use at least two details from the passage and three unit words to support your view.

2. According to a 2005 Gallup Poll, most Americans consider electricity as the greatest invention of all time, with the automobile and the printing press ranking well behind. Do you agree? Write an essay of at least three paragraphs in which you explain what your top choice is and why. Support your answer with specific examples from your observations, studies, reading (refer to pages 22–23), or personal experience. Use at least three words from this unit in your essay.

Writing prompt #2 is modeled on that of standardized tests.

CCSS Vocabulary: 6; Writing: 2.d., 3.d. (See pp. T14–15.)

Vocabulary in Context: Informational Text for Unit 2 is available online at **vocabularyworkshop.com**.

Vocabulary in Context

Literary Text

The following excerpts are from Theodore Dreiser's novels Sister Carrie *and* Jennie Gerhardt. *Some of the words you have studied in this unit appear in* **boldface** *type. Complete each statement below the excerpt by circling the letter of the correct answer.*

1. For Carrie, as we well know, the stage had a great attraction. She had never forgotten her one **histrionic** achievement in Chicago. *(Sister Carrie)*

Something **histrionic** involves

a. moneymaking **c.** acting and emotions
b. education **d.** ambitions and goals

2. Though often disillusioned, she was still waiting for that **halcyon** day when she would be led forth among dreams become real. Ames had pointed out a farther step, but on and on beyond that, if accomplished, would lie others for her. *(Sister Carrie)*

Something that is **halcyon** is NOT

a. peaceful **c.** happy
b. turbulent **d.** calm

3. Hanson jumped out of bed with more **celerity** than he usually displayed and looked at the note. *(Sister Carrie)*

Celerity is

a. nervousness **c.** determination
b. irritability **d.** swiftness

The 1952 film *Carrie*, based on Dreiser's novel *Sister Carrie*, stars Laurence Olivier and Jennifer Jones.

4. Her support was assured, for her income was paid to her through a trust company. She had no desire for speculation or for the **devious** ways of trade. The care of flowers, the nature of children, the ordering of a home were more in her province. *(Jennie Gerhardt)*

If something is **devious**, it is

a. unhealthy **c.** respectable
b. shifty **d.** defiant

5. He had never really been healed of the wound that his father had given him. He had never been comfortable in his mind since Robert had deserted him so **summarily**. *(Jennie Gerhardt)*

Something done **summarily** is done

a. abruptly **c.** gradually
b. predictably **d.** sarcastically

Snap the code, or go to **vocabularyworkshop.com**

CCSS Vocabulary: 4.c.; Reading (Literature): 4. (See pp. T14–15.)

Note that not all of the 20 unit words are used in this passage. *Cavort*, *distraught*, *eulogy*, *verdant*, and *viscous* are not included in the passage.

Read the following selection, taking note of the ***boldface*** *words and their contexts. These words are among those you will be studying in Unit 3. As you complete the exercises in this unit, it may help to refer to the way the words are used below.*

CCSS Vocabulary: 4; Reading (Informational Text): 4, 6. (See pp. T14–15.)

Third Parties in American Politics

<Encyclopedia Entry>

The two-party system has been in effect since the **primordial** days of American politics and the Founding Fathers. At that time, the two opposing parties were known as the Federalists and the Anti-Federalists. Democrats and Republicans dominate United States politics now, but smaller third parties have addressed **substantive** issues, challenged the two-party orthodoxy, and **evinced** signs of success at local, state, and national levels.

Background and Perspective

A modern-day third-party candidate has yet to wrest the presidency from the Republicans or Democrats. However, many third-party positions have been adopted by the major parties, whose **propinquity** has been **decried** by voters who want clearer divisions.

Sometimes, after Democrats or Republicans have embraced the ideas of a third party, that third party has faded away. Other times—although not since the nineteenth century—a third party has become so powerful that it supplants one of the major parties. This happened in 1856 when the Republican Party, a third party at the time, replaced the Whig Party.

A campaign ribbon for the Know-Nothing party from 1856

Some third parties have clear-cut platforms and strong nominees, while others have been criticized for **murky** views or **feckless** leadership or for having more **utopian** than real-world positions. Still others are essentially single-issue parties—like the Prohibition Party—known for its opposition to the sale or consumption of alcohol.

Significant Third Parties in U.S. History

The Know-Nothing Party This party rose with **unwonted** rapidity in the mid-1800s. Among other things, its leaders spread **nefarious** misinformation to increase opposition to Catholic immigration from countries such as Ireland and Germany. The name came about because members, when asked about the party's activities, **dissembled** and said they "knew nothing." The party shortly died out, but modern candidates **exhume** parts of its platform from time to time, for example, calling for restrictions on liquor sales.

Teddy Roosevelt and the Bull Moose Party In 1912, former President Theodore Roosevelt tried to win back the presidency by challenging incumbent

Teddy Roosevelt's Bull Moose Party captured the imagination of the voting public in 1912.

William Howard Taft for the Republican nomination. Roosevelt lost, but a rolling stone gathers no moss, and he formed the Progressive Party, soon nicknamed the Bull Moose Party. This development split the Republican vote, and the Democrat, Woodrow Wilson, was elected President. Although Roosevelt, known for his colorful **verbiage** in speeches and **piquant** ideas, lost, much of his platform later became public policy.

Recent Third-Party Candidates

Some contenders, like H. Ross Perot in 1992 and 1996 and Ralph Nader in two of his bids—in 2000 and 2004—won enough votes to give **credence** to the idea of a third party in the United States. Some have viewed third-party candidates as "spoilers": They cannot win, but they'll siphon off enough votes to impact the election.

H. Ross Perot This billionaire businessman and folksy populist threw his hat into the presidential ring in 1992 as a Reform Party candidate. He received almost 20 million votes, more than any other third-party candidate since Theodore Roosevelt in 1912.

Ralph Nader A trailblazing consumer advocate and four-time presidential candidate, Nader ran for president in 2000 on the Green Party ticket. Some Democrats feared he would draw votes from their candidate, Al Gore. Nader won just under three percent of the vote.

Legacy

The United States has the longest-surviving two-party system of any country. However, roughly one-third of voters today are not affiliated with either of the two major parties, and that number is growing. Many people are registering as Independents, which may signal an opportunity for the next third party.

Snap the code, or go to **vocabularyworkshop.com**

Definitions

Note the spelling, pronunciation, part(s) of speech, and definition(s) of each of the following words. Then write the word in the blank spaces in the illustrative sentence(s) following. Finally, study the lists of synonyms and antonyms.

1. cavort (kə vôrt′)
(*v.*) to romp or prance around exuberantly; to make merry
The actors in the musical **cavort(ed)** on stage.
SYNONYM: gambol

2. credence (krēd′ əns)
(*n.*) belief, mental acceptance
The government and the public failed to give **credence** to the reports of an impending water shortage.
SYNONYMS: credit, trust, confidence
ANTONYMS: disbelief, skepticism, incredulity

3. decry (di krī′)
(*v.*) to condemn, express strong disapproval; to officially depreciate
Every arm of government and every educational institution should **decry** bigotry in all its forms.
SYNONYMS: denounce, censure, devalue
ANTONYMS: tout, commend, extol, laud, praise

4. dissemble (di sem′ bəl)
(*v.*) to disguise or conceal, deliberately give a false impression
The young man was unable to **dissemble** his feelings and admitted to having committed the crime.
SYNONYMS: dissimulate, mask, feign

5. distraught (dis trôt′)
(*adj.*) very much agitated or upset as a result of emotion or mental conflict
The workforce became **distraught** in the wake of the 1929 stock market crash.
SYNONYM: distracted
ANTONYMS: calm, collected

6. eulogy (yü′ lə jē)
(*n.*) a formal statement of commendation; high praise
The best friend and longtime law partner of the deceased delivered the **eulogy** at the funeral.
SYNONYMS: panegyric, encomium, tribute
ANTONYMS: philippic, invective

7. evince (i vins′)
(*v.*) to display clearly, to make evident, to provoke
The crowd did not **evince** any signs of panic but moved in an orderly fashion to the nearest exits.
SYNONYMS: exhibit, manifest, occasion

CCSS Vocabulary: 4.c., 4.d. (See pp. T14–15.)

8. exhume (eks hyüm′)

(*v.*) to remove from a grave; to bring to light

Suspecting foul play, the coroner issued an order to ______**exhume**______ the body immediately.

SYNONYMS: disinter, unearth, uncover
ANTONYMS: bury, inter

9. feckless (fek′ ləs)

(*adj.*) lacking in spirit and strength; ineffective, weak; irresponsible, unreliable

Although a ______**feckless**______ youth, he eventually matured into a hard-working and responsible citizen.

SYNONYMS: feeble, incompetent, ineffectual
ANTONYMS: competent, capable, effective

10. murky (mər′ kē)

(*adj.*) dark and gloomy, obscure; lacking in clarity and precision

Many visitors have claimed to see a mysterious creature in the ______**murky**______ waters of Loch Ness in Scotland.

SYNONYMS: dim, cloudy
ANTONYMS: clear, transparent, lucid, limpid

11. nefarious (nə fâr′ ē əs)

(*adj.*) wicked, depraved, devoid of moral standards

Brutus and Cassius hatched a ______**nefarious**______ plot to assassinate Julius Caesar on the steps of the Roman Senate.

SYNONYMS: iniquitous, reprehensible
ANTONYMS: virtuous, honorable, praiseworthy, meritorious

12. piquant (pē′ kənt)

(*adj.*) stimulating to the taste or mind; spicy, pungent; appealingly provocative

The chef was an expert in making those ______**piquant**______ dishes that are characteristic of South Indian cooking.

SYNONYMS: zestful, tangy
ANTONYMS: bland, insipid, tasteless, mild

13. primordial (prī môr′ dē əl)

(*adj.*) developed or created at the very beginning; going back to the most ancient times or earliest stage; fundamental, basic

The ______**primordial**______ stages of most civilizations are founded on common needs met by common goals.

SYNONYMS: original, primal

14. propinquity (prō piŋ′ kwə tē)

(*n.*) nearness in place or time; kinship

The ______**propinquity**______ of the two cities has created a greater metropolitan area that in effect is one city.

SYNONYM: similarity
ANTONYMS: remoteness, distance

15. substantive (səb′ stən tiv)

(*adj.*) real, having a solid basis; considerable in number or amount; meaningful and on topic

The candidate dismissed the silly questions but took the time to answer the most ___**substantive**___ ones.

SYNONYMS: firm, substantial, meaty
ANTONYMS: imaginary, unreal, meaningless

16. unwonted (un wōn′ tid)

(*adj.*) not usual or expected; not in character

The listless student answered with ___**unwonted**___ spirit when the subject of military tactics was raised.

SYNONYMS: unusual, uncommon, unexpected, atypical
ANTONYMS: usual, customary, typical

17. utopian (yü tō′ pē ən)

(*adj.*) founded upon or involving a visionary view of an ideal world; impractical

A number of American religious groups like the Shakers have built separate communities based on ___**utopian**___ schemes.

SYNONYM: idealistic
ANTONYMS: realistic, pragmatic

18. verbiage (vər′ bē ij)

(*n.*) language that is too wordy or inflated in proportion to the sense or content, wordiness; a manner of expression

The contract was full of meaningless ___**verbiage**___ that seemed designed to confuse the lay person.

SYNONYMS: prolixity, diction, jargon

19. verdant (vər′ dənt)

(*adj.*) green in tint or color; immature in experience or judgment

The tourists on safari traveled over the ___**verdant**___ grasslands of Kenya in search of native wildlife.

SYNONYMS: artless, naïve
ANTONYMS: scorched, sere, barren

20. viscous (vis′ kəs)

(*adj.*) having a gelatinous or gluey quality, lacking in easy movement or fluidity

The varnish left a ___**viscous**___ residue on the wood that was hard to remove.

SYNONYMS: sticky, thick
ANTONYMS: watery, aqueous

CCSS Vocabulary: 4.c. (See pp. T14–15.)

Choosing the Right Word

*Select the **boldface** word that better completes each sentence. You might refer to the selection on pages 32–33 to see how most of these words are used in context.*

Mozart composed his first minuet at the age of five.

1. The extraordinary musical talents of Wolfgang Amadeus Mozart (**evinced, dissembled**) themselves at an amazingly early age.
2. From the deck of our luxury liner, we occasionally caught sight of schools of porpoises (**cavorting, evincing**) playfully in the waves.
3. Far from being unpleasant, her slight foreign accent added an extra dash of spice to her already (**primordial, piquant**) personality.
4. The new mayor is a curious mixture of the hardheaded pragmatist and the (**utopian, murky**) reformer.
5. Not surprisingly, the address was a notably evenhanded affair in which the speaker cleverly mixed (**eulogy, verbiage**) with admonition.
6. When life was easy he was all dash and confidence, but in times of trouble his essentially (**piquant, feckless**) character came to the fore.
7. Unfortunately, the (**nefarious, verdant**) hopes and aspirations of my youth have been somewhat blighted by the icy blasts of reality.
8. Trying to read your (**viscous, utopian**) prose is just like trying to swim upstream through custard.
9. Because the playwright had hurried through her first draft, she had to make (**substantive, nefarious**) changes as she revised the dialogue.
10. His (**viscous, unwonted**) interest in the state of my finances strengthened my suspicions that he was about to ask for a loan.
11. The book has an interesting plot, but the author has practically smothered it in endless (**verbiage, eulogy**).
12. Despite all the reports of "miraculous" cures, you would be well advised to withhold (**verbiage, credence**) until the drug has been fully tested.
13. (**Exhumed, Distraught**) with grief, they sat motionless for hours, staring blankly into space.
14. An accomplished hypocrite usually finds it very easy to (**dissemble, decry**) his or her true feelings as circumstances dictate.
15. The behavior of armies in wartime often evinces the (**murky, primordial**) blood lust that civilized people have not yet fully overcome.

CCSS Vocabulary: 4.d. (See pp. T14–15.)

16. The United States is cooperating with the other nations of the world in an effort to check the (**feckless, nefarious**) trade in narcotics.

17. The (**credence, propinquity**) of our ideas on handling the problem made it very easy for my colleague and me to produce the report in record time.

18. The investigating committee (**decried, dissembled**) the use of substandard materials and slovenly workmanship in the housing project.

19. From the bridge, the rescue team could just make out the blurred image of a car beneath the (**murky, unwonted**) waters of the river.

20. Though the work hadn't seen the light of day for over a century, a daring impresario (**cavorted, exhumed**) and staged it to great public acclaim.

21. In my opinion, the columnist's observations about contemporary media and popular culture are humorous and wonderfully (**piquant, viscous**).

22. Members of Congress were relieved to learn that the current peace negotiations involve (**murky, substantive**) discussion of key issues.

23. Given my birthday's (**eulogy, propinquity**) to July 4th, my mother customarily decorates my wrapped gifts with red, white, and blue ribbons.

24. Plato's (**utopian, verdant**) description of the ideal society and its politics in *The Republic* exerted great influence on later philosophers like Aristotle.

25. The (**feckless, piquant**) efforts of our new quarterback caused the team to lose.

Synonyms

*Choose the word from this unit that is the same or most nearly the same in meaning as the **boldface** word or expression in the phrase. Write that word on the line. Use a dictionary if necessary.*

1. some **actual** doubt — substantive
2. **primeval** history — primordial
3. a **blossoming** garden — verdant
4. delivered an emotional **testimonial** — eulogy
5. a slightly **gummy** coating of wax — viscous
6. **played** in the wading pool — cavorted
7. feared for the **helpless** child — feckless
8. an unwelcome **proximity** — propinquity
9. tried to calm the **frantic** parents — distraught
10. could not make out the **unclear** image — murky

CCSS Vocabulary: 5. (See pp. T14–15.)

The synonyms and antonyms here do not appear on the Definitions page.

Choose the word from this unit that is most nearly opposite in meaning to the ***boldface*** *word or expression in the phrase. Write that word on the line. Use a dictionary if necessary.*

1. watered the **arid** lawn ______verdant______
2. spent the summer **being serious** ______cavorting______
3. feeling **composed** after the accident ______distraught______
4. make **minor** repairs ______substantive______
5. published her lengthy **diatribe** ______eulogy______

Completing the Sentence

From the words in this unit, choose the one that best completes each of the following sentences. Write the word in the space provided.

1. An educated citizenry will not give ______credence______ to wild charges of extremists seeking to undermine our political and economic system.
2. Although Aimée is usually quiet in class, her contribution to our political discussion yesterday was ______substantive______.
3. The NCAA has in recent years cracked down hard on such ______nefarious______ practices as "shaving points."
4. I have always regarded the man as something of a daredevil, but on this occasion he approached the problem with ______unwonted______ caution.
5. In the hands of our hopelessly ______feckless______ producer, what should have been a surefire hit turned into a resounding fiasco.
6. Even at an early age, my sister ______evinced______ a strong interest in studying medicine.
7. Such spices as red pepper make many of the sauces used in Cajun cooking delightfully ______piquant______.
8. Since my apartment is in such close ______propinquity______ to my office, I usually walk to work.
9. For as far as the eye could see, ______verdant______ fields of unripe corn swayed gently in the morning breeze.
10. How could we draw any clear ideas from a talk that was so disorganized, confused in language, and generally ______murky______?

11. Sadly, the ___utopian___ schemes of high-minded idealists usually founder on the rocks of practical realities.

12. I believe there is an overall design to the universe that has been visible ever since the first thing crawled out of the ___primordial___ ooze.

13. When new evidence turned up in the case, the court ordered the coroner to ___exhume___ the victim's body and reexamine it.

14. Every Memorial Day, the mayor delivers a(n) ___eulogy___ extolling the selfless devotion of those who have died in defense of this country.

15. When news of the fire ran through town, ___distraught___ residents rushed to the scene of the blaze.

16. Though diesel fuels are not as thick as motor oil, they are a good deal more ___viscous___ than regular gasoline.

17. The new chairman ___decried___ what she called the "deplorable tendency of so many Americans to try to get something for nothing."

18. Though I prefer to be as open and aboveboard as possible, I have learned that it is sometimes wiser or more tactful to ___dissemble___.

19. He clothes his puny ideas in such highfalutin ___verbiage___ that they resemble gnats in top hats and tails.

20. When Bill was told that he had made the varsity wrestling team, he began to ___cavort___ around the gym like a young colt.

Writing: Words in Action

Answers to both prompts will vary.

1. Look back at "Third Parties in American Politics" (pages 32–33), and think about the idea of a third party that focuses on a single issue. Suppose you are a third-party candidate running for president in the next election. What one issue would you want to focus on? Write a brief essay that explains your view of the issue and its importance to you and to the country in general. Use at least two details from the passage and three unit words to support your view.

2. Being the U.S. President is, arguably, one of the most challenging and powerful jobs in the world. Think of the range of particular qualities and skills someone needs to be an effective President. If you had to narrow those characteristics down to two, what would they be? Write at least three paragraphs explaining your answer. Support your ideas with specific details from your own experience and observations, as well as information you have gained from your reading, studies, or media viewing. Use three or more words from this unit in your answer.

Writing prompt #2 is modeled on that of standardized tests.

CCSS Vocabulary: 6; Writing: 2.d., 3.d. (See pp. T14–15.)

Vocabulary in Context: Informational Text for Unit 3 is available online at **vocabularyworkshop.com**.

Vocabulary in Context

Literary Text

The following excerpts are from Herman Melville's novel Moby-Dick. *Some of the words you have studied in this unit appear in* ***boldface*** *type. Complete each statement below the excerpt by circling the letter of the correct answer.*

1. Of all the pre-adamite whales yet **exhumed**, by far the largest is the Alabama one mentioned in the last chapter, and that was less than seventy feet in length in the skeleton.

When something is **exhumed**, it is

a. displayed in a museum
b. removed from a grave
c. examined by scientists
d. documented by records

2. But even stripped of these supernatural surmisings, there was enough in the earthly make and incontestable character of the monster to strike the imagination with **unwonted** power.

If something is **unwonted**, it is

a. unusual
b. frightening
c. expected
d. undesirable

Large sections of *Moby-Dick* focus on the American whaling industry in the nineteenth century.

3. It needs scarcely to be told, with what feelings, on the eve of a Nantucket voyage, I regarded those marble tablets, and by the **murky** light of that darkened, doleful day read the fate of the whalemen who had gone before me.

Something that is **murky** is NOT

a. dim
b. cloudy
c. gloomy
d. clear

4. Yet without power to kill, or change, or shun the fact; he likewise knew that to mankind he did now long **dissemble**; in some sort, did still. But that thing of his dissembling was only subject to his perceptibility, not to his will determinate.

To **dissemble** is to

a. disappoint
b. inspire
c. conceal
d. deride

5. For as this appalling ocean surrounds the **verdant** land, so in the soul of man there lies one insular Tahiti, full of peace and joy, but encompassed by all the horrors of the half known life.

Something **verdant** is

a. barren
b. green
c. inhabited
d. enduring

Snap the code, or go to **vocabularyworkshop.com**

CCSS Vocabulary: 4.c.; Reading (Literature): 4. (See pp. T14–15.)

Vocabulary for Comprehension

*Read the following selection in which some of the words you have studied in Units 1–3 appear in **boldface** type. Then answer the questions on page 43.*

Although the Chicago fire caused enormous destruction, the city recovered quickly, as this passage shows.

(Line)

On the evening of October 8, 1871, at around 9 o'clock, the city of Chicago went up in flames. The exact **incendiary** agent remains unknown, but historians have **substantiated** the Chicago Fire Department's discovery that the blaze began in or near the barn of Mr. and Mrs. Patrick O'Leary, on the southwest side of the city. Official **credence**, however, has not been extended to the popular belief that it all started when the O'Learys' cow knocked over a lighted lantern.

Whatever the initial spark, the city was a tinderbox. That summer had been unusually dry, and almost all the buildings, bridges, and even the sidewalks were made of wood. Construction over the previous years had proceeded rapidly and with little attention to fire safety. The **feckless** city council ignored all pleas to improve the level of fire protection, either by bolstering the fire department or by passing zoning laws. As a result of this inaction, the city of Chicago averaged about two fires a day.

Driven by a strong wind out of the southwest, the October 8 fire was already out of control by the time the exhausted Chicago firefighters (who had been working the day before on another large fire) arrived. The wind carried the flames to the center of the city, where they consumed nearly every structure in their path. In a panic, the **distraught** population fled northward toward Lincoln Park and Lake Michigan. The fire raged for more than twenty-four hours until it rained on the morning of October 10.

In the days that followed, **reconnaissance** missions were conducted over the rubble that remained of homes, businesses, and tunnels. Three hundred were dead, nearly 100,000 were homeless, and property damage amounted to $200 million. Yet, four years later, Chicago was almost completely rebuilt. And today, the Chicago Fire Academy stands on the site of the O'Leary cowshed.

CCSS Vocabulary: 4.a.; Reading (Informational Text): 2, 4, 6. (See pp. T14–15.)

1. The primary purpose of the passage is to
   - (a.) tell the story of the Chicago fire of 1871
   - b. compare the Chicago fire with the San Francisco earthquake of 1906
   - c. highlight the geography of Chicago
   - d. focus on the heroism of the firefighters
   - e. expose the incompetence of the city council

2. The meaning of **incendiary** (line 4) is
   - a. criminal
   - b. causative
   - c. subversive
   - (d.) inflammatory
   - e. foreign

3. **Substantiated** (line 6) most nearly means
   - a. disputed
   - b. analyzed
   - c. ignored
   - (d.) verified
   - e. dismissed

4. From the passage, it is clear that
   - a. the fire started when the O'Learys' cow knocked over a lighted lantern
   - b. no one really knows how or where the fire started
   - (c.) the fire started in or near the O'Learys' barn
   - d. the fire spread slowly but steadily
   - e. Mr. and Mrs. O'Leary were responsible for setting the fire

5. **Credence** (line 11) is best defined as
   - a. pardon
   - (b.) acceptance
   - c. condemnation
   - d. mourning
   - e. enthusiasm

6. Which of the following best describes the organizational structure of paragraph 2 (lines 15–28)?
   - a. comparison and contrast
   - b. spatial order
   - (c.) cause and effect
   - d. chronological order
   - e. order of importance

7. The meaning of **feckless** (line 22) is
   - a. corrupt
   - b. effective
   - c. popular
   - d. conservative
   - (e.) incompetent

8. From the passage, you can reasonably infer that all of the following played a role in the spread of the fire EXCEPT
   - (a.) the fleeing population
   - b. the minimal attention to safety in construction
   - c. the exhaustion of the firefighters
   - d. a strong wind
   - e. the unusually dry summer

9. **Distraught** (line 39) is best defined as
   - a. disheveled
   - b. angry
   - (c.) frantic
   - d. bemused
   - e. frightened

10. **Reconnaissance** (line 45) is best defined as
    - a. detailed analysis
    - b. calm evacuation
    - (c.) scouting expedition
    - d. slow deliberation
    - e. court decision

11. The effect of the last sentence in the passage (lines 52–55) might best be described as
    - a. fanciful
    - b. melancholy
    - (c.) ironic
    - d. tragic
    - e. farcical

12. Which of the following best describes the author's attitude toward the subject of the passage?
    - a. disillusioned
    - (b.) factual
    - c. satiric
    - d. skeptical
    - e. enthusiastic

CCSS Vocabulary: 4.a.; Reading (Informational Text): 2, 4, 6. (See pp. T14–15.)

Two-Word Completions

Select the pair of words that best complete the meaning of each of the following passages.

1. Someone with a ____________ nature is generally very good at ____________, while more honest people give off unconscious cues that they are not telling the truth.

a. distraught . . . emulating
b. devious . . . dissembling
c. ubiquitous . . . strategizing
d. acquisitive . . . decrying

2. Despite the somewhat strident ____________ of some professional critics and the inane ____________ of a few literary pedants, the work enjoyed a notable popular success.

a. encomiums . . . largesse
b. verbiage . . . eulogies
c. animadversions . . . carping
d. gambits . . . sacrilege

3. For what must have been the first and only time in his life, the overly cautious general did not ____________ or vacillate but committed his troops to battle with ____________ celerity.

a. arrogate . . . overt
b. temporize . . . unwonted
c. carp . . . myopic
d. dissemble . . . feckless

4. From the top of the mountain that summer afternoon, I looked out on a(n) ____________ panorama of fields and pasturelands through which countless streams and rivulets ____________ like so many serpents slithering lazily across a carpet.

a. substantive . . . exhumed
b. avid . . . congealed
c. verdant . . . undulated
d. primordial . . . cavorted

5. Someone who is by nature as skeptical as I am usually refuses to give any ____________ to the kinds of wild allegations thrown about in an election until they have been ____________ by solid evidence.

a. credence . . . substantiated
b. celerity . . . decried
c. largesse . . . exhumed
d. propriety . . . eschewed

6. Little did we realize, as we ____________ blithely on the beach during those ____________ and cloudless days of spring 1914, that the world was moving inexorably into the maelstrom of total war.

a. evinced . . . piquant
b. belabored . . . utopian
c. emulated . . . insatiable
d. cavorted . . . halcyon

7. The senator hoped his colleagues would find his ____________ argument about the deficit to be ____________ .

a. histrionic . . . invidious
b. germane . . . murky
c. coherent . . . tenable
d. viscous . . . nefarious

CCSS Vocabulary: 4.a. (See pp. T14–15.)

In one of the letters about women's suffrage (see pages 12–13), the writer predicts that after Wyoming's decision to allow women to vote, other Western states and territories will "follow suit."

"Follow suit" is an idiom. An **idiom** is a group of words whose meaning is different from the literal meanings of each word considered individually. For example, "follow suit" means "do the same as has been done previously." Speakers and writers often use idioms to add interest and an air of informality to their style and tone. While it is sometimes possible to determine the meaning of an idiom from its context, you should memorize the meanings of common idioms. For others, you may need to consult a dictionary.

Choosing the Right Idiom

*Read each sentence. Use context clues to figure out the meaning of each idiom in **boldface** print. Then write the letter of the definition for the idiom in the sentence.*

1. To her older colleagues, the new personal trainer seemed **wet behind the ears** on her first day. h
2. After tiring in the first half of the race, Bryan and Phil got a **second wind** in the last few laps. e
3. I was **fit to be tied** when the airline lost my suitcases. a
4. Any library **worth its salt** has a variety of both print and digital encyclopedias. j
5. Because the Smiths suspected that the rental contract was not **on the up and up,** they refused to sign it. i
6. One recently hired employee left the engineering department last week for **greener pastures.** d
7. Although we read the directions twice, we couldn't **make heads or tails of** them. g
8. The homeowners and the real estate agent tried to remain polite, but they were clearly **at odds**. f
9. The bride hoped that **down the line** the groom would begin helping her address the wedding invitations. b
10. Although I once doubted I would make the varsity team, now I believe it is **in the cards.** c

a. furious
b. in the future
c. likely to happen
d. a better situation
e. renewed energy
f. in disagreement
g. understand
h. inexperienced and young
i. legal
j. deserving of respect

CCSS Vocabulary: 5.a. (See pp. T14–15.)

WORD STUDY

Writing with Idioms

Find the meaning of each idiom. (Use an online or print dictionary if necessary.) Then write a sentence for each idiom. **Answers will vary.**

1. done in **Sample answer: The flight attendants looked done in as they exited the plane after the nine-hour flight.**

2. gain ground

3. by the book

4. a full plate

5. set up shop

6. in a nutshell

7. sound bite

8. ax to grind

9. bite the bullet

10. par for the course

11. get wind of

12. with bated breath

 CCSS Vocabulary: 5. (See pp. T14–15.)

Denotation and Connotation

The literal meaning of a word is its **denotation**, or the definition of the word found in a dictionary. In contrast, a word's **connotation** is its implied meaning. Many words have connotations that are either *positive* or *negative*.

For example, a writer could describe one character looking at another as *watching, staring, gazing, leering, scrutinizing, ogling,* and so on. Each of these different words conveys a different set of associations or images in a reader's mind. Writers choose the particular word that will help them best communicate a precise mood or message.

Consider these synonyms for the word *utopian:*

idealistic *sublime* *quixotic* *illusory*

Idealistic and *sublime* have positive connotations, suggesting noble-minded or lofty ideas, values, and behaviors. *Quixotic* and *illusory* have negative connotations, suggesting foolish impracticality or deception.

Think: Residents would welcome an idealistic or sublime vision of community reform but would criticize or reject calls for quixotic or illusory changes.

Look at these examples of words that are similar in denotation but have different connotations.

NEUTRAL	POSITIVE	NEGATIVE
dwell on	**emphasize**	**belabor**
avid	**enthusiastic**	**coveting**
unwonted	**extraordinary**	**aberrant**

Skilled writers and readers need to understand the emotional power that certain words have and pay attention to the differing nuances of words with similar denotations.

Shades of Meaning

Write a plus sign (+) in the box if the word has a positive connotation. Write a minus sign (–) if the word has a negative connotation. Put a zero (0) if the word is neutral.

1. decry –
2. congeal 0
3. propinquity 0
4. distraught –
5. murky –
6. germane +
7. brackish –
8. animadversion –
9. accost –
10. devious –
11. eulogy +
12. coherent +
13. overt 0
14. sacrilege –
15. undulate 0
16. pejorative –

CCSS Vocabulary: 5.b. (See pp. T14–15.)

Expressing the Connotation

Read each sentence. Select the word in parentheses that expresses the connotation (positive, negative, or neutral) given at the beginning of the sentence.

negative **1.** I have enjoyed several of the author's previous novels, but the (**diction, verbiage**) used throughout this one made reading it tedious.

negative **2.** With one rap of his gavel, the judge (**rudely, summarily**) ordered the defense attorneys to leave his chambers.

positive **3.** Featuring a variety of (**piquant, suitable**) seafood salads, the buffet was well worth the cost.

negative **4.** The ineffective advertisement relied on (**common, banal**) descriptive phrases and images.

positive **5.** We had tears in our eyes after hearing the (**encomium, sermon**) to the injured firefighters.

neutral **6.** During the play's final act, the tearful heroine questions her sister's (**dubious, nefarious**) behavior.

neutral **7.** Predictably, the newspaper's (**unfortunate, invidious**) headline stirred up controversy in the community.

positive **8.** With a stunning view of the castle and elegant decor, the hotel room offered a(n) (**halcyon, agreeable**) atmosphere.

Challenge: Using Connotation

Choose vocabulary words from Units 1–3 to replace the highlighted words in the sentences below. Then explain how the connotation of the replacement word changes the tone of the sentence. Answers will vary.

largesse	**histrionic**	**acquisitive**
talisman	**carping**	**suppliant**

1. Hearing his unexpectedly **critical** carping comments changed the team's opinion of their new coach. Sample response: The unfavorable connotation of *carping* suggests that the coach's comments were harsh and that the team's opinion became more negative.

2. The film review emphasized the **dramatic** histrionic manner in which the lead actor delivered his lines in the final scene. Sample response: The negative connotation of *histrionic* reveals that the reviewer was critical of the actor's melodramatic performance.

3. The minister remarked on the surprising **gift** largesse to the church building fund given by an anonymous donor. Sample response: The positive connotation of *largesse* makes it clear the gift was generous and lavish; one can infer that the minister was grateful for it.

 CCSS Vocabulary: 5. (See pp. T14–15.)

Classical Roots

cred—to believe

The root *cred* appears in **credence** (page 34). The literal meaning is "belief," but the word now suggests a belief that is accepted. Some other words based on the same root are listed below.

accreditation	**credibility**	**creditor**	**credulity**
credentials	**creditable**	**credo**	**credulous**

From the list of words above, choose the one that corresponds to each of the brief definitions below. Write the word in the blank space in the illustrative sentence below the definition. Use an online or print dictionary if necessary.

1. a person or an organization to which money is owed
The bank denied her request for a loan when they saw that she had made late payments to a past ___creditor___.

2. an undue readiness to believe; a lack of critical judgment
The wily con artists exploited their victim's ___credulity___.

3. a statement or summary of faith or fundamental belief; an authoritative statement of religious belief *("I believe")*
The ___credo___ of our hiking club is "Take only pictures; leave only footprints."

4. inclined to believe very readily, gullible
The naïve young man seemed as ___credulous___ as a child.

5. official authorization or approval (often used in regard to academic affairs)
The college received ___accreditation___ as an institution of higher learning.

6. bringing or deserving credit or honor
Despite limited rehearsal time, the cast did a(n) ___creditable___ job on that play.

7. references, testimonials, or other (usually written) evidence of identity or status ("that which provides a basis for belief")
The security guard demanded to see their ___credentials___ before they could enter the building.

8. worthiness of belief
At the hearing, a panel of experts questioned the ___credibility___ of the advertisement.

Note that not all of the 20 unit words are used in this passage. *Incarcerate*, *jocular*, *pusillanimous*, and *recumbent* are not included in the passage.

*Read the following selection, taking note of the **boldface** words and their contexts. These words are among those you will be studying in Unit 4. As you complete the exercises in this unit, it may help to refer to the way the words are used below.*

C CCSS Vocabulary: 4; Reading (Informational Text): 4, 6. (See pp. T14–15.)

Reforming the Security Council

<Newspaper Editorial>

For more than a decade, diplomats and politicians the world over have sought to reform the United Nations Security Council. While everyone seems to agree that reform could increase the Council's effectiveness, there is less **concord** as to how to bring it about. Many nations favor changes that suit their own interests and **grouse** about their rivals' points of view. As the debate drags on, proposals for reform pile up like **flotsam** on the shore, each idea thwarted by a barrage of **mordant** objections. So the process of reform has proven less efficient than the Security Council itself, and hope for change threatens to **atrophy**.

The Security Council was created to serve as a **bastion** of peace and security in the world. It has the power to mediate disputes and to authorize peacekeeping operations, sanctions, and military action. Its members include representatives from fifteen nations, five of which hold permanent seats. A minimum of nine votes is required for the Council to pass a resolution, but the five permanent members have the lion's share of influence over important decisions. If any permanent member votes against a proposed measure, the resolution does not pass.

This veto power held by the permanent members is the chief source of the Council's inefficacy. When there is disagreement among permanent members, a single "no" vote is enough to prevent the Council from taking action. Just the threat of a veto can throw negotiations into **disarray**, holding the Council hostage to the slow workings of diplomacy. This cumbersome process prevents the Council from reacting quickly to the **exigencies** of political crises. Accordingly, many critics

A meeting of the UN Security Council

The UN building in New York City, as seen from the East River

claim it is **incumbent** upon reformers to amend the Council's voting procedures. Others demand that the number of non-permanent members be increased to limit the permanent members' power. While there is wisdom in both of these suggestions, debate as to how the U.N. can implement such measures remains **frenetic**, with no end to the **stratagems** by which each nation hopes to gain advantage.

An increasing number of critics have suggested doing away with permanent membership entirely and making all members of the Council temporary officials. While proponents of this reform may **glean** support from some corners, there is little chance of its coming to pass. The permanent members will not willingly give up their privileged positions: Since they have the power to veto the proposal, it is **ludicrous** to expect that such a resolution could ever be enacted. Moreover, permanent membership is designed to reflect the realities of global politics. In theory, permanent members consist of the nations that contribute the most **pecuniary** and military support to the U.N. and that have the greatest power to influence world affairs by diplomatic, economic, or other means.

That is not necessarily the case today. The list of permanent members was drawn up just after World War II and no longer reflects the balance of global power. The fortunes of many nations have changed, for better or worse, in the past six decades. To better reflect today's world, influential nations such as Germany and Japan should be made permanent members, along with emerging regional powers like India, South Africa, and Brazil. And the Council's voting process must be improved. Achieving these aims will require an unusual degree of compromise and **consummate** diplomatic tact, and there is no doubt that some nations will be **nettled** by the result. But the only alternative is to allow the Council to remain an ineffective institution—and this is an outcome that benefits no one.

Snap the code, or go to **vocabularyworkshop.com**

A UN peacekeeper monitors the border between Israel and Lebanon.

Definitions

Note the spelling, pronunciation, part(s) of speech, and definition(s) of each of the following words. Then write the word in the blank spaces in the illustrative sentence(s) following. Finally, study the lists of synonyms and antonyms.

1. atrophy (a′ trə fē)

(*n.*) the wasting away of a body organ or tissue; any progressive decline or failure; (*v.*) to waste away

The **atrophy** of the downtown business district began when two huge malls opened.

The patient's muscles have **atrophied**.

SYNONYMS: (*n.*) degeneration, deterioration; (*v.*) wither
ANTONYMS: (*n.*) growth; (*v.*) mature

2. bastion (bas′ chən)

(*n.*) a fortified place, stronghold

Contrary to popular belief, the military is not always a **bastion** of political conservatism.

SYNONYMS: citadel, rampart, parapet

3. concord (kän′ kôrd)

(*n.*) a state of agreement, harmony, unanimity; a treaty, pact, covenant

A spirit of **concord** was restored when the company compensated its employees.
ANTONYMS: disagreement, strife, discord

4. consummate (*v.*, kän′ sə māt; *adj.*, kən′ sə mət)

(*adj.*) complete or perfect in the highest degree; (*v.*) to bring to a state of completion or perfection

Michelangelo's paintings on the ceiling of the Sistine Chapel in the Vatican are works of **consummate** artistry.

The lawyers could not **consummate** the settlement until the two parties met face to face.

SYNONYMS: (*adj.*) masterful; (*v.*) clinch, conclude
ANTONYMS: (*v.*) launch, initiate, begin, kick off

5. disarray (dis ə rā′)

(*n.*) disorder, confusion; (*v.*) to throw into disorder

The burgled home was in a state of **disarray**.

If you leave the window open, a breeze may **disarray** the papers on the desktop.

SYNONYMS: (*n.*) disorganization; (*v.*) dishevel, mess up
ANTONYMS: (*n.*) organization, order, tidiness

6. exigency (ek′ sə jən sē)

(*n.*, often *pl.*) urgency, pressure; urgent demand, pressing need; an emergency

He emphasized the **exigency** of the situation by requesting the immediate dispatch of rescue teams.

SYNONYMS: requirement, crisis

CCSS Vocabulary: 4.c., 4.d. (See pp. T14–15.)

7. flotsam (flät′ səm)

(*n.*) floating debris; homeless, impoverished people

After the two ships collided, the survivors clung to various pieces of ___flotsam___ and hoped for rescue.

SYNONYM: floating wreckage

8. frenetic (frə net′ ik)

(*adj.*) frenzied, highly agitated

When a court order was issued, the social services department made a ___frenetic___ search for the missing report.

SYNONYMS: frantic, overwrought
ANTONYMS: calm, controlled, relaxed, leisurely

9. glean (glēn)

(*v.*) to gather bit by bit; to gather small quantities of grain left in a field by the reapers

By means of painstaking investigation, the detectives will eventually ___glean___ the truth.

SYNONYMS: cull, pick up

10. grouse (graůs)

(*n.*) a type of game bird; a complaint; (*v.*) to complain, grumble

The patient's latest ___grouse___ was that he did not get any dessert with his dinner the night before.

Those who just stand around and ___grouse___ about their low salaries are not likely to get raises.

SYNONYMS: (*v.*) kvetch, bellyache

11. incarcerate (in kär′ sə rāt)

(*v.*) to imprison, confine, jail

They will ___incarcerate___ the convicted felon at the state penitentiary.

SYNONYM: intern; ANTONYMS: liberate, free

12. incumbent (in kəm′ bənt)

(*adj.*) obligatory, required; (*n.*) one who holds a specific office at the time spoken of

Voting on election day is a duty ___incumbent___ on all Americans who value a democratic government.

The ___incumbent___ has the advantage when standing for reelection but does not have a guarantee of victory.

SYNONYMS: (*adj.*) mandatory, necessary
ANTONYMS: (*adj.*) optional, unnecessary

13. jocular (jäk′ yə lər)

(*adj.*) humorous, jesting, jolly, joking

After receiving the news that she was ahead in the polls, the candidate was in a delightfully ___jocular___ mood.

SYNONYMS: waggish, facetious, droll
ANTONYMS: solemn, grave, earnest, grim

CCSS Vocabulary: 4.c. (See pp. T14–15.)

14. ludicrous (lüd′ ə krəs)

(*adj.*) ridiculous, laughable, absurd

Her comment was so ___ludicrous___ that we finally understood that she was joking.

SYNONYMS: risible, preposterous
ANTONYMS: heartrending, poignant, pathetic

15. mordant (môr′ dənt)

(*adj.*) biting or caustic in thought, manner, or style; sharply or bitterly harsh

The actor was upset by the ___mordant___ criticism of the gossip columnist who seemed out to ruin his reputation.

SYNONYMS: acrimonious, acidulous, sardonic, scathing
ANTONYMS: bland, mild, gentle, soothing

16. nettle (net′ əl)

(*n.*) a prickly or stinging plant; (*v.*) to arouse displeasure, impatience, or anger; to vex or irritate severely

If you are pricked by a ___nettle___, aloe cream will soothe and reduce the sting.

The principal was ___nettled___ by the student's disrespectful behavior.

SYNONYMS: (*v.*) peeve, annoy, incense, gall
ANTONYMS: (*v.*) please, delight, soothe, pacify

17. pecuniary (pi kyü′ nē er ē)

(*adj.*) consisting of or measured in money; of or related to money

The couple was forced by ___pecuniary___ considerations to sell their large home and buy a smaller one.

SYNONYM: monetary

18. pusillanimous (pyü sə lan′ ə məs)

(*adj.*) contemptibly cowardly or mean-spirited

It is often said that bullies, when tested, are the most ___pusillanimous___ people of all.

SYNONYM: lily-livered
ANTONYMS: stouthearted, courageous

19. recumbent (ri kəm′ bənt)

(*adj.*) in a reclining position, lying down, in the posture of one sleeping or resting

The tired toddlers were ___recumbent___ on the couch after playing all afternoon in the yard.

SYNONYMS: prone, supine, inactive
ANTONYMS: erect, energetic, dynamic

20. stratagem (strat′ ə jəm)

(*n.*) a scheme to outwit or deceive an opponent or to gain an end

The defense attorney used a clever ___stratagem___ to curry sympathy for her client.

SYNONYMS: trick, ploy, subterfuge

C CCSS Vocabulary: 4.c. (See pp. T14–15.)

Choosing the Right Word

*Select the **boldface** word that better completes each sentence. You might refer to the selection on pages 50–51 to see how most of these words are used in context.*

1. In Victorian times, fashionable ladies (**disarrayed, incarcerated**) their waists in tight corsets to achieve a chic "hourglass" figure.

2. During the 19th century, it was fashionable to spend a few weeks in the fall hunting (**grouse, nettles**), pheasants, and other game birds.

3. Comfortably (**recumbent, frenetic**) in the shade of the elm tree, I watched the members of the football team go through a long, hard workout.

4. The affairs of our city are in such (**disarray, flotsam**) that the state may have to intervene to restore some semblance of order.

5. Before the ceremony began, we all bowed our heads and hoped for unity, peace, and (**concord, atrophy**) among all nations.

Victorian dress with a high neckline and long, full skirt

6. We were fascinated by the (**mordant, frenetic**) scene on the floor of the stock exchange as brokers struggled to keep up with sudden price changes.

7. I have always regarded our schools and colleges as citadels of learning and (**bastions, stratagems**) against ignorance and superstition.

8. Do you really think that those (**jocular, recumbent**) remarks are appropriate on such a solemn occasion?

9. In the shelter, I saw for the first time people who'd been beaten and discouraged by life—the so-called derelicts and (**flotsam, incumbents**) of the great city.

10. The only way we'll really be able to increase productivity is to offer our employees a few solid (**frenetic, pecuniary**) incentives to work harder.

11. We were able to (**consummate, glean**) only a few shreds of useful information from his long, pretentious speech.

12. Of the ten Congressional seats in our state, only one was won by a new member; all the other winners were (**incumbents, bastions**).

13. There are few things in life as (**frenetic, ludicrous**) as an unqualified person trying to assume the trappings of authority.

14. The huge influx of wealth that resulted from foreign conquests led in part to the physical and moral (**atrophy, flotsam**) of the Roman ruling class.

15. What we need to cope with this crisis is not cute (**grouses, stratagems**) but a bold, realistic plan and the courage to carry it out.

CCSS Vocabulary: 4.d. (See pp. T14–15.)

16. All that I needed to (**consummate, nettle**) the most important deal of my career was her signature on the dotted line.

17. To feel fear in difficult situations is natural, but to allow one's conduct to be governed by fear is (**jocular, pusillanimous**).

18. I noticed with approval that his (**pecuniary, mordant**) remarks were intended to deflate the pompous and unmask the hypocritical.

19. It has been said that the only way to handle a (**nettle, stratagem**), or any difficult problem, without being stung is to grasp it firmly and decisively.

20. A born leader is someone who can rise to the (**incumbents, exigencies**) of any crisis that he or she may be confronted with.

21. Why did my grandparents feel it necessary to show the (**pecuniary, ludicrous**) photo of me dressed as a chicken to my new girlfriend?

22. Although most of the diners' comments were favorable, several (**grouses, concords**) about the soggy salads dismayed the chef.

23. Recent polls confirm a widespread (**atrophy, nettle**) in small business owners' abilities to secure bank loans at reasonable rates.

24. In his 1907 painting *The Sick Child*, Edvard Munch's depiction of a (**jocular, recumbent**) adolescent creates a mood of despair.

25. The undisciplined puppy (**disarrayed, consummated**) the boxes in the garage.

Choose the word from this unit that is the same or most nearly the same in meaning as the ***boldface*** *word or expression in the phrase. Write that word on the line. Use a dictionary if necessary.*

1. **gripes** about every change in the routine _grouses_
2. received **financial** compensation _pecuniary_
3. the ill-conceived **ruse** _stratagem_
4. **collected** tidbits of information _gleaned_
5. a longtime **bulwark** of resistance _bastion_
6. **prostrate** on a hospital bed _recumbent_
7. **craven** behavior _pusillanimous_
8. a **witty** conversation _jocular_
9. **immured** for years in a dank dungeon _incarcerated_
10. **irks** her coworkers with senseless chatter _nettles_

 CCSS Vocabulary: 5. (See pp. T14–15.)

Antonyms

*Choose the word from this unit that is most nearly opposite in meaning to the **boldface** word or expression in the phrase. Write that word on the line. Use a dictionary if necessary.*

1. made a **daring** attempt ______pusillanimous______
2. enthusiasm that **developed** ______atrophied______
3. stayed **upright** without moving ______recumbent______
4. **release** the trapped bat ______incarcerate______
5. a **humorless** manner ______jocular______

Completing the Sentence

From the words in this unit, choose the one that best completes each of the following sentences. Write the word in the space provided.

1. The defeated army fled in such ______disarray______ that before long it had become little more than a uniformed mob.
2. People who are used to the unhurried atmosphere of a country town often find it hard to cope with the ______frenetic______ pace of big-city life.
3. Almost every case of muscle or tissue ______atrophy______ is the result of disease, prolonged disuse, or changes in cell nutrition.
4. I have yet to meet an adult who did not ______grouse______ about the taxes he or she had to pay.
5. I get my best ideas while lying down; the ______recumbent______ position seems to stimulate my brain.
6. The ______exigencies______ of my present financial situation demand that I curtail all unnecessary expenses for at least a month.
7. Even critics of our penal system admit that as long as hardened criminals are ______incarcerated______, they can't commit further crimes.
8. Shakespeare's Timon of Athens is a disillusioned misanthrope who spends his time hurling ______mordant______ barbs at the rest of mankind.
9. As soon as he struck the opening chords of the selection, we realized that we were listening to a(n) ______consummate______ master of the piano.
10. The ______flotsam______ that we observed here and there in the harbor bore mute testimony to the destructive power of the storm.

11. I regret that Nancy was **nettled** by my unfavorable review of her short story, but I had to express my opinion honestly.

12. Most people regarded the government's attempt to avert a war by buying off the aggressor as not only shameful but **pusillanimous**.

13. It was pleasant to see the usually quiet and restrained Mr. Baxter in such a(n) **jocular** and expansive mood.

14. It is **incumbent** on all of us to do whatever we can to help our community overcome this crisis.

15. Since I had had only one year of high-school French, my attempts to speak that language on my trip to Paris were pretty **ludicrous**.

16. Peace is not just the absence of war but a positive state of **concord** among the nations of the world.

17. Despite all their highfalutin malarkey about helping the poor, I suspect that their interest in the project is purely **pecuniary**.

18. Though next to nothing is known about Homer, historians have been able to **glean** a few odd facts about him from studying his works.

19. The high ground east of the river formed a natural **bastion**, which we decided to defend with all the forces at our disposal.

20. The purpose of our **stratagem** was to draw in the safety so that Tom could get behind him to receive a long pass.

Writing: Words in Action

Answers to both prompts will vary.

1. Look back at "Reforming the Security Council" (pages 50–51). Think about how the U.N. Security Council could become more effective. Which one of the possible changes to the Council that the author mentions do you think makes the most sense? Write a persuasive essay explaining the single most important change to the Security Council that you would like to see made. Use at least two details from the passage and three unit words to support your argument.

2. *"Nearly all men can stand adversity, but if you want to test a man's character, give him power."—Abraham Lincoln*

   Do you agree with Lincoln's statement? How does having power bring out the best or the worst in a person? Write an essay that explains your opinion, using specific examples from your reading (refer to pages 50–51), your studies, or your own experience and observations to clarify and support your ideas. Write at least three paragraphs, and use three or more words from this unit.

Writing prompt #2 is modeled on that of standardized tests.

CCSS Vocabulary: 6; Writing: 2.d., 3.d. (See pp. T14–15.)

Vocabulary in Context: Informational Text for Unit 4 is available online at **vocabularyworkshop.com**.

Vocabulary in Context

Literary Text

The following excerpts are from Thomas Hardy's novels Jude the Obscure *and* Tess of the d'Urbervilles. *Some of the words you have studied in this unit appear in* **boldface** *type. Complete each statement below the excerpt by circling the letter of the correct answer.*

1. The sight of it [a milestone], unimpaired, within its screen of grass and **nettles**, lit in his soul a spark of the old fire. Surely his plan should be to move onward through good and ill—to avoid morbid sorrow even though he did see uglinesses in the world? (*Jude the Obscure*)

Nettles are

a. tiny pebbles
b. thick roots
c. prickly plants
d. crumbling rocks

2. As a set-off against such discussions as these there had come an improvement in their **pecuniary** position, which earlier in their experience would have made them cheerful. (*Jude the Obscure*)

A **pecuniary** position is related to

a. money
b. emotions
c. family
d. taxes

The 1998 TV version of *Tess of the d'Urbervilles* stars Justine Waddell.

3. To have suggested such a story was certainly not very exhilarating, in a serious view of their position. However, in a few minutes Sue seemed to see that their position this morning had a **ludicrous** side, and wiping her eyes she laughed. (*Jude the Obscure*)

Something **ludicrous** is

a. pathetic
b. arbitrary
c. fleeting
d. absurd

4. She musingly turned to withdraw, passing near an altar-tomb, the oldest of them all, on which was a **recumbent** figure. In the dusk she had not noticed it before, and would hardly have noticed it now but for an odd fancy that the effigy moved. (*Tess of the d'Urbervilles*)

Someone who is **recumbent** is NOT

a. talkative
b. hideous
c. sturdy
d. standing

5. They [the mountain summits] had a low and unassuming aspect from this upland, though as approached on the other side from Blackmoor in her childhood they were as lofty **bastions** against the sky. (*Tess of the d'Urbervilles*)

Bastions are

a. strongholds
b. benedictions
c. shadows
d. omens

Interactive Quiz

Snap the code, or go to **vocabularyworkshop.com**

CCSS Vocabulary: 4.c.; Reading (Literature): 4. (See pp. T14–15.)

Note that not all of the 20 unit words are used in this passage. *Figment* and ignominy are not included in the passage.

Read the following selection, taking note of the ***boldface*** *words and their contexts. These words are among those you will be studying in Unit 5. As you complete the exercises in this unit, it may help to refer to the way the words are used below.*

CCSS Vocabulary: 4; Reading (Informational Text): 4, 6. (See pp. T14–15.)

What Is Pop Art?

<Essay>

Roy Lichtenstein's "In the Car," 1963, looks like a comic strip but measures more than 6 feet wide.

What is pop art? The simple answer: Art based on popular culture. Beginning in the mid-1950s and continuing for more than a decade, pop artists borrowed images directly from everyday popular culture. Drawing upon this seemingly **mundane** content, pop artists created bold, overpowering images. With great **acuity**, their canvases detailed such familiar things as comic strips, American flags, race cars, popular movie stars, and even boxes of laundry detergent.

In many ways, pop art was a reaction to abstract expressionism, the dominant style of painting during the 1940s and 1950s. Abstract expressionist paintings were nonrepresentational; they did not **delineate** objects directly. Instead, artists used abstract shapes and **nuances** in color to express personal ideas and feelings. Pop artists viewed abstract expressionism as elitist—too **esoteric** to be appreciated by most museum goers. In response, they returned to representational art. This was a time when consumerism was booming in the United States and advertising had become **ubiquitous**. So the world around the pop artists became a **fecund** source of images.

At first, pop art **garnered** much negative criticism. Some critics complained that pop art's **penchant** for reproducing existing images—such as painting a portrait of a can of soup—was too easy. Others claimed the pop artist's love of commercial images **enervated** traditional artistic values. A few critics even implied that pop art was **depraved**, or at least was

Warhol, Andy (1928–1987). *Vegetarian Vegetable from Campbell's Soup II*. 1969. Screenprint, $35\frac{1}{8}$ x $23\frac{1}{16}$ in. Gift of Mr. and Mrs. Peter Eider-Orley, 1972 (1972.724.3). The Metropolitan Museum of Art, New York, NY.

devoid of aesthetic principles. Pop artists dismissed these arguments as so much **sophistry**. Why should traditional art be **hallowed** and commercial art be dismissed as vulgar? Was it a declaration of truth or a mere **fiat** when a critic pronounced one piece art and another trash?

No doubt reminding themselves that beauty is in the eye of the beholder, pop artists ignored the critics and continued to explore the relationship between the two types of art, playing around with commercial images and presenting them as works of art. Roy Lichtenstein, for example, chose comic strips as his main subject. Reproducing all the **idiosyncrasies** of this format, including voice balloons and printing dots, he chose frames that showed violent action or sentimental romance. The images, enlarged to monumental size and completely out of context, took on a new significance.

Andy Warhol is **reputed** to have eaten soup for lunch every day for twenty years. Perhaps that explains why he, the best-known of the pop artists, first became famous for his images of soup cans and other consumer products. Later, glamour and fame became a central theme of his work, and he produced **sumptuous** silkscreens of celebrities, such as Marilyn Monroe and Elvis Presley. Thanks to an **overweening** desire for publicity, Andy Warhol helped make pop art a household term, and he became one of the wealthiest artists of all time.

Pop art sculptors were also active, again taking consumer products as their starting point. Claes Oldenburg stuffed and painted cloth to produce giant hamburgers, toothpaste tubes, and ice cream bars. Like so much pop art, Oldenburg's "soft sculptures" remind us that, in pop art, the ordinary things of life become strange and things that we take for granted are seen anew, as if for the first time.

Pop art outlived its critics, and today, a half century later, its seriousness is not in doubt. As a movement, pop art ended, but not before greatly expanding the range of subjects, attitudes, and techniques available to all artists. Thanks to the pop artists, younger generations of painters, sculptors, and photographers now explore the world in more imaginative and thought-provoking ways.

Snap the code, or go to vocabularyworkshop.com

Note the spelling, pronunciation, part(s) of speech, and definition(s) of each of the following words. Then write the word in the blank spaces in the illustrative sentence(s) following. Finally, study the lists of synonyms and antonyms.

1. acuity (ə kyü′ ə tē)

(*n.*) sharpness (particularly of the mind or senses)

The **acuity** of most people's hearing diminishes as they grow older.

SYNONYM: acuteness
ANTONYMS: dullness, obtuseness

2. delineate (di lin′ ē āt)

(*v.*) to portray, sketch, or describe in accurate and vivid detail; to represent pictorially

The architects will **delineate** the main features of their plan at the next client meeting.

SYNONYMS: picture, render

3. depraved (di prāvd′)

(*adj.*) marked by evil and corruption, devoid of moral principles

Oscar Wilde's novel *The Picture of Dorian Gray* is about a **depraved** man whose portrait reveals his wickedness.

SYNONYMS: perverted, degenerate, vicious, corrupt
ANTONYMS: moral, virtuous, upright, uncorrupted

4. enervate (en′ ər vāt)

(*v.*) to weaken or lessen the mental, moral, or physical vigor of; enfeeble, hamstring

Unfortunately, the great musician's mind was **enervated** by disease in the last decade of her life.

SYNONYMS: impair, cripple, paralyze
ANTONYMS: invigorate, strengthen, buttress

5. esoteric (es ə ter′ ik)

(*adj.*) intended for or understood by only a select few, private, secret

The fraternity developed a set of **esoteric** rites that had to be performed by anyone seeking membership.

SYNONYMS: cryptic, arcane, recondite
ANTONYMS: accessible, comprehensible, intelligible

6. fecund (fek′ und)

(*adj.*) fruitful in offspring or vegetation; intellectually productive

The remarkably **fecund** mind of Albert Einstein produced theories that revolutionized the science of physics.

SYNONYMS: fertile, teeming, prolific
ANTONYMS: infertile, barren, unproductive

CCSS Vocabulary: 4.c., 4.d. (See pp. T14–15.)

7. fiat
(fē ət)

(*n.*) an arbitrary order or decree; a command or act of will or consciousness

The ruler instituted several new ___fiats___.

SYNONYMS: dictum, ukase

8. figment
(fig′ mənt)

(*n.*) a fabrication of the mind; an arbitrary notion

The silhouette of a man on the porch was a mere ___figment___ of your overheated imagination.

SYNONYMS: invention, fancy

9. garner
(gär′ nər)

(*v.*) to acquire as the result of effort; to gather and store away, as for future use

Over the years, the writer was able to ___garner___ some wisdom that she passed on to others in her books.

SYNONYMS: collect, accumulate, accrue
ANTONYMS: scatter, squander, waste, dissipate

10. hallow
(hal′ ō)

(*v.*) to set apart as holy or sacred, sanctify, consecrate; to honor greatly, revere

In the Gettysburg Address, Lincoln ___hallowed___ the battlefield on which the Union soldiers fought and died.

SYNONYMS: venerate, bless
ANTONYMS: defile, profane

11. idiosyncrasy
(id ē ə siŋ′ krə sē)

(*n.*) a peculiarity that serves to distinguish or identify

The fact that the plurals of some nouns are formed irregularly is an ___idiosyncrasy___ of English grammar.

SYNONYMS: quirk, mannerism

12. ignominy
(ig′ nə min ē)

(*n.*) shame and disgrace

He went from glory to ___ignominy___.

SYNONYMS: humiliation, disrepute, odium
ANTONYMS: honor, acclaim

13. mundane
(mən dān′)

(*adj.*) earthly, worldly, relating to practical and material affairs; concerned with what is ordinary

The painter left all ___mundane___ concerns to her sister while she single-mindedly pursued her artistic goals.

SYNONYMS: prosaic, humdrum, routine, sublunary
ANTONYMS: heavenly, spiritual, transcendental

CCSS Vocabulary: 4.c. (See pp. T14–15.)

14. nuance (nü′ äns)

(*n.*) a subtle or slight variation (as in color, meaning, quality), delicate gradation or shade of difference

In his writing, the poet paid close attention to every ____**nuance**____ of meaning in the words he chose.

SYNONYMS: shade, nicety, refinement

15. overweening (ō vər wē ′niŋ)

(*adj.*) conceited, presumptuous; excessive, immoderate

It was the ____**overweening**____ confidence of the candidate that prevented her from acknowledging her weaknesses.

SYNONYMS: arrogant, unbridled, inflated
ANTONYMS: restrained, understated, meek

16. penchant (pen′ chənt)

(*n.*) a strong attraction or inclination

A teacher with a ____**penchant**____ for belaboring the obvious is bound to be boring.

SYNONYMS: proclivity, predilection
ANTONYMS: disinclination, aversion

17. reputed (ri pyüt′ id)

(*adj.*) according to reputation or general belief; having widespread acceptance and good reputation; (*part.*) alleged

Although he is the ____**reputed**____ head of a crime syndicate, he has never spent time in jail.

SYNONYMS: putative, reputable
ANTONYMS: proven, corroborated, authenticated

18. sophistry (säf′ ə strē)

(*n.*) reasoning that seems plausible but is actually unsound; a fallacy

The couple was beguiled into buying a bigger house than they needed by the clever ____**sophistry**____ of the broker.

SYNONYM: specious reasoning

19. sumptuous (səmp′ chü əs)

(*adj.*) costly, rich, magnificent

The ____**sumptuous**____ feast honoring the king's birthday was followed by musical entertainment.

SYNONYMS: lavish, munificent, opulent, splendid
ANTONYMS: skimpy, stingy, niggardly, spartan

20. ubiquitous (yü bik′ wə təs)

(*adj.*) present or existing everywhere

The ____**ubiquitous**____ eye of the TV camera threatens to rob citizens of any sense of privacy.

SYNONYMS: pervasive, universal
ANTONYMS: restricted, limited, rare, scarce

CCSS Vocabulary: 4.c. (See pp. T14–15.)

Choosing the Right Word

*Select the **boldface** word that better completes each sentence. You might refer to the selection on pages 60–61 to see how most of these words are used in context.*

A relief of Cleopatra, the last ruler of ancient Egypt (51 BC–30 BC).

1. Cleopatra took her own life rather than suffer the (**figment, ignominy**) of being led through the streets of Rome in chains.
2. Her imagination is like a (**fecund, depraved**) field in which new ideas spring up like so many ripe ears of corn.
3. Scandal and corruption may so (**enervate, delineate**) an administration that it can no longer function effectively.
4. Two synonyms are rarely exactly the same because (**fiats, nuances**) of tone or applicability make each of the words unique.
5. Few writers have J. D. Salinger's remarkable ability to (**delineate, garner**) the emotions and aspirations of the average teenager.
6. It is only in superior mental powers, not in physical strength or (**ignominy, acuity**) of the senses, that human beings surpass other living things.

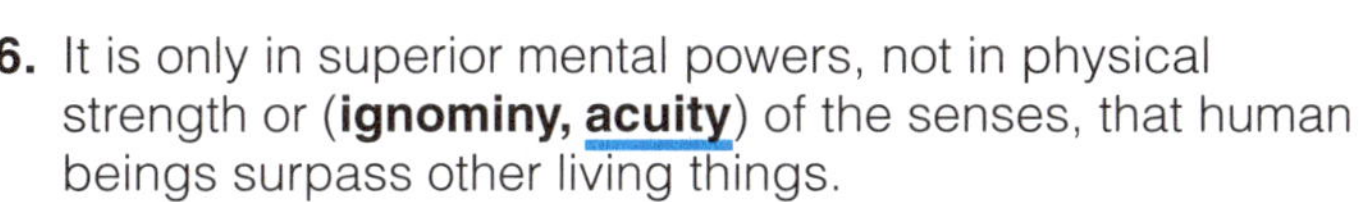

7. Your language is indeed clever and amusing, but your argument is nothing but a piece of outright (**sophistry, idiosyncrasy**).
8. Someone with a pronounced (**penchant, figment**) for saying the wrong thing might justly be described as a victim of "foot-in-mouth" disease.
9. The (**sumptuous, ubiquitous**) banquet was a pleasant change of pace from the spartan fare to which I had become accustomed.
10. He means well, but we cannot tolerate his highly (**idiosyncratic, fecund**) behavior in an organization that depends on discipline and teamwork.
11. Like a true fanatic, he considers anyone who disagrees with him on any issue to be either feebleminded or (**depraved, mundane**).
12. A true sign of intellectual maturity is the ability to distinguish the (**figments, penchants**) of wishful thinking from reality.
13. In a democracy, the government must rule by persuasion and consent—not by mere (**fiat, sophistry**).
14. How I'd love to knock the wind out of the sails of that lout's (**fecund, overweening**) conceit!
15. The conversation between the computer programmers was so (**esoteric, ubiquitous**) that I wasn't sure they were speaking English.

CCSS Vocabulary: 4.d. (See pp. T14–15.)

16. In that rarefied atmosphere, I was afraid to ask about anything quite so (**sumptuous, mundane**) as the location of the rest room.

17. I appreciate all those kind expressions of gratitude for my services, but I had hoped also to (**garner, nuance**) some cash.

18. The alert defense put up by our team completely neutralized our opponents' (**reputedly, sumptuously**) unstoppable passing attack.

19. We will never abandon a cause that has been (**garnered, hallowed**) by the achievements and sacrifices of so many noble people.

20. Probably no complaint of young people is more (**ubiquitous, depraved**) than "My parents don't understand me!"

21. In Shakespeare's *Othello* and *King Lear*, the (**overweening, sumptuous**) pride of the title characters contributes to their tragic downfalls.

22. Eight White Sox players in the 1919 World Series were banned from baseball for throwing games and forced to live with the (**fiat, ignominy**) of their actions.

23. The orator who is most able to recognize and rebut his or her opponent's persuasive (**figments, sophistry**) consistently will win the debate.

24. Weary of her (**mundane, ubiquitous**) day-to-day life, the woman embarked on a summer-long bicycle adventure across the continental United States.

25. Given my (**penchant, nuance**) for spicy food, I should enjoy the cayenne pepper.

Synonyms

Choose the word from this unit that is the same or most nearly the same in meaning as the ***boldface*** *word or expression in the phrase. Write that word on the line. Use a dictionary if necessary.*

1. known for his **propensity** for exaggeration — penchant

2. as a result of a general **edict** — fiat

3. a **supposed** heir to a huge fortune — reputed

4. an **eccentricity** of speech — idiosyncrasy

5. **depicted** the view from the balcony — delineated

6. sought **occult** knowledge in ancient books — esoteric

7. the latest **creation** of his imagination — figment

8. their **omnipresent** sense of dread — ubiquitous

9. known for the **keenness** of her wit — acuity

10. the **dishonor** of plagiarism — ignominy

CCSS Vocabulary: 5. (See pp. T14–15.)

Antonyms

*Choose the word from this unit that is most nearly opposite in meaning to the **boldface** word or expression in the phrase. Write that word on the line. Use a dictionary if necessary.*

1. a man of **modest** aspirations ____overweening____
2. the **other worldly** side of life ____mundane____
3. made a **meager** meal ____sumptuous____
4. the **glory** of her situation ____ignominy____
5. believed the story was **reality** ____(a) figment____

Completing the Sentence

From the words in this unit, choose the one that best completes each of the following sentences. Write the word in the space provided.

1. The marathon not only brought in huge sums of money for Africa's starving masses, but also ____garnered____ much sympathy for their plight.

2. Beneath the man's cultivated manner and impeccable grooming there lurked the ____depraved____ mind of a brutal sadist.

3. The man is ____reputed____ to have mob connections, but so far no one has actually substantiated the allegation.

4. May I interrupt this abstruse discussion and turn your attention to more ____mundane____ matters—like what's for dinner?

5. Most people I know are so busy dealing with the ordinary problems of life that they have no time for ____esoteric____ philosophical speculation.

6. During the eleven years of his "personal rule," King Charles I bypassed Parliament and ruled England by royal ____fiat____.

7. Analysis will show that his "brilliant exposition" of how we can handle the pollution problem without cost to anyone is sheer ____sophistry____.

8. I was so ____enervated____ by the oppressive heat and humidity of that awful afternoon that I could barely move.

9. The phonograph is but one of the wonderful new devices that sprang from the ____fecund____ mind of Thomas Edison, our most prolific inventor.

10. "Your suspicion that I am constantly making fun of you behind your back is a mere ____figment____ of your overheated brain," I replied.

CCSS Vocabulary: 4.a. (See pp. T14–15.)

11. The ground in which those soldiers are buried was **hallowed** by the blood they shed on it.

12. He was a changed young man after he suffered the **ignominy** of expulsion from West Point for conduct unbecoming a gentleman.

13. His constant use of the word *fabulous*, even for quite ordinary subjects, is a(n) **idiosyncrasy** that I could do without.

14. There is quite a difference between the austere furnishings of my little apartment and the **sumptuous** accommodations of a luxury hotel.

15. His **overweening** sense of superiority dominates his personality in much the same way as his beetling brow dominates his face.

16. You may have many good traits, but I do not admire your **penchant** for borrowing things and failing to return them.

17. The passing years lessened her physical vigor but in no way diminished the **acuity** of her judgment.

18. Music can often express a(n) **nuance** of mood or feeling that would be difficult to put into words.

19. The artist's sketch not only **delineated** the model's appearance accurately, but also captured something of her personality.

20. American-style fast-food shops have gained such popularity all over the world that they are now truly **ubiquitous**.

Writing: Words in Action

Answers to both prompts will vary.

1. Look back at "What Is Pop Art?" (pages 60–61). Think about the kinds of art and music that are popular today. How have styles of art and music changed over the years? How do they reflect the social values and issues of a specific time period? Write a brief essay in which you analyze one or two current trends in art or music, explaining what they reveal about contemporary society. Use at least two details from the passage and three unit words in your analysis.

2. For centuries, people have tried to answer this question: "Is some art actually better than other art, or is the quality of a work of art really just a matter of personal taste?" What is your opinion? If there is good and bad art, then what makes good art good, and what makes bad art bad? Write at least three paragraphs explaining your viewpoint. Support your ideas with specific details from your reading (pages 60–61), your prior knowledge, and your personal experience and observations.

Writing prompt #2 is modeled on that of standardized tests.

CCSS Vocabulary: 6; Writing: 2.d., 3.d. (See pp. T14–15.)

Vocabulary in Context: Informational Text for Unit 5 is available online at **vocabularyworkshop.com**.

Vocabulary in Context
Literary Text

The following excerpts are from Charles Dickens's novel David Copperfield. *Some of the words you have studied in this unit appear in* ***boldface*** *type. Complete each statement below the excerpt by circling the letter of the correct answer.*

1. By and by, when we had dined in a **sumptuous** manner off boiled dabs, melted butter, and potatoes, with a chop for me, a hairy man with a very good-natured face came home.

Something that is **sumptuous** is

a. casual
b. magnificent
c. protracted
d. companionable

2. "The victim, from my cradle, of pecuniary liabilities to which I have been unable to respond, I have ever been the sport and toy of debasing circumstances. **Ignominy,** Want, Despair, and Madness, have, collectively or separately, been the attendants of my career."

Ignominy is

a. disgrace
b. poverty
c. larceny
d. imprisonment

A scene from the 1935 film version of *David Copperfield*, starring W.C. Fields as Mr. Micawber and Freddie Bartholomew as David Copperfield.

3. "Miss Dartle," I returned, "you deepen the injury... you do him a great wrong."

"I do him no wrong," she returned. "They are a **depraved**, worthless set."

Someone who is **depraved** is definitely NOT

a. reasonable
b. dynamic
c. cheerful
d. moral

4. Before this boy, who was **reputed** to be a great scholar, and was very good-looking, and at least half-a-dozen years my senior, I was carried as before a magistrate.

A person who is **reputed** to be a scholar is

a. generally believed to be one
b. expected to become one
c. humble about his abilities
d. devoted to his studies

5. What other changes have come upon me, besides the changes in my growth and looks, and in the knowledge I have **garnered** all this while?

When something is **garnered**, it is

a. verified
b. gathered
c. utilized
d. dispersed

Snap the code, or go to **vocabularyworkshop.com**

Note that not all of the 20 unit words are used in this passage. *Agnostic*, *effigy*, and *sylvan* are not included in the passage.

Read the following selection, taking note of the ***boldface*** *words and their contexts. These words are among those you will be studying in Unit 6. As you complete the exercises in this unit, it may help to refer to the way the words are used below.*

CCSS Vocabulary: 4; Reading (Informational Text): 4, 6. (See pp. T14–15.)

Your Papers, Please

<Debate>

Today's debate question is: *Should every citizen of the United States be required to have a national identity card?*

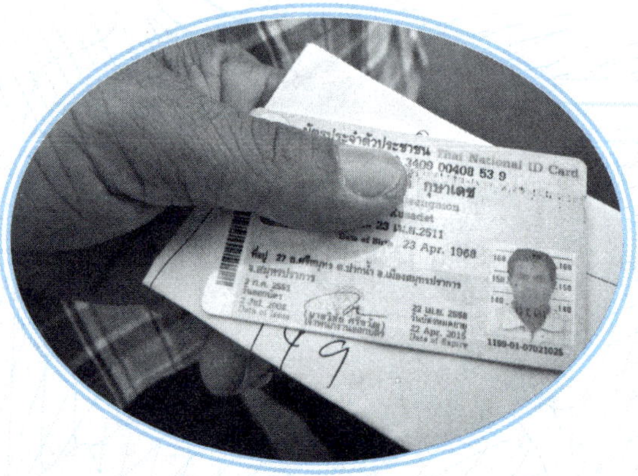

Tessa: The United States should implement a national identity card system without delay. Failure to do so would make the government **derelict** in its duty to protect citizens, as well as constitute a **travesty** of common sense. The most compelling argument favoring national ID cards is the crucial, ongoing effort to forestall any terrorist attacks against the United States. Advocates of national ID cards have noted with **perspicacity** that our existing system of **surveillance** has been proved inadequate and has failed in the past to detect the **complicity** of the terrorists in plots against the Unites States.

Tyrone: All that glitters is not gold, Tessa, and establishment of a national ID card would be an **abject** surrender of civil liberties and our citizens' right to privacy. At the risk of sounding **testy**, I firmly dispute the implicit assumption that an ID card system would have foiled previous terrorist attacks. That conjecture is an illusion in this high-tech world, where forgery, hacking, and identity theft might well have equipped terrorists with fake cards.

Tessa: I believe a national ID card would have several **indubitable** benefits, Tyrone. First, it would offer consistency, in contrast to the varying requirements of the states for the issue of driver's licenses. Second, an ID card system could be administered with **equity**. Despite the **diatribes** of privacy advocates against such a system, an effective ID card setup could operate with only five basic elements: name, address, Social Security number, photograph, and a finger or retinal print matching a chip on the card. Even a civil liberties **neophyte** would hesitate before raising an **indictment** of such requirements.

Tyrone: Tessa, people's right to privacy is the most important **motif** in my critique of a national ID card system, as there are numerous unresolved questions about the elements, requirements, and circumstances of an ID card program. All these questions would affect privacy: Would the program be voluntary or mandatory, for example? Who could lawfully demand presentation of the card, and on what occasions? Should the card be local, federal, or international? How much information could the government collect?

To ignore the risk of a slippery slope here would be **inane**. In the information age, everyone knows the extent to which giant institutions tend to assemble more and more data on citizens, sometimes for illegitimate purposes.

Tessa: I have several more arguments, Tyrone—the first of which is with a national ID card system concerns about racial and ethnic profiling would no longer be **moot**, because such concerns would be nullified by the uniformities of the card system. **Intermittent** harassment of minority groups would thus in all likelihood decline. Finally, many other countries, especially in Europe, use national ID cards successfully, so why not here?

Tyrone: A national ID card system would grant a single institution, the federal government, **plenary** powers to accrue information on all American citizens, so the potential for abuse is discernible. Contrary to your assertion, Tessa, racial profiling might actually increase. In other parts of the world with this system, the police are often entitled to demand presentation of the card on the threat of arrest. The misuse of ID cards under totalitarian governments such as in South Africa, the former Soviet Union, and China has long been known. Let's consider carefully before we go down that path.

Snap the code, or go to **vocabularyworkshop.com**

Left: A foreign national ID card; Right: fraudulent government documents seized by U.S. Customs in New York

Note the spelling, pronunciation, part(s) of speech, and definition(s) of each of the following words. Then write the word in the blank spaces in the illustrative sentence(s) following. Finally, study the lists of synonyms and antonyms.

1. abject (ab′ jekt)

(*adj.*) degraded; base, contemptible; cringing, servile; complete and unrelieved

In the American dream, those who work hard can escape lives of **abject** poverty.

SYNONYMS: wretched, miserable, ignoble, sheer, utter
ANTONYMS: noble, exalted

2. agnostic (ag näs′ tik)

(*n.*) one who believes that nothing can be known about God; a skeptic; (*adj.*) without faith, skeptical

Although he was a confirmed **agnostic**, he supported the rights of others to practice their religion.

Her **agnostic** tendencies made it difficult for her to subscribe to any set of religious beliefs.

SYNONYM: (*n.*) doubter
ANTONYM: (*n.*) believer

3. complicity (kəm plis′ ə tē)

(*n.*) involvement in wrongdoing; the state of being an accomplice

If you know a crime is going to be committed but do nothing to prevent it, you may be accused of **complicity**.

SYNONYMS: connivance, collusion
ANTONYMS: noninvolvement, innocence

4. derelict (der′ ə likt)

(*n.*) someone or something that is abandoned or neglected; (*adj.*) left abandoned; neglectful of duty

The family complained about the unsightly collection of **derelict** cars in its neighbor's driveway.

SYNONYMS: (*n.*) vagrant; (*adj.*) delinquent
ANTONYMS: (*adj.*) punctilious, conscientious, scrupulous

5. diatribe (dī′ ə trīb)

(*n.*) a bitter and prolonged verbal attack

The senator's speech was more of a **diatribe** than a reasoned address.

SYNONYMS: harangue, tirade
ANTONYMS: panegyric, encomium, eulogy

6. effigy (ef′ ə jē)

(*n.*) a crude image of a despised person

The night before the battle, the troops burned the despised enemy leader in **effigy**.

SYNONYMS: figure, figurine

CCSS Vocabulary: 4.c., 4.d. (See pp. T14–15.)

7. equity
(ek′ wət ē)

(*n.*) the state or quality of being just, fair, or impartial; fair and equal treatment; something that is fair; the money value of a property above and beyond any mortgage or other claim

Prompted by considerations of ___**equity**___, the father decided to divide his estate equally among his children.

SYNONYMS: justice, fairness, impartiality
ANTONYMS: unfairness, bias, prejudice

8. inane
(in ān′)

(*adj.*) silly, empty of meaning or value

The politician made an ___**inane**___ reply to the interviewer's probing question.

SYNONYMS: idiotic, moronic, fatuous
ANTONYMS: sensible, meaningful, profound

9. indictment
(in dīt′ mənt)

(*n.*) the act of accusing; a formal accusation

The grand jury delivered the ___**indictment**___.

SYNONYMS: charge, accusation

10. indubitable
(in dü′ bə tə bəl)

(*adj.*) certain, not to be doubted or denied

You cannot argue with ___**indubitable**___ truths.

SYNONYMS: unquestionable, indisputable
ANTONYMS: questionable, debatable, dubious

11. intermittent
(in tər mit′ ənt)

(*adj.*) stopping and beginning again, sporadic

She had ___**intermittent**___ back pains for a week.

SYNONYMS: fitful, spasmodic, random
ANTONYM: uninterrupted

12. moot
(müt)

(*adj.*) open to discussion and debate, unresolved; (*v.*) to bring up for discussion; (*n.*) a hypothetical law case argued by students

The class agreed that the question of whether Jefferson should have retaliated sooner against the Barbary pirates was a ___**moot**___ point.

The committee members decided to ___**moot**___ the issue to the full Congress at the earliest opportunity.

The law student prepared for the ___**moot**___.

SYNONYMS: (*adj.*) debatable, questionable; (*v.*) broach
ANTONYMS: (*adj.*) undebatable, indisputable, self-evident

13. motif
(mō tēf′)

(*n.*) a principal idea, feature, theme, or element; a repeated or dominant figure in a design

The collector admired the unusual Asian ___**motif**___ woven into the tapestry.

CCSS Vocabulary: 4.c. (See pp. T14–15.)

14. neophyte (nē′ ə fīt)

(*n.*) a new convert, beginner, novice

In comparison to an experienced wilderness hiker, he is a mere ____**neophyte**____ in the woods.

SYNONYMS: tenderfoot, tyro
ANTONYMS: veteran, past master, expert, pro

15. perspicacity (pər spə kas′ ət ē)

(*n.*) keenness in observing and understanding

The bird watcher scans the surrounding trees and fields with the same ____**perspicacity**____ as a hawk looking for prey.

SYNONYMS: acumen, discernment
ANTONYMS: dullness, obtuseness

16. plenary (plēn′ ə rē)

(*adj.*) complete in all aspects or essentials; absolute; attended by all qualified members

Because of its importance, the case was presented at a ____**plenary**____ session of the Superior Court.

SYNONYM: unrestricted
ANTONYMS: limited, restricted, incomplete

17. surveillance (sər vā′ ləns)

(*n.*) a watch kept over a person; careful, close, and disciplined observation

The police kept the suspect under strict ____**surveillance**____ after she was released.

SYNONYMS: observation, monitoring

18. sylvan (sil′ vən)

(*adj.*) pertaining to or characteristic of forests; living or located in a forest; wooded, woody

Once upon a time, Hansel and Gretel walked down a ____**sylvan**____ path, leaving only bread crumbs.

SYNONYM: arcadian

19. testy (tes′ tē)

(*adj.*) easily irritated; characterized by impatience and exasperation

The lawyer's ____**testy**____ remarks during cross-examination probably affected her credibility with the jury.

SYNONYMS: irritable, peevish, waspish, petulant
ANTONYMS: imperturbable, unexcitable

20. travesty (trav′ ə stē)

(*n.*) a grotesque or grossly inferior imitation; a disguise, especially the clothing of the opposite sex; (*v.*) to ridicule by imitating in a broad or burlesque fashion

Instead of modernizing Shakespeare's *Twelfth Night*, they made a ____**travesty**____ of it.

The new song ____**travesties**____ the original version.

SYNONYMS: (*n.*) burlesque, caricature, farce

CCSS Vocabulary: 4.c. (See pp. T14–15.)

Choosing the Right Word

*Select the **boldface** word that better completes each sentence. You might refer to the selection on pages 70–71 to see how most of these words are used in context.*

1. Human and animal forms carved in stucco and stone are a common (**motif, neophyte**) in ancient Aztec art.

The Aztec calendar marked a sacred year of 260 days.

2. Though the book was written by an avowed (**agnostic, derelict**), it enjoyed a certain popularity with religious types.

3. As he sat before the fire reading his newspaper, Grandfather seemed the very epitome of (**plenary, sylvan**) contentment.

4. Because she is a fair-minded woman, I'm sure she will present both sides of the controversy with admirable (**equity, effigy**).

5. Though I can sometimes be as (**testy, derelict**) as an irate wasp, I normally do not lose my temper very easily.

6. Today's forecast calls for variable cloudiness with (**abject, intermittent**) periods of rain.

7. My studies have convinced me that the one dominant (**motif, diatribe**) in American history has been the expansion of democracy.

8. Bag ladies and other homeless (**neophytes, derelicts**) roam our streets in increasing numbers.

9. The awkward pause in the conversation became even more painful when he interjected his (**plenary, inane**) attempts at humor.

10. All of a sudden, a strange young man rushed onto the speaker's platform and launched into a (**travesty, diatribe**) against "big government."

11. After over 30 years in Congress, he retains the idealism of the (**agnostic, neophyte**) but has gained the practical wisdom of the veteran.

12. His disgraceful behavior since he left college is in itself a(n) (**indictment, surveillance**) of the lax, overindulgent upbringing he received.

13. What qualities will he have to fall back on when his (**indubitable, testy**) charm and good looks begin to wear thin?

14. His extraordinary ability to (**moot, travesty**) the works of popular writers is largely due to his keen eye for the ridiculous.

15. The picture shows the three Graces dancing in a forest clearing, while nymphs, satyrs, and other (**sylvan, indubitable**) creatures cavort among the trees.

CCSS Vocabulary: 4.d. (See pp. T14–15.)

16. According to that village's custom, one can get rid of an enemy by making a tiny (**effigy, motif**) of him and sticking it full of pins.

17. Observers on the ground keep close (**surveillance, equity**) on air traffic at a busy airport by means of various electronic devices, such as radar.

18. Only an (**intermittent, abject**) coward would stand idly by while a defenseless old woman was mugged in the street.

19. The historian had long been noted for the soundness of his scholarship and the (**complicity, perspicacity**) of his judgment.

20. "I vetoed that idea when it was first (**mooted, indicted**) years ago," the governor said, "and I have never regretted my decision."

21. How can I be accused of (**indictment, complicity**) in that plot when I did not even know the conspirators?

22. To some readers, the dark and (**intermittent, sylvan**) setting of Hawthorne's short story "Young Goodman Brown" symbolizes the unknown.

23. We laughed at Grandmother's confession that she can be (**testy, moot**) before she has her morning cup of coffee.

24. Several theology professors have given provocative reviews of the new book by Mr. Stuart, who readily admits he is an (**effigy, agnostic**).

25. The sleeping security guard was (**derelict, plenary**) in his duties.

Synonyms

*Choose the word from this unit that is the same or most nearly the same in meaning as the **boldface** word or expression in the phrase. Write that word on the line. Use a dictionary if necessary.*

1. a crude **likeness** — effigy
2. put under **scrutiny** — surveillance
3. their level of **involvement** — complicity
4. the **forested** slopes of the Rockies — sylvan
5. admired for his uncommon **acuity** — perspicacity
6. was given **unlimited** power to govern — plenary
7. indoctrinated the **rookie** — neophyte
8. a questioning **nonbeliever** — agnostic
9. **remiss** in discharging her responsibilities — derelict
10. the **vapid** chatter of thoughtless critics — inane

CCSS Vocabulary: 5. (See pp. T14–15.)

Antonyms

Choose the word from this unit that is most nearly opposite in meaning to the ***boldface*** *word or expression in the phrase. Write that word on the line. Use a dictionary if necessary.*

1. **nonparticipation** as partners ____complicity____
2. being very **clever** ____inane____
3. painted the **treeless** landscape ____sylvan____
4. pleased the **devout** ____agnostic____
5. noticed the **flattering copy** ____effigy____

Completing the Sentence

From the words in this unit, choose the one that best completes each of the following sentences. Write the word in the space provided.

1. During the emergency, the mayor assumed ____plenary____ authority and did whatever was needed to provide essential services.

2. Those who saw the young woman being assaulted and did nothing to help her were guilty of ____complicity____ in the crime.

3. The ____perspicacity____ of her analysis not only clarified the nature of the problem but also suggested its most promising solution.

4. Though some writers have emphasized Jefferson's human weaknesses, his greatness is also a(n) ____indubitable____ part of the historical record.

5. I would be ____derelict____ in my duty to you if I did not warn you against the pernicious effects of smoking cigarettes.

6. For years, we carried on a(n) ____intermittent____ correspondence, sometimes allowing months to pass before a letter was answered.

7. How could a mere ____neophyte____ in the teaching profession question the judgment of so experienced an educator?

8. The fact that so many released prisoners return to a life of crime is in itself a terrifying ____indictment____ of our penal system.

9. Throughout the period that the spy thought he had gone undetected, he was actually under close ____surveillance____ by the CIA.

10. Since the accused was never really given a chance to defend himself, his so-called trial was nothing but a(n) ____travesty____ of justice.

CCSS Vocabulary: 4.a. (See pp. T14–15.)

11. "Simple **equity** demands that we distribute the tax burden as fairly as possible among the populace," the senator remarked.

12. Since he neither affirms nor denies the existence of God, I'd classify him as a(n) **agnostic** rather than an atheist.

13. Every time we did something to anger him, he delivered an intemperate **diatribe** lambasting our "hopeless irresponsibility."

14. It was such a(n) **inane** remark that I couldn't keep myself from laughing derisively when I heard it.

15. I'd say that the phrase "having a short fuse" aptly describes my boss's decidedly **testy** disposition.

16. In her garland of leaves and acorns, the child looked very much like some **sylvan** spirit from an Arthurian myth.

17. The overthrown dictator was hanged in **effigy** before a vast throng in the town square.

18. At the slightest sound of thunder, my dog Rover dives under the bed in a state of **abject** terror.

19. In Wagner's operas, brief musical **motifs** associated with the characters or their actions recur again and again.

20. How can you call that a(n) **moot** question when it is quite clearly a simple matter of right and wrong?

Writing: Words in Action

Answers to both prompts will vary.

1. Look back at "Your Papers, Please" (pages 70–71). Think about the arguments offered by each side in the debate. Do you believe every U.S. citizen should be required to have a national identity card? Write a persuasive essay that identifies and supports your position on this issue. Use at least two details from the passage and three unit words to support your argument.

2. Legal and ethical concerns about a person's right to privacy that are part of the debate about a national ID also extend into issues in the workplace. For example, do employers have the right to monitor their employees' workplace use of the Internet (such as email and social media)? Write an essay of at least three paragraphs in which you discuss the advantages and disadvantages of such monitoring. Draw on specific examples from your own observations, studies, reading (refer to pages 70–71), or personal experiences, and use three or more words from this unit.

Writing prompt #2 is modeled on that of standardized tests.

CCSS Vocabulary: 6; Writing: 2.d., 3.d. (See pp. T14–15.)

Vocabulary in Context: Informational Text for Unit 6 is available online at **vocabularyworkshop.com**.

6

Vocabulary in Context

Literary Text

The following excerpts are from Joseph Conrad's novels Victory *and* Nostromo. *Some of the words you have studied in this unit appear in* **boldface** *type. Complete each statement below the excerpt by circling the letter of the correct answer.*

1. He felt intensely aware of her personality, as if this were the first moment of leisure he had found to look at her since they had come together. The peculiar timbre of her voice, with its modulations of audacity and sadness, would have given interest to the most **inane** chatter. But she was no chatterer. (*Victory*)

Something that is **inane** is definitely NOT

a. enjoyable
b. meaningful
c. surprising
d. boring

2. He leaned his back against one of the lofty uprights which still held up the company's signboard above the mound of **derelict** coal. Nobody could have guessed how much his blood was up. (*Victory*)

Something that is **derelict** is

a. filthy
b. primeval
c. useless
d. abandoned

3. But Don Jose, disregarding the general **indictment** as though he had not heard a word of it, took up the defense of Barrios. The man was competent enough for his special task in the plan of campaign. (*Nostromo*)

An **indictment** is a(n)

a. perspective
b. strategy
c. slander
d. accusation

Considered a great English novelist and short story writer, the Polish-born Joseph Conrad began learning English at age twenty.

4. Not to have bound and gagged him seemed to Decoud now the height of improvident folly. As long as the miserable creature had the power to raise a yell he was a constant danger. His **abject** terror was mute now, but there was no saying from what cause it might suddenly find vent in shrieks. (*Nostromo*)

Terror that is **abject** is

a. unjustified
b. sporadic
c. unrelieved
d. conspicuous

5. The necessity of winding round his little finger, almost daily, the pompous and **testy** self-importance of the old seaman had grown irksome with use to Nostromo. (*Nostromo*)

Someone who is **testy** is

a. sly
b. exasperating
c. greedy
d. dull

Snap the code, or go to **vocabularyworkshop.com**

CCSS Vocabulary: 4.c.; Reading (Literature): 4. (See pp. T14–15.)

Vocabulary for Comprehension

*Read the following selection in which some of the words you have studied in Units 4–6 appear in **boldface** type. Then answer the questions on page 81.*

As this passage shows, zoos have served a wide range of purposes during their long history.

(Line)

Zoos, or at least collections of **incarcerated** animals, have existed for millennia. The purpose of capturing and caging animals, however, has changed over time. In ancient Egypt, certain animals were deified or else considered very closely connected to gods. These animals were held in cages in temple complexes and treated as objects of worship. In a sense, these ancient zoos were **hallowed** grounds, but it is difficult not to see them as existing more for the benefit of humans than for animals. In the classical world, private menageries, or collections of exotic animals, were **ubiquitous** among **overweening** rulers who wished to advertise their power and wealth.

The modern conception of a zoo emerged in Victorian England. In fact, the word *zoo* derives from the London zoological garden, which was established in the late nineteenth century. The purpose of this zoo, according to its founder Sir Stamford Raffles, was scientific study, not the "vulgar admiration" of animals. Despite Raffles's **fiat**, however, zoos on both sides of the Atlantic soon focused on entertaining the large crowds that paid money to view the animals. While exposure to both rare and commonplace creatures benefited many zoo patrons, the animals often suffered. The creatures, which had been either taken captive in the wild or bred in captivity, were usually housed singly in tiny metal cages or other bare enclosures, where they paced nervously or lay **recumbent** in a bored stupor.

Finally, with the rise of ecological consciousness in the 1970s, the bars began to come down in zoos all over the world. Increasingly, captive animals were placed in roomier, more natural environments not only for their own well-being but also as a way of educating the public about the need to preserve wild habitats.

CCSS Vocabulary: 4.a.; Reading (Informational Text): 2, 4, 6. (See pp. T14–15.)

1. The meaning of **incarcerated** (line 2) is
   a. imaginary
   (b.) confined
   c. immense
   d. exotic
   e. dangerous

2. The primary purpose of the passage is
   (a.) to present some aspects of the historical development of zoos
   b. to offer insights into the religion of ancient Egypt
   c. to compare modern zoos with ancient ones
   d. to argue that zoos unjustifiably deprive wild animals of their freedom
   e. to expose the shocking conditions in modern zoos

3. **Hallowed** (line 12) most nearly means
   a. forbidden
   b. breeding
   c. fertile
   (d.) sacred
   e. neutral

4. **Ubiquitous** (line 17) is best defined as
   a. prohibited
   (b.) pervasive
   c. coveted
   d. traditional
   e. unusual

5. The meaning of **overweening** (line 18) is
   a. weak
   b. benevolent
   c. feuding
   (d.) arrogant
   e. brutal

6. According to the author, in the classical world private menageries of exotic animals served to
   a. entertain large crowds of visitors
   b. strengthen traditional religious attitudes
   (c.) advertise the power and wealth of rulers
   d. celebrate foreign conquests
   e. insure the progress of science

7. The author states that the modern conception of a zoo emerged
   a. in China around 1900
   b. during the late Middle Ages in France
   (c.) in Victorian England
   d. in the United States during the late nineteenth century
   e. during the Italian Renaissance

8. From paragraph 2 (lines 21–44), one can reasonably infer that the author
   a. rejects the techniques of captive breeding
   b. thinks that zoos are vital for scientific progress
   c. thinks that zoos should be abolished
   d. believes that zoo admission should be free
   (e.) sympathizes with the animals' suffering

9. **Fiat** (line 30) most nearly means
   (a.) decree
   b. opinion
   c. title
   d. request
   e. wealth

10. The organization of the passage as a whole is best defined as
    a. comparison and contrast
    (b.) chronological order
    c. cause and effect
    d. spatial order
    e. order of importance

11. **Recumbent** (line 43) most nearly means
    a. contented
    b. ignored
    c. injured
    (d.) prostrate
    e. relaxed

12. The tone of the final paragraph (lines 45–53) is best described as
    a. humorous
    b. philosophical
    (c.) positive
    d. satirical
    e. skeptical

CCSS Vocabulary: 4.a.; Reading (Informational Text): 2, 4, 6. (See pp. T14–15.)

Two-Word Completions

Select the pair of words that best complete the meaning of each of the following passages.

1. I'm extremely circumspect about what I say or do in the office because my boss is so ____________ that it is easy to ____________ or exasperate him.

a. mordant . . . disarray
b. abject . . . moot
c. testy . . . nettle
d. jocular . . . enervate

2. Edward R. Murrow will hold a place in history as a journalist who saw in 1950s television the potential to educate, and not simply to entertain. He felt it was the ____________ responsibility of all journalists to act as a(n) ____________ against both zealotry and indifference.

a. consummate . . . fiat
b. plenary . . . grouse
c. overweening . . . indictment
d. incumbent . . . bastion

3. Vincent van Gogh was indeed a(n) ____________ technician, able to ____________ every nuance of nature's variegated panorama with a mere stroke of the brush.

a. ubiquitous . . . hallow
b. indubitable . . . enervate
c. consummate . . . delineate
d. sylvan . . . travesty

4. Despite the harried officer's ____________ attempts to steady his troops after the left flank had been turned, they fled from the field in such ____________ that their departure was more of a rout than a retreat.

a. consummate . . . ignominy
b. ludicrous . . . equity
c. intermittent . . . concord
d. frenetic . . . disarray

5. After the battle, the officer who had failed to carry out his orders was arrested by the military police, charged with ____________ of duty, and ____________ in the stockade, pending a court-martial.

a. atrophy . . . garnered
b. dereliction . . . incarcerated
c. travesty . . . mooted
d. ignominy . . . hallowed

6. Although the man is certainly thought to have been involved in the crime, no ____________ has yet been brought against him because the authorities have not been able to assemble enough evidence to establish his ____________ beyond a reasonable doubt.

a. indictment . . . complicity
b. surveillance . . . equity
c. exigency . . . acuity
d. figment . . . perspicacity

7. The wealthy widow had a(n) ____________ for fine clothes and ____________ meals.

a. stratagem . . . pecuniary
b. flotsam . . . fecund
c. acuity . . . recumbent
d. penchant . . . sumptuous

CCSS Vocabulary: 4.a. (See pp. T14–15.)

Adages

In the essay "What Is Pop Art?" (see pages 60–61), the author uses the old saying "Beauty is in the eye of the beholder."

"Beauty is in the eye of the beholder" is an example of an adage. An **adage** is a traditional saying that many people accept as true. Adages offer a condensed, general observation about human nature and experience. They may be humorous or profound and frequently use memorable figures of speech. The adage "Beauty is in the eye of the beholder" emphasizes that each individual's perception of beauty is unique. It suggests that a person's judgment that something or someone is beautiful is subjective. What one person finds beautiful, another might not.

Choosing the Right Adage

Read each sentence. Use context clues to figure out the meaning of each adage in ***boldface*** *print. Then write the letter of the definition for the adage in the sentence.*

1. When Kim missed the bus a second time, she muttered, "**When it rains, it pours**." f
2. "**Mind your p's and q's**," called Mr. Rose to his three young children as they began pulling boxes from the grocery store shelves. i
3. I told my best friend, "**Don't put the cart before the horse**; get a job before you buy a new car." g
4. If Erin will **let bygones be bygones**, she can save her friendship with Alex. a
5. The housepainter was tempted to rush, but he knew that **a stitch in time saves nine**. b
6. After the election, the losing candidate's daughter whispered to her father, "**Keep your chin up**." d
7. When my grandfather said he wanted to start blogging, my grandmother laughed and reminded him that **you can't teach an old dog new tricks**. h
8. After ignoring residents' concerns about traffic, the mayor finally pledged to **grab the bull by the horns**. c
9. It would be risky to appoint a new general since the war is not over; **do not change horses midstream**. j
10. Uncle John said he knew Jennifer would receive the scholarship because **cream always rises to the top**. e

a. Forget about past disagreements.
b. Doing things right initially will save time later.
c. Tackle the problem directly and confidently.
d. Remain cheerful during difficult times.
e. Something very good will eventually attract attention.
f. Misfortunes rarely come alone.
g. Do things in the proper order.
h. As people age, it becomes harder to learn new skills.
i. Behave properly.
j. It's unwise to change leaders during a crisis.

CCSS Vocabulary: 5.a. (See pp. T14–15.)

Writing with Adages

Find the meaning of each adage. (Use an online or print dictionary if necessary.) Then write a sentence for each adage. **Answers will vary.**

1. Virtue is its own reward. **Sample answer: Andrew did not expect any praise for returning the lost wallet because virtue is its own reward.**

2. Charity begins at home.

3. Waste not, want not.

4. Drastic times call for drastic measures.

5. The proof of the pudding is in the eating.

6. When the cat's away, the mice will play.

7. Don't cut off your nose to spite your face.

8. Every rose has its thorn.

9. Money doesn't grow on trees.

10. An empty purse frightens away friends.

11. It's no use crying over spilt milk.

12. Let the chips fall where they may.

 CCSS Vocabulary: 5. (See pp. T14–15.)

Denotation and Connotation

The **denotation** of a word—its definition—is objective. It can be found in the dictionary. Many words, however, have one or more subjective meanings. They are the emotional associations, or **connotations**, of a word. Connotations can be positive or negative.

By using words with different shades of meaning and connotations, writers and speakers can create and convey a precise mood or message. For instance, to emphasize the cleverness of two characters, a writer could describe them as *ingenious, astute,* or *resourceful.* To convey not only intelligence but also suggest a lack of candor, a writer might instead describe the characters as *cunning, sly,* or *wily.*

Consider these synonyms for the neutral word *intermittent:*

sporadic *variable* *desultory* *spasmodic*

Sporadic and *variable* have neutral or positive connotations, describing something occurring at irregular intervals. The negative connotations of *desultory* and *spasmodic* suggest that the lack of regularity is unfortunate, disappointing, or even violent.

> **Think:** An insomniac might look forward to taking sporadic or variable rests the next day, not desultory or spasmodic naps.

Look at these examples of words that are similar in denotation but have different connotations.

NEUTRAL	POSITIVE	NEGATIVE
utterance	**tribute**	**diatribe**
timid	**retiring**	**pusillanimous**
reasoning	**sagacity**	**sophistry**

Understanding the connotations of words with similar denotations is an important skill. It enables writers and speakers to get across their point more effectively and allows readers and listeners to understand meaning more precisely.

Shades of Meaning

Write a plus sign (+) in the box if the word has a positive connotation. Write a minus sign (–) if the word has a negative connotation. Put a zero (0) if the word is neutral.

1. disarray –	**2.** incumbent 0	**3.** equity +	**4.** grouse –
5. sylvan 0	**6.** atrophy –	**7.** overweening –	**8.** incarcerate –
9. jocular +	**10.** mordant –	**11.** pecuniary 0	**12.** hallow +
13. enervate –	**14.** fecund +	**15.** perspicacity +	**16.** abject –

CCSS Vocabulary: 5.b. (See pp. T14–15.)

Expressing the Connotation

Read each sentence. Select the word in parentheses that expresses the connotation (positive, negative, or neutral) given at the beginning of the sentence.

positive **1.** In last Sunday's recital, the cellist's (**terminal, consummate**) performance of a Beethoven concerto surprised the audience.

neutral **2.** The hotel staff worked at a (**frenetic, bustling**) pace as the wedding guests began to arrive.

negative **3.** As they spilled into the streets, angry protestors displayed (**effigies, embodiments**) of the tyrannical dictator.

neutral **4.** The newspaper report hinted at the elderly woman's (**participation, complicity**) in the recent police investigation.

negative **5.** The girl is planning to (**imitate, travesty**) Shakespeare's sonnet by rewriting it as a limerick.

positive **6.** The chaperone was pleased by the cooperation and (**demeanor, concord**) her young students displayed on the field trip.

neutral **7.** One (**idiosyncrasy, flaw**) of William Faulkner's writing style is his use of long sentences with multiple independent and dependent clauses.

positive **8.** Sean's (**whimsical, inane**) comments about the film made me appreciate his unique wit.

Challenge: Using Connotation

Choose vocabulary words from Units 4–6 to replace the highlighted words in the sentences below. Then explain how the connotation of the replacement word changes the tone of the sentence. Answers will vary.

fiat	**agnostic**	**sumptuous**
ignominy	**penchant**	**testy**

1. The busy librarian responded to the child's question in a **distracted**
testy manner. Sample response:
The negative connotation of *testy* suggests that the librarian's response revealed irritation and exasperation, not just a lack of focus.

2. It has taken my brother years to live down the **embarrassment**
ignominy of failing his driver's test the first three times he took it.
Sample response: The negative connotation of *ignominy* reveals that the brother was more than embarrassed by his failures; he felt disgraced and ashamed.

3. Guidebooks agree that the hotel's accommodations are among the most **expensive**
sumptuous in London.
Sample response: The positive connotation of *sumptuous* makes it clear that the hotel furnishings are lavish and splendid, not simply costly.

 CCSS Vocabulary: 5. (See pp. T14–15.)

Classical Roots

gno(s)—to know

The Greek root *gno(s)* appears in **agnostic** (page 72). The literal meaning is "one who does not know." In modern usage the word refers to an individual who believes that nothing can be known about God, or a skeptic.

cognate	**cognizant**	**gnostic**	**prognosis**
cognition	**diagnose**	**ignore**	**recognize**

From the list of words above, choose the one that corresponds to each of the brief definitions below. Write the word in the blank space in the illustrative sentence below the definition. Use an online or print dictionary if necessary.

1. a prediction of the probable course of a disease; a probable forecast or estimate

With modern treatment options, patients who contract this once-fatal disease now have an excellent **prognosis** for full recovery.

2. to identify a disease or condition based on observation, examination, and analysis

A podiatrist is trained to **diagnose** and treat a range of problems of the foot.

3. of, relating to, or possessing intellectual or spiritual knowledge

Many religions observe a **gnostic** doctrine, where emphasis is placed on the pursuit of spiritual and intellectual knowledge.

4. to disregard deliberately; to pay no attention to; to refuse to consider

If we just **ignore** Rover, he will eventually stop begging for food at the table.

5. related by family or origin; related in nature, character, quality, or function; a person or thing related to another

The Sanskrit word for king—*rajah*—is a **cognate** of the Latin *rex.*

6. the broad mental process by which knowledge is acquired, including aspects of awareness, perception, reasoning, judgment, memory, and intuition; knowledge

After a serious blow to the head, her **cognition** was impaired for several weeks.

7. to know, identify, or show awareness of something from past experience or knowledge; to accept as a fact; to acknowledge a thing's existence, validity, or authority; to approve of or appreciate

The school board has come to **recognize** the positive impact of art and music classes.

8. fully informed; conscious; aware

As a result of a 1966 court decision, all arrested suspects must be made **cognizant** of their Miranda rights.

CCSS Vocabulary: 4.c. (See pp. T14–15.)

UNIT 7

Note that not all of the 20 unit words are used in this passage. *Bestial*, *furtive*, and *misanthrope* are not included in the passage.

Read the following selection, taking note of the ***boldface*** *words and their contexts. These words are among those you will be studying in Unit 7. As you complete the exercises in this unit, it may help to refer to the way the words are used below.*

CCSS Vocabulary: 4; Reading (Informational Text): 4, 6. (See pp. T14–15.)

John Lennon's Legacy

<Biographical Sketch>

John Lennon in 1961

John Lennon was born in Liverpool, England, on October 9, 1940, at the height of World War II. Forty years later, on December 8, 1980, he was shot dead by a mentally unstable fan outside his Manhattan apartment. During his short life, as a musician, artist, poet, and political activist, Lennon transcended his time. "If someone thinks that love and peace is a cliché that must have been left behind in the '60s, that's his problem," he said. "Love and peace are eternal."

Lennon's father left his wife and young son before World War II ended. Poor but never **indigent**, Lennon's mother, Julia, entrusted the boy to her sister, Mimi, one of a **coterie** of "five strong, intelligent sisters," as Lennon later recalled. During his childhood, Lennon spent an **inordinate** amount of time with **convivial** female relatives. In later years, he said that this was his "first feminist education" and that living apart from his parents enabled him "to see that parents are not gods" but were human and had flaws just like everyone else.

Despite their living apart, Julia Lennon maintained a close relationship with her son. She encouraged his interest in music, rather than demand that he **jettison** his musical aspirations (as his Aunt Mimi hoped he would do), even giving him his first guitar when he was fifteen. The gift was **felicitous**, as Lennon dove into music with **pertinacious** ambition. His belief that it would bring him lasting fame was as strong as Aunt Mimi's conviction that his hopes were **illusory**.

Lennon soon realized his dream of fame, thanks to the success of the Beatles, the band he formed with his songwriting **counterpart**, Paul McCartney. The band rocketed to fame in the early 1960s, propelled by energetic pop songs like "Love Me Do," simple variations on the time-honored theme of teenage love.

With age comes wisdom. As Lennon's artistic vision matured, he led the Beatles toward new horizons, and his lyrics increasingly contained intricate metaphors and political themes. Lennon's humor, free spirit, and politics soon permeated the band's image and music, a transformation marked by the album *Sgt. Pepper's Lonely Hearts Club Band*. The album cover ridicules military formality, presenting the bandmates in **garish** uniforms, **raiment** that was absurd even for its era. Lennon's maturing talents shine in songs like "A Day in the Life," which weaves themes of class and political

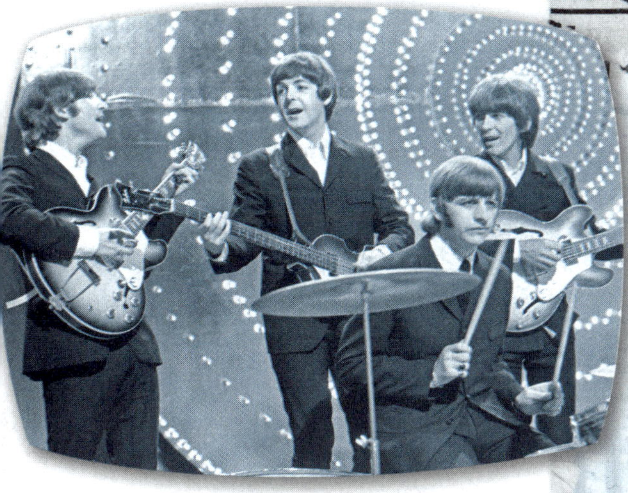

The Beatles in the BBC's *Top of the Pops* television show in June 1966

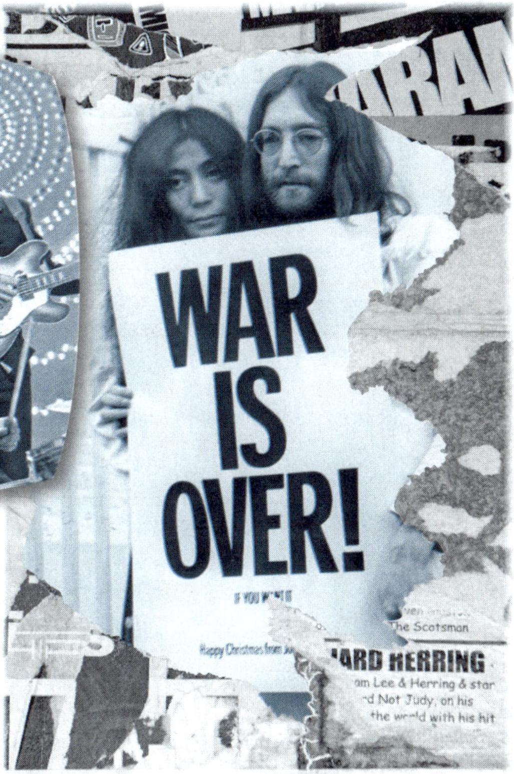

power with images of mundane and tragic moments in life; the lyrics are a dreamlike tapestry **embellished** with metaphor. Critics soon acknowledged Lennon as a worthy moden poet.

Politics and poetry remained at the fore of Lennon's songwriting as he became a high-profile social activist. U.S. leaders, mired in the Vietnam War, objected to the **effrontery** of this popular British "peacenik," and had him monitored by the FBI, which diligently collected **picayune** details for his file. Lennon did little to **allay** their concerns. Many of his lyrics, such as those in "All You Need Is Love" and later, "Imagine," rallied those who **demurred** violence. As a group, the Beatles proved more **ephemeral** than their fame, and personal tensions broke up the band. Yet Lennon continued to speak passionately against violence and enmity with solo works like "Give Peace a Chance."

"We're not being unreasonable. Just saying 'give it a chance,' " said Lennon in 1980 when discussing his desire for a world without war. With "Imagine," he was asking for a world without hate, greed, or hunger. "It's the same message over and over. And it's positive," he said of his work. Lennon's devotion to such positive messages, his willingness to use his art and fame to promote love and peace among all people, is his most enduring legacy.

John Lennon and Yoko Ono, his wife, in a war protest, London, 1969.

Note the spelling, pronunciation, part(s) of speech, and definition(s) of each of the following words. Then write the word in the blank spaces in the illustrative sentence(s) following. Finally, study the lists of synonyms and antonyms.

1. allay (ə lā′)

(*v.*) to calm or pacify, set to rest; to lessen or relieve

The politician made a speech in order to _____**allay**_____ his constituents' fears.

SYNONYMS: reduce, alleviate, moderate
ANTONYMS: aggravate, exacerbate, intensify

2. bestial (bes′ chəl)

(*adj.*) beastlike; beastly, brutal; subhuman in intelligence and sensibility

In beating their prisoner, the guards were guilty of a truly _____**bestial**_____ act.

SYNONYMS: animalistic, loathsome
ANTONYMS: human, clement, virtuous, upright

3. convivial (kən viv′ ē əl)

(*adj.*) festive, sociable, having fun together, genial

Thanksgiving dinner at Grandmother's house is always a _____**convivial**_____ family gathering.

SYNONYMS: fun-loving, jovial, merry
ANTONYMS: dour, sullen, unsociable

4. coterie (kō′ tə rē)

(*n.*) a circle of acquaintances; a close-knit, often exclusive, group of people with a common interest

Robert Browning and his _____**coterie**_____ had ideas about poetry that seemed revolutionary in their day.

SYNONYMS: clique, set

5. counterpart (kau̇nt′ ər pärt)

(*n.*) a person or thing closely resembling or corresponding to another; a complement

I have to admit I was frightened of my _____**counterpart**_____ on the other team because she held the high-jump record.

SYNONYM: match

6. demur (di mər′)

(*v.*) to object or take exception to; (*n.*) an objection

The rank and file will _____**demur**_____ if they are not consulted regularly by the union leadership.

The speech in favor of the proposal was drowned out by a chorus of _____**demurs**_____ from the senate floor.

SYNONYMS: (*v.*) protest, object to
ANTONYMS: (*v.*) assent to, consent to, accept, agree to

CCSS Vocabulary: 4.c., 4.d. (See pp. T14–15.)

7. effrontery (ə frən′ tə rē)

(*n.*) shameless boldness, impudence

After having been suspended for disrespectful behavior, the student had the **effrontery** to talk back to his teacher again.

SYNONYMS: chutzpah, nerve, impertinence, cheek
ANTONYMS: shyness, diffidence, timidity

8. embellish (em bel′ ish)

(*v.*) to decorate, adorn, touch up; to improve by adding details

The best storytellers **embellish** their tales in ways that help readers visualize the setting.

SYNONYM: garnish
ANTONYMS: strip, mar, disfigure

9. ephemeral (i fem′ ər əl)

(*adj.*) lasting only a short time, short-lived

Only the greatest of writers and artists achieve anything other than **ephemeral** popularity.

SYNONYMS: transient, evanescent, transitory
ANTONYMS: durable, long-lasting, permanent, perpetual

10. felicitous (fə lis′ ə təs)

(*adj.*) appropriate, apt, well chosen; marked by well-being or good fortune, happy

In view of the high prices for home heating oil, the mild winter was a **felicitous** turn of events.

SYNONYMS: fortunate, well-put
ANTONYMS: inappropriate, inept, graceless, unhappy

11. furtive (fər′ tiv)

(*adj.*) done slyly or stealthily, sneaky, secret, shifty; stolen

The girl was caught taking a **furtive** glance at the test paper of the student sitting next to her.

SYNONYMS: covert, surreptitious
ANTONYMS: aboveboard, open

12. garish (gar′ ish)

(*adj.*) glaring; tastelessly showy or overdecorated in a vulgar or offensive way

The storefront was painted in **garish** colors so that it would attract the attention of passersby.

SYNONYMS: gaudy, flashy, tawdry
ANTONYMS: subdued, muted, understated, quiet

13. illusory (i lü′ sə rē)

(*adj.*) misleading, deceptive; lacking in or not based on reality

Police state tactics provide an **illusory** sense of security in an unjust society.

SYNONYMS: specious, spurious, imaginary
ANTONYMS: actual, real, factual, objective

CCSS Vocabulary: 4.c. (See pp. T14–15.)

14. indigent (in′ də jənt)

(*adj.*) needy, impoverished

The number of homeless and ___indigent___ persons has increased since the economy took a downturn.

SYNONYMS: penniless, poverty-stricken, destitute
ANTONYMS: affluent, prosperous

15. inordinate (in ôr′ də nət)

(*adj.*) far too great, exceeding reasonable limits, excessive

The press showered the popular actor with ___inordinate___ praise for what seemed a rather ordinary performance.

SYNONYMS: exorbitant, extravagant
ANTONYMS: reasonable, equitable

16. jettison (jet′ ə sən)

(*v.*) to cast overboard, get rid of as unnecessary or burdensome

The captain ordered the crew to ___jettison___ the ballast so the ship could move more quickly through the water.

SYNONYMS: cast off, discard, dump, junk
ANTONYMS: conserve, retain, hold on to, keep

17. misanthrope (mis′ ən thrōp)

(*n.*) a person who hates or despises people

The millionaire ___misanthrope___ left all her money to an animal shelter and not a penny to a single human being.

SYNONYM: people-hater

18. pertinacious (pər tə nā′ shəs)

(*adj.*) very persistent; holding firmly to a course of action or a set of beliefs; hard to get rid of, refusing to be put off or denied

The defense attorney was as ___pertinacious___ as a bulldog in his cross-examination of the witness.

SYNONYMS: stubborn, determined

19. picayune (pik ē yün′)

(*adj.*) of little value or importance, paltry, measly; concerned with trifling matters, small-minded

A supervisor who fusses about every ___picayune___ fault of the workers will lower morale and productivity.

SYNONYMS: piddling, trifling
ANTONYMS: important, significant, huge, gigantic

20. raiment (rā′ mənt)

(*n.*) clothing, garments

When the chorus in the Greek tragedy hears that the king has died, they tear their ___raiment___ in anguish.

SYNONYMS: apparel, attire

CCSS Vocabulary: 4.c. (See pp. T14–15.)

Choosing the Right Word

*Select the **boldface** word that better completes each sentence. You might refer to the selection on pages 88–89 to see how most of these words are used in context.*

In the 1840s, Ralph Waldo Emerson founded and contributed to *The Dial*, a magazine that explored transcendental philosophy.

1. Ralph Waldo Emerson and a(n) (**coterie, effrontery**) of like-minded friends led the American transcendentalism movement in the mid-nineteenth century.

2. Though the federal government does much to help the (**indigent, illusory**), private charities play no small part in their welfare.

3. To anyone as fond of horses as I am, the stable and the tack room provide as (**indigent, convivial**) an atmosphere as one could wish for.

4. I can always come up with the crushing rejoinder, the dazzling witticism, or the (**furtive, felicitous**) phrase—about an hour after I need it!

5. When I returned to the office earlier than expected, I caught the little snoop (**felicitously, furtively**) going through the papers on my desk.

6. The presidency is the "toughest job in the world" because it makes such (**bestial, inordinate**) demands on a person's time, energy, and ingenuity.

7. Nothing we could say seemed to (**demur, allay**) her grief over the loss of her dog.

8. If installment buying is not carefully controlled, the benefits that can accrue from it may prove wholly (**illusory, inordinate**).

9. The atrocities committed by the (**garish, bestial**) commanders of such concentration camps as Auschwitz appalled the civilized world.

10. As the rock star's popularity began to skyrocket, what had been a small (**coterie, raiment**) of admirers became an unruly mob.

11. I am flattered that you want me to chair the meeting, but I must (**demur, embellish**) on the grounds of my youth and inexperience.

12. The famous sleuth pursued his investigation with all the (**pertinacity, conviviality**) of a lion stalking its dinner.

13. The kind of (**garish, picayune**) theatrical makeup used by circus clowns is not suitable for an elegant fashion model.

14. Often the antonym of a given English word is not so much its opposite as its (**embellishment, counterpart**)—for example, *actor* and *actress*.

15. "You mean you had the (**effrontery, demur**) to ask for a raise when everyone knows you've been goofing off lately?" I asked in amazement.

CCSS Vocabulary: 4.d. (See pp. T14–15.)

16. The proofreader didn't notice any significant flaws in the writing, but he did find a few (**ephemeral, picayune**) errors in the punctuation.

17. When the facts of a matter speak so plainly for themselves, we shouldn't seek to (**embellish, jettison**) them.

18. She has neither the starry-eyed optimism of the idealist nor the mordant cynicism of the (**misanthrope, coterie**).

19. Every dynamic and successful society must be able to (**allay, jettison**) ideas and institutions that have outlived their usefulness.

20. Somehow, it depresses me to think that with the approach of winter this magnificent old tree will surrender all its leafy (**raiment, effrontery**).

21. An emotion so fickle and (**ephemeral, pertinacious**) does not deserve to be categorized as "love."

22. Not surprisingly, my sister's solemnly made commitment to daily clarinet practice for one month was (**garish, ephemeral**), lasting only five days.

23. Sadly, in our celebrity-obsessed culture, professional athletes make (**pertinacious, inordinate**) amounts of money while professional educators make little.

24. To celebrate their fiftieth anniversary, my grandfather described the (**felicitous, indigent**) choice he made to ask my grandmother for a first date.

25. Effective coaches are able to (**allay, embellish**) the doubts of their players.

*Choose the word from this unit that is the same or most nearly the same in meaning as the **boldface** word or expression in the phrase. Write that word on the line. Use a dictionary if necessary.*

1. the **dogged** researcher — pertinacious
2. a **clandestine** midnight meeting — furtive
3. willingly **abandoned** their prejudices — jettisoned
4. had the **gall** to demand an apology — effrontery
5. prone to **fanciful** get-rich-quick schemes — illusory
6. condemned the militia's **depraved** behavior — bestial
7. a well-known **despiser of mankind** — misanthrope
8. **ornamented** with high-sounding phrases — embellished
9. ignore those **inconsequential** objections — picayune
10. the **fleeting** nature of power — ephemeral

 CCSS Vocabulary: 5. (See pp. T14–15.)

The synonyms and antonyms here do not appear on the Definitions page.

Antonyms

*Choose the word from this unit that is most nearly opposite in meaning to the **boldface** word or expression in the phrase. Write that word on the line. Use a dictionary if necessary.*

1. their **forthright** attempt to withdraw ____furtive____
2. **moderate** increases in profits ____inordinate____
3. the **social** inhabitants of the big cities ____misanthropic____
4. a very **grim** lunch meeting ____convivial____
5. **humane** behavior ____bestial____

Completing the Sentence

From the words in this unit, choose the one that best completes each of the following sentences. Write the word in the space provided.

1. When Charles V retired to a Spanish monastery, he exchanged the costly ____raiment____ of a king for the simple habit of a monk.
2. Since we all agreed that the proposal seemed to offer the best solution to our problem, it was accepted without ____demur____.
3. A busy administrator in today's high-pressure business world just doesn't have time to deal with such ____picayune____ concerns as making coffee.
4. He is entitled to reasonable compensation for the damage to his car, but the demands he has made are totally ____inordinate____.
5. The man's features suddenly contorted into a(n) ____bestial____ mask, more reminiscent of a hobgoblin than a human being.
6. Jonathan Swift so came to loathe human folly, vice, and hypocrisy that he died a virtual ____misanthrope____.
7. The ____furtive____ manner in which he sidled into the room and tried to avoid being noticed actually drew attention to his presence.
8. The disastrous stock market crash of 1929 left many a wealthy speculator as ____indigent____ as the proverbial church mouse.
9. Who wouldn't have had fun among such a(n) ____convivial____ group of people?
10. The crew of the freighter ____jettisoned____ most of its cargo in a desperate effort to keep the sinking ship afloat.

CCSS Vocabulary: 4.a. (See pp. T14–15.)

11. The "Old 400" was a very small and exclusive **coterie** of prominent families that dominated East Coast society for decades.

12. Recent developments in that part of the world have intensified rather than **allayed** our fears of a renewed conflict.

13. At the Casablanca Conference in 1943, President Roosevelt and his military aides met with their British **counterparts** to map military strategy for the Western Allies.

14. A good deal of sad experience has taught me that my youthful hopes of getting something for nothing are entirely **illusory**.

15. Though I don't consider myself much of a diplomat, I think I handled that delicate situation in a particularly **felicitous** manner.

16. "If at first you don't succeed, try, try again" seems to be the motto of that **pertinacious** young woman.

17. In the Victorian era, designers **embellished** women's dresses with all sorts of elaborate frills and flounces.

18. The **garish** movie palaces of an earlier era have given way to smaller theaters, decorated in a simpler, more austere style.

19. Many a now-forgotten "movie great" has discovered to his or her chagrin that fame may indeed be as **ephemeral** as a passing shower.

20. He had the **effrontery** to come into my own home to tell me what I should do to help him.

Writing: Words in Action

Answers to both prompts will vary.

1. Look back at "John Lennon's Legacy" (pages 88–89). In it, the author mentions Lennon's "dream of fame" and his confidence that he would achieve it through his music. How important is fame to you? Would you include it as part of your definition of being successful or happy? Write an essay in which you explain your opinion of fame. Use at least two details from the passage and three unit words to explain your ideas.

2. Think about the power celebrities have to influence individual people as well as society as a whole. Do you think celebrities—including singers, actors, and professional athletes—should become politically active, or should they stay out of politics? In a brief essay, support your opinion with specific examples from current events, your reading (refer to pages 88–89), your media viewing, or your personal observations and experience. Write at least three paragraphs, and use three or more words from this unit.

Writing prompt #2 is modeled on that of standardized tests.

 CCSS Vocabulary: 6; Writing: 2.d., 3.d. (See pp. T14–15.)

Vocabulary in Context: Informational Text for Unit 7 is available online at **vocabularyworkshop.com**.

Vocabulary in Context

Literary Text

The following excerpts are from Henry James's novels The Bostonians *and* Roderick Hudson. *Some of the words you have studied in this unit appear in* **boldface** *type. Complete each statement below the excerpt by circling the letter of the correct answer.*

1. Ransom could see for himself that the occasion was not crudely festive; there was a want of **convivial** movement, and, among most of the visitors, even of mutual recognition. (*The Bostonians*)

   Convivial movement is

   a. energetic **c.** knowledgeable
   b. purposeful **d.** sociable

2. Basil Ransom wondered whether it were **effrontery** or innocence that enabled Miss Tarrant to meet with such complacency the aloofness of the elder lady. (*The Bostonians)*

   Effrontery is

   a. experience **c.** serenity
   b. impudence **d.** sympathy

Christopher Reeve stars as Mississippi lawyer Basil Ransom in the 1984 film version of James's *The Bostonians*.

3. She was silent for a few minutes; then at last, "In that, then, we are better than Europe," she said. To a certain point Rowland agreed with her, but he **demurred**, to make her say more. (*Roderick Hudson*)

   If you have **demurred,** you have

   a. remained silent **c.** raised your voice
   b. asked a question **d.** made an objection

4. Her daughter had come lawfully by her loveliness, but Rowland mentally made the distinction that the mother was silly and that the daughter was not. The mother had a very silly mouth—a mouth, Rowland suspected, capable of expressing an **inordinate** degree of unreason. (*Roderick Hudson*)

   Something **inordinate** is NOT

   a. admirable **c.** moderate
   b. necessary **d.** predictable

5. Her mouth was larwge, fortunately for the principal grace of her physiognomy was her smile, which displayed itself with magnificent amplitude. Rowland, indeed, had not yet seen her smile, but something assured him that her rigid gravity had a radiant **counterpart**. (*Roderick Hudson*)

   A **counterpart** is a(n)

   a. authority **c.** extension
   b. complement **d.** component

Snap the code, or go to **vocabularyworkshop.com**

UNIT 8

Note that not all of the 20 unit words are used in this passage. *Allege* and *saturnine* are not included in the passage.

Read the following selection, taking note of the ***boldface*** *words and their contexts. These words are among those you will be studying in Unit 8. As you complete the exercises in this unit, it may help to refer to the way the words are used below.*

CCSS Vocabulary: 4; Reading (Informational Text): 4, 6. (See pp. T14–15.)

A Passage to Power

<Interview>

Whoever is Speaker of the U.S. House of Representatives sets House rules, adjudicates procedural conflicts, and strives to maintain civility during debates. The Speaker also exerts behind-the-scenes powers by appointing committee chairs and setting the timetables for legislative votes. To learn more about the post and its evolution, we asked the noted congressional scholar, Bill T. Kanoho, about one of the most powerful government posts.

Q: What are the requirements for the Speaker's job?

A: You must be at least 25 years old, a U.S. citizen for the previous seven years, and an inhabitant of the state you are to represent at the time of election.

Q: That's it?

A: That's what the Constitution requires. Another aspect of the post—it's slightly **macabre**—is that the Speaker is second in line, after the Vice President, to the presidency if the President can no longer serve.

Q: How do other representatives view the Speaker?

A: It's **irrefutable** that the House reveres its Speaker. After all, it's a very important position. Money talks: From the First Congress onwards, the Speaker always made more money than members of Congress. For example, in 2011, the Speaker was paid $223,500 and members of Congress $174,000.

Q: Was the role of the Speaker always as influential as it is today?

A: Actually, no. The first speaker, Frederick Muhlenberg of Pennsylvania, did little that would **portend** the post would ever grow in importance. It has become **saturated** with power, but I would say a **paucity** of change marked the role until the Twelfth Congress (1811–1813).

Q: Why so little change in those early years?

A: It wasn't that the Speakers were **lackadaisical**, and in fact I believe they all saw the expanding nation as a **juggernaut** on the world stage. But it seems the first Speakers wanted to **conciliate** the members, perhaps because in the early

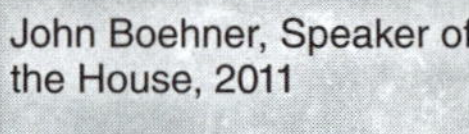

John Boehner, Speaker of the House, 2011

days of our republic fistfights could erupt when one member refused to **recant** a position that angered another.

Q: Why did the job start to change?

A: Henry Clay of Kentucky stirred the pot when he served six nonconsecutive terms as Speaker, from 1811 through 1825, and made a **litany** of changes. The biggest were that he participated in debates, and he enforced strict rules of order to **slough** off attempts to **countermand** his efforts to raise the office to a new **echelon**.

Q: Is that when the job's scope became as powerful as it is today?

A: Well, after Clay left, the office returned to its original scope until 1880, when the Speaker's role was expanded to include being Chairman of the Committee on Rules, a power-filled position.

Q: Then what happened?

A: Maine's Thomas Brackett Reed is what happened. While serving as Speaker from 1889 to 1891, then again from 1895 to 1899, he made **arrant** and successful bids to increase the Speaker's power. The most notable change occurred when he masterminded how to prevent the minority party from using parliamentary maneuvers—that is, exploiting legal technicalities—to block majority party decisions.

Q: Is that when the post became truly powerful?

A: It's been evolving since then. However, it would be **fatuous** not to mention the post's current partisan profile: Republicans and Democrats sometimes have a hard time working together, so a powerful Speaker is needed in order to get things done. And sometimes problems in Congress are **exacerbated** by talking heads—talk show guests and politicians who talk in sound bites that tell only half the story and thus misrepresent an issue.

Q: What can the Speaker do to solve that problem?

A: He or she can be fair. Though politicians may pontificate and argue and attack others' positions, many voters fail to realize this is part of the game. These officials strike a pose to appeal to their constituents, then they get down to business. A lot of friendly **badinage** goes on in the House. Our elected officials are not about to **raze** the Capitol building. The Speaker wouldn't allow it!

Frederick Muhlenberg, circa 1790, was the first Speaker of the House and represented Pennsylvania.

Snap the code, or go to **vocabularyworkshop.com**

Speaker Henry Clay served six nonconsecutive two-year terms as Speaker and made changes that started the post's evolution to what it is today.

Definitions

Note the spelling, pronunciation, part(s) of speech, and definition(s) of each of the following words. Then write the word in the blank spaces in the illustrative sentence(s) following. Finally, study the lists of synonyms and antonyms.

1. allege (ə lej′)
(*v.*) to assert without proof or confirmation

The newspaper tabloid **alleged** that the movie star and the director were having creative differences.

SYNONYM: contend
ANTONYM: prove

2. arrant (ar′ ənt)
(*adj.*) thoroughgoing, out-and-out; shameless, blatant

In Shakespeare's tragedy the audience sees clearly that Iago is an **arrant** scoundrel, but Othello is blind to his treachery.

SYNONYMS: egregious, unmitigated

3. badinage (bad ə näzh′)
(*n.*) light and playful conversation

I enjoy the delightful **badinage** between stars like Spencer Tracy and Katharine Hepburn in 1940s movies.

SYNONYMS: banter, persiflage, repartee
ANTONYM: sermon

4. conciliate (kən sil′ ē āt)
(*v.*) to overcome the distrust of, win over; to appease, pacify; to reconcile, make consistent

Because of the weakness of our army, we had to try to **conciliate** the enemy.

SYNONYMS: mollify, propitiate
ANTONYMS: antagonize, alienate, estrange

5. countermand (kau̇n′ tər mand)
(*v.*) to cancel or reverse one order or command with another that is contrary to the first

Today's directive clearly **countermanded** all previous instructions on how to exit the building in case of fire.

SYNONYMS: recall, revoke
ANTONYMS: reaffirm, reassert

6. echelon (esh′ ə län)
(*n.*) one of a series of grades in an organization or field of activity; an organized military unit; a steplike formation or arrangement

Although the civil servant began in the lower **echelon** of government service, he rose quickly through the ranks.

SYNONYM: rank

CCSS Vocabulary: 4.c., 4.d. (See pp. T14–15.)

7. exacerbate (eg zas′ ər bāt)

(*v.*) to make more violent, severe, bitter, or painful

Shouting and name-calling are sure to **exacerbate** any quarrel.

SYNONYMS: intensify, worsen
ANTONYMS: alleviate, mitigate, ameliorate

8. fatuous (fach′ ü əs)

(*adj.*) stupid or foolish in a self-satisfied way

In order to discredit the candidate, the columnist quoted some of his more **fatuous**, self-serving remarks.

SYNONYMS: silly, vapid, inane, doltish, vacuous
ANTONYMS: intelligent, perceptive, bright

9. irrefutable (ir i fyü′ tə bəl)

(*adj.*) impossible to disprove; beyond argument

The jury felt the prosecution presented it with **irrefutable** evidence of the defendant's guilt.

SYNONYMS: indisputable, incontrovertible, undeniable
ANTONYMS: disputable, indefensible, untenable

10. juggernaut (jəg′ ər nôt)

(*n.*) a massive and inescapable force or object that crushes whatever is in its path

Any population that has experienced the **juggernaut** of war firsthand will not easily forget its destructive power.

11. lackadaisical (lak ə dā′ zə kəl)

(*adj.*) lacking spirit or interest, halfhearted

The team's performance in the late innings was **lackadaisical** because they were so far ahead.

SYNONYMS: indolent, indifferent, lax
ANTONYMS: energetic, vigorous, wholehearted

12. litany (lit′ ə nē)

(*n.*) a prayer consisting of short appeals to God recited by the leader alternating with responses from the congregation; any repetitive chant; a long list

Whenever she talks about her childhood, she recites an interminable **litany** of grievances.

SYNONYMS: catalog, megillah

13. macabre (mə käb′)

(*adj.*) grisly, gruesome; horrible, distressing; having death as a subject

The continuing popularity of horror movies suggests that one way to score at the box office is to exploit **macabre** situations.

SYNONYMS: grim, ghoulish

CCSS Vocabulary: 4.c. (See pp. T14–15.)

14. paucity (pô′ sə tē)

(*n.*) an inadequate quantity, scarcity, dearth

The senate campaign was marred by a **paucity** of original ideas.

SYNONYM: lack
ANTONYMS: glut, plenitude, deluge

15. portend (por tənd′)

(*v.*) to indicate beforehand that something is about to happen; to give advance warning of

In Shakespeare's plays, disturbances in the heavens usually **portend** disaster or trouble in human affairs.

SYNONYMS: bode, foretell, suggest

16. raze (rāz)

(*v.*) to tear down, destroy completely; to cut or scrape off or out

The town **razed** the old schoolhouse to make room for a larger, more modern school complex.

SYNONYMS: pull down, demolish, shave off
ANTONYMS: build, construct, raise, erect

17. recant (ri kant′)

(*v.*) to withdraw a statement or belief to which one has previously been committed, renounce, retract

On the stand, the defendant **recanted** the guilty admissions she had made in her confession to the police.

SYNONYMS: repudiate, disavow
ANTONYM: reassert

18. saturate (sach′ ə rāt)

(*v.*) to soak thoroughly, fill to capacity; to satisfy fully

A sponge that is **saturated** with water swells up but does not drip.

SYNONYMS: drench, flood, imbue; ANTONYM: drain

19. saturnine (sat′ ər nīn)

(*adj.*) of a gloomy or surly disposition; cold or sluggish in mood

Ebenezer Scrooge, of Dickens's *A Christmas Carol*, has a decidedly **saturnine** temperament.

SYNONYM: morose; ANTONYMS: cheerful, vivacious

20. slough (sləf)

(*v.*) to cast off, discard; to get rid of something objectionable or unnecessary; to plod through as if through mud; (*n.*) a mire; a state of depression

At New Year's time, many people resolve to **slough** off bad habits and live better.

The advancing line of tanks became bogged down in a **slough**.

SYNONYMS: (*v.*) shed, slog
ANTONYMS: (*v.*) take on, acquire, assume

CCSS Vocabulary: 4.c. (See pp. T14–15.)

Choosing the Right Word

*Select the **boldface** word that better completes each sentence. You might refer to the selection on pages 98–99 to see how most of these words are used in context.*

A French solider protects himself from shrapnel in a trench during World War I.

1. On the Western Front in August 1914, the French army steeled itself against the oncoming (**badinage, juggernaut**) that was the German Second Army.

2. Not surprisingly, the committee's final report was an incongruous mixture of the astute and the (**irrefutable, fatuous**).

3. By (**portending, sloughing**) off the artificiality of her first book, the novelist arrived at a style that was simple, genuine, and highly effective.

4. What possible purpose will be served by setting up yet another hamburger stand in an area already (**saturated, sloughed**) with fast-food shops?

5. Our excitement at visiting the world-famous ruins was dampened by the (**lackadaisical, arrant**) attitude of the bored and listless guide.

6. The authority of the student council is not absolute because the principal can (**countermand, exacerbate**) any of its decisions.

7. It is a good deal easier to (**raze, allege**) an old building than it is to destroy a time-honored social institution.

8. I never ask anyone, "How are you?" anymore because I am afraid I will be treated to an endless (**litany, badinage**) of symptoms and ailments.

9. His debating technique is rooted in the firm belief that anything bellowed in a loud voice is absolutely (**saturnine, irrefutable**).

10. The views of the two parties involved in this dispute are so diametrically opposed that it will be almost impossible to (**conciliate, saturate**) them.

11. Only a(n) (**arrant, macabre**) knave would be capable of devising such an incredibly underhanded and treacherous scheme.

12. In earlier times, people whose views conflicted with "received opinion" often had to (**recant, portend**) their ideas or face the consequences.

13. Stephen King's book *Danse* (***Macabre, Lackadaisical***) surveys popular and obscure horror fiction of the twentieth century.

14. Over the years, hard work and unstinting devotion to duty have raised me from one (**echelon, paucity**) of company management to the next.

15. She excused herself from lending me the money I so desperately needed by (**conciliating, alleging**) that she had financial troubles of her own.

CCSS Vocabulary: 4.d. (See pp. T14–15.)

16. By denying your guilt without offering any explanation of your actions, you will only (**recant, exacerbate**) an already bad situation.

17. Economists believe that the drop in automobile sales and steel production (**countermands, portends**) serious problems for business in the future.

18. His attempts at casual (**badinage, echelon**) did not conceal the fact that he was acutely embarrassed by his blunder.

19. We have many capable and well-meaning people in our organization, but it seems to me that there is a (**paucity, juggernaut**) of real leadership.

20. Someone with such a (**fatuous, saturnine**) outlook on life doesn't make an agreeable traveling companion, especially on a long journey.

21. With incredible unconcern, the nobles of Europe immersed themselves in social frivolities as the fearful (**juggernaut, litany**) of World War I steamrolled ineluctably toward them.

22. Ever a bit of a melancholic, Mr. Smithers sank into a (**litany, slough**) in the wintertime.

23. The defense attorney succeeded in portraying the genial witness as a(n) (**arrant, saturnine**) liar, whose testimony was never credible.

24. The dog's owner (**exacerbated, razed**) the situation when he flagrantly encouraged the terrier to romp in the neighbor's petunias.

25. A plunge in atmospheric pressure (**conciliates, portends**) an oncoming storm.

*Choose the word from this unit that is the same or most nearly the same in meaning as the **boldface** word or expression in the phrase. Write that word on the line. Use a dictionary if necessary.*

1. seemed in a **sullen** mood — saturnine

2. **claimed** that a crime had been committed — alleged

3. **foreshadows** dangers to come — portends

4. an idea that **permeates** all aspects of society — saturates

5. will **aggravate** tensions between the rivals — exacerbate

6. a long **rigmarole** of questions and answers — litany

7. a **listless** response from voters — lackadaisical

8. the upper **levels** of power — echelons

9. tried to **placate** both sides in the dispute — conciliate

10. wore a very **grotesque** mask — macabre

CCSS Vocabulary: 5. (See pp. T14–15.)

Antonyms

Choose the word from this unit that is most nearly opposite in meaning to the ***boldface*** *word or expression in the phrase. Write that word on the line. Use a dictionary if necessary.*

1. a growing **abundance** of cheap labor — paucity
2. given to **lighthearted** predictions — saturnine
3. known for his **sensible** opinions — fatuous
4. has **reaffirmed** her support of free trade — recanted
5. **deny** involvement in the burglary — allege

Completing the Sentence

From the words in this unit, choose the one that best completes each of the following sentences. Write the word in the space provided.

1. The breaking news story concerned corruption among the highest ___echelons___ of politics.
2. We object to the policy of ___razing___ historic old buildings to make way for unsightly parking lots.
3. Ms. Ryan's warnings to the class to "review thoroughly" seemed to me to ___portend___ an unusually difficult examination.
4. The seriousness of the matter under discussion left no room for the type of lighthearted ___badinage___ encountered in the locker room.
5. At first I thought it would be easy to shoot holes in their case, but I soon realized that their arguments were practically ___irrefutable___.
6. As a snake ___sloughs___ off its old skin, so he hoped to rid himself of his weaknesses and develop a new and better personality.
7. Though some "home remedies" appear to alleviate the symptoms of a disease, they may in fact ___exacerbate___ the condition.
8. After he made that absurd remark, a(n) ___fatuous___ grin of self-congratulation spread like syrup across his face.
9. The men now being held in police custody are ___alleged___ to have robbed eight supermarkets over the last year.
10. Only someone with a truly ___macabre___ sense of humor would decide to use a hearse as the family car or a coffin as a bed.

11. My shirt became so **saturated** with perspiration on that beastly day that I had to change it more than once during the match.

12. You are not going to do well in your job if you continue to work in such a(n) **lackadaisical** and desultory manner.

13. No sooner had the feckless tsar decreed a general mobilization than he **countermanded** his order, only to reissue it a short time later.

14. Her friendly manner and disarming smile helped to **conciliate** those who opposed her views on the proposal.

15. The enemy's lines crumpled before the mighty **juggernaut** of our attack like so much wheat before a harvester.

16. "I find it terribly depressing to be around people whose dispositions are so **saturnine** and misanthropic," I remarked.

17. His four disastrous years in office were marked by a plenitude of promises and a(n) **paucity** of performance.

18. The service in honor of the miners trapped in the underground collapse included prayers and **litanies**.

19. However much it may cost me, I will never **recant** the principles to which I have devoted my life.

20. "It seems to me that such **arrant** hypocrisy is indicative of a thoroughly opportunistic approach to running for office," I said sadly.

Writing: Words in Action

Answers to both prompts will vary.

1. Look back at "A Passage to Power" (pages 98–99). Think about the three requirements for the Speaker's job—the Speaker must be at least 25 years old, a United States citizen for the previous seven years, and a resident in the state that he or she represents. In a brief essay, explain which of those three requirements you believe is the most important. Use at least two details from the passage and three unit words to support your answer.

2. *"Compromise is usually a sign of weakness, or an admission of defeat. Strong men don't compromise, it is said, and principles should never be compromised." –Andrew Carnegie*

   One challenge for the Speaker is deciding if and when to compromise with other members. Do you agree with businessman Andrew Carnegie that compromise is often a sign of weakness? Would you ever compromise your principles? Write an expository essay that explains your view. Support your ideas with specific examples from your personal experience or from your studies. Write at least three paragraphs, and use three or more unit words.

Writing prompt #2 is modeled on that of standardized tests.

CCSS Vocabulary: 6; Writing: 2.d., 3.d. (See pp. T14–15.)

Vocabulary in Context: Informational Text for Unit 8 is available online at **vocabularyworkshop.com**.

Vocabulary in Context

Literary Text

The following excerpts are from William Makepeace Thackeray's novels Vanity Fair *and* The History of Henry Esmond. *Some of the words you have studied in this unit appear in* **boldface** *type. Complete each statement below the excerpt by circling the letter of the correct answer.*

1. "When she comes to tea here she does not speak a word during the whole evening. She is but a poor **lackadaisical** creature, and it is my belief has no heart at all. It is only her pretty face which all you gentlemen admire so." (*Vanity Fair*)

Someone who is **lackadaisical** is NOT

a. vigorous
b. ordinary
c. intelligent
d. kind

2. And so having easily won the daughter's good-will, the indefatigable little woman bent herself to **conciliate** the august Lady Southdown. As soon as she found her Ladyship alone, Rebecca attacked her on the nursery question at once and said that her own little boy was saved, actually saved, by calomel, freely administered, when all the physicians in Paris had given the dear child up. *(Vanity Fair)*

To **conciliate** is to

a. exonerate
b. demean
c. appease
d. bewilder

3. O, my dear brethren and fellow-sojourners in Vanity Fair, which among you does not know and suffer under such benevolent despots? It is in vain you say to them, "Dear Madam, I took Podgers' specific at your orders last year, and believe in it. Why, why am I to **recant** and accept the Rodgers' articles now?" (*Vanity Fair*)

To **recant** is to

a. renounce
b. proclaim
c. apologize
d. sacrifice

A scene from the 2004 film version of *Vanity Fair*, starring Reese Witherspoon as Becky Sharp.

4. Although Mr. Esmond had told Jack Lockwood to get horses and they would ride for Winchester that night, when he heard this news he **countermanded** the horses at once; his business lay no longer in Hanta; all his hope and desire lay within a couple of miles of him in Kensington Park wall. (*The History of Henry Esmond*)

Something **countermanded** is

a. summoned
b. restrained
c. recalled
d. scattered

5. There was a fire in the room where the cloths were drying for the baths, and there lay a heap in a corner **saturated** with the blood of my dear lord's body. Esmond went to the fire, and threw the paper into it. *(The History of Henry Esmond)*

Something that is **saturated** is

a. tossed carelessly
b. mangled badly
c. soaked completely
d. stained lightly

Snap the code, or go to **vocabularyworkshop.com**

CCSS Vocabulary: 4.c.; Reading (Literature): 4. (See pp. T14–15.)

UNIT 9

Note that not all of the 20 unit words are used in this passage. *Bucolic*, *dilettante*, *increment*, *refulgent*, and *vacillate* are not included in the passage.

*Read the following selection, taking note of the **boldface** words and their contexts. These words are among those you will be studying in Unit 9. As you complete the exercises in this unit, it may help to refer to the way the words are used below.*

CCSS Vocabulary: 4; Reading (Informational Text): 4, 6. (See pp. T14–15.)

Security Status: It's Complicated

<Persuasive Essay>

To great **acclamation**, social networking sites, websites that allow connected groups of individuals to interact online, burst onto the scene in the late 1990s. Since then, tell-all social networking sites have increased in popularity exponentially. With some sites boasting hundreds of millions of users disclosing information with total strangers and friends alike, there now exists an extensive online community sharing ideas, interests, and activities.

Social networking is, in theory, an excellent, appealing concept, but risks abound with every online **peregrination**. Sites provide ready access to personal information, so even the most **imperturbable** and experienced users must recognize and be mindful of the hazards.

Social networking sites allow users to keep in touch and build connections without much effort, but who else is effortlessly monitoring their correspondences? Corporations are, for one. Looking for market advantages, businesses use personal information to evaluate potential customers. The companies that own the social networks are, in a sense, in **collusion** with those corporations when they collect data to sell to their advertisers. But the infringements of advertisers are **paltry** problems, more **redolent** of annoying telephone marketing, than of the serious crimes committed by those who prey on social network users. For, unfortunately, along with the rapid growth of sites and their many beneficial applications, there has also emerged a veritable **paroxysm** of criminal activity associated with those sites.

Yes, there are unsavory individuals out there who are very interested in collecting the information that people post. There are identity thieves and those who **vituperatively** harass or stalk people online, or who infect computers with malware; scam artists looking to take advantage of **tyros** and veterans alike. It is another sad truth that there is a growing number of bullying teens who use social networks to cruelly **calumniate** and isolate classmates. In a few cases, cyber-bullying has led to tragedy as victims try to escape their tormentors.

Fortunately, available tools and strategies minimize risks when using social networks. Users must remain as **unremitting** in their efforts to protect their privacy as the malefactors are in theirs to breach it.

The old **shibboleth**, "Leave no stone unturned," is a **mandate** in this war against cyber criminals and against as yet unforeseen issues. Above all, users must be **chary** in what they post, providing only necessary information that errs on the side of caution and good sense. Social networkers should limit personal data in postings and provide more details in secure areas. Nobody really wants strangers to have his or her phone number or address. Remember, personal data are valuable to crooks, identity thieves, spammers, and advertisers.

Furthermore, users should familiarize themselves with a site's privacy settings and be alert to changes in them. It is a good practice to reject requests to connect with strangers looking for money. If a social network account is compromised, it should be reported to the site and the account should be closed. Protective strategies are not **pedantry**, but key components of a prudent approach to safe social networking. Social networkers must proceed with caution and common sense to enjoy the many benefits of cyber-communities.

Snap the code, or go to vocabularyworkshop.com

Note the spelling, pronunciation, part(s) of speech, and definition(s) of each of the following words. Then write the word in the blank spaces in the illustrative sentence(s) following. Finally, study the lists of synonyms and antonyms.

1. acclamation (ak lə mā′ shən)

(*n.*) a shout of welcome; an overwhelming verbal vote of approval

It is very rare for a presidential candidate to be nominated by **acclamation** from the convention floor.

SYNONYMS: ovation, cheering, plaudits
ANTONYMS: booing, hissing, jeers, catcalls

2. bucolic (byü käl′ ik)

(*adj.*) characteristic of the countryside, rural; relating to shepherds and cowherds, pastoral

The Elizabethans who wrote of shepherds in ideal country settings were imitating the Greek **bucolic** poets.

SYNONYM: rustic
ANTONYM: metropolitan

3. calumniate (kə ləm′ nē āt)

(*v.*) to slander; to accuse falsely and maliciously

Not only did the artist's enemy seek to discredit her while she was alive but tried to **calumniate** her memory as well.

SYNONYMS: defame, libel
ANTONYMS: flatter, whitewash, praise

4. chary (châr′ ē)

(*adj.*) extremely cautious, hesitant, or slow (to); reserved, diffident

Since so many funds had been spent with so few results, they were **chary** about appropriating more money.

SYNONYM: skittish
ANTONYMS: heedless, reckless, incautious

5. collusion (kə lü′ zhən)

(*n.*) secret agreement or cooperation

Years later, it was discovered that senior members of the company had been in **collusion** with the enemy.

SYNONYMS: conspiracy, plot, connivance

6. dilettante (dil′ ə tänt)

(*n.*) a dabbler in the arts; one who engages in an activity in an amateurish, trifling way; (*adj.*) superficial

Many people dismissed the poster artists of the 1960s as mere **dilettantes** with nothing serious to say about life or art.

SYNONYM: amateur
ANTONYM: professional

CCSS Vocabulary: 4.c., 4.d. (See pp. T14–15.)

7. imperturbable (im pər tər′ bə bəl)
(*adj.*) not easily excited; emotionally steady

The witness remained ___imperturbable___ throughout the grueling cross-examination.

SYNONYMS: unflappable, unexcitable, serene, unruffled
ANTONYM: excitable

8. increment (in′ krə mənt)
(*n.*) an enlargement, increase, addition

Employees were added to the work force in ___increments___ of five to reduce training costs.

SYNONYM: accretion
ANTONYMS: reduction, decrease

9. mandate (man′ dāt)
(*n.*) an authoritative command, formal order, authorization; (*v.*) to issue such an order

The peacekeepers were sent into the war-torn country under a UN ___mandate___ to protect civilians.

The environmental protection agency has ___mandated___ that all automobiles pass an annual emissions test.

SYNONYM: (*n.*) directive
ANTONYMS: (*v.*) forbid, ban, outlaw

10. paltry (pôl′ trē)
(*adj.*) trifling, insignificant; mean, despicable; inferior, trashy

The billionaire was so greedy that he contributed only a ___paltry___ sum of money to charity each year.

SYNONYMS: measly, meager, piddling, trivial
ANTONYMS: gigantic, immense

11. paroxysm (par′ ək siz əm)
(*n.*) a sudden outburst; a spasm, convulsion

The children greeted the clown with a ___paroxysm___ of laughter when he began making his funny faces.

SYNONYMS: fit, seizure

12. pedantry (ped′ ən trē)
(*n.*) a pretentious display of knowledge; overly rigid attention to rules and details

The fussy music professor was distinguished more for her ___pedantry___ than her true scholarship.

SYNONYMS: nit-picking, pettifoggery

13. peregrination (per ə grə nā′ shən)
(*n.*) the act of traveling; an excursion, especially on foot or to a foreign country

After returning from my ___peregrination___ throughout South America, I wrote a book about my experiences.

SYNONYMS: journey, wandering, odyssey

CCSS Vocabulary: 4.c. (See pp. T14–15.)

14. redolent (red′ ə lənt)

(*adj.*) fragrant, smelling strongly; tending to arouse memories or create an aura

My grandmother's kitchen was always **redolent** with the smells of baking.

SYNONYMS: evocative, reminiscent, aromatic
ANTONYMS: unevocative, odorless

15. refulgent (ri fəl′ jənt)

(*adj.*) shining, radiant, resplendent

The swift-flowing stream beside our house was **refulgent** in the morning light.

SYNONYM: splendid
ANTONYMS: dim, dark, obscure, dingy, dull

16. shibboleth (shib′ ə leth)

(*n.*) a word, expression, or custom that distinguishes a particular group of persons from all others; a commonplace saying or truism

By the time Election Day rolls around, most voters are tired of hearing the same old promises and **shibboleths**.

SYNONYMS: password, slogan

17. tyro (tī′ rō)

(*n.*) a beginner, novice; one with little or no background or skill

You cannot expect a mere **tyro** to perform like a veteran in his first season of major league play.

SYNONYM: neophyte
ANTONYMS: veteran, past master, expert

18. unremitting (ən ri mit′ iŋ)

(*adj.*) not stopping, maintained steadily, never letting up, relentless

The social laws in Edith Wharton's novels are **unremitting**.

SYNONYMS: incessant, unrelenting
ANTONYMS: desultory, intermittent

19. vacillate (vas′ ə lāt)

(*v.*) to swing indecisively from one idea or course of action to another; to waver weakly in mind or will

Someone who **vacillates** in a crisis should not be in a position of leadership.

SYNONYMS: fluctuate, oscillate
ANTONYM: persevere

20. vituperative (vī tü′ pər ə tiv)

(*adj.*) harshly abusive, severely scolding

That **vituperative** speech in which she blamed others for her own mistakes may have cost her the election.

SYNONYMS: abusive, scurrilous, insulting
ANTONYMS: complimentary, laudatory, flattering

CCSS Vocabulary: 4.c. (See pp. T14–15.)

Choosing the Right Word

*Select the **boldface** word that better completes each sentence. You might refer to the selection on pages 108–109 to see how most of these words are used in context.*

1. Many of the most well-known paintings of Grandma Moses portray rural scenes that are (**redolent, vituperative**) of her childhood in upstate New York.

2. Because my teacher is usually so (**chary, imperturbable**) of giving compliments, I felt really good when she spoke well of my essay.

3. Isn't it sheer (**pedantry, refulgence**) on his part to use terms like *Proustian* and *Kafkaesque* when he knows they mean nothing to his audience?

4. Although he has been in this business for 20 years, he still has the sublime innocence of the most helpless (**tyro, shibboleth**).

Born in 1860, Anna Mary Robertson, better known as "Grandma Moses," began painting in her seventies.

5. Not satisfied with the slow (**increment, peregrination**) of his savings in a bank account, he turned to speculation in the stock market.

6. Are we to try to make a realistic analysis of our alternatives or let ourselves be distracted by slogans and (**tyros, shibboleths**)?

7. Once the senator's nomination became a certainty, all opposition to him evaporated, and he was named by (**vituperation, acclamation**).

8. Perhaps he would be less lyrical about the delights of the (**bucolic, redolent**) life if, like me, he had grown up on a farm in Kansas.

9. The gambler's predictions of the game scores were so incredibly accurate that we suspected some form of (**acclamation, collusion**).

10. The same difficulties that serve as a challenge to the true professional will be a crushing discouragement to the typical (**mandate, dilettante**).

11. I'm not sure if Tom's (**imperturbable, collusive**) spirit is due to toughness or to an inability to understand the dangers of the situation.

12. Since she comes from a rural area, she expresses herself in language that is (**redolent, paltry**) of the farm and of country life in general.

13. During the course of my (**peregrinations, paroxysms**) through the world of books, I have picked up all kinds of useful information.

14. Clad in the (**refulgent, dilettante**) armor of moral rectitude, he sallied forth to do battle with the forces of evil.

15. I am perfectly willing to listen to a reasonable complaint, but I will not put up with that kind of (**bucolic, vituperative**) backbiting.

CCSS Vocabulary: 4.d. (See pp. T14–15.)

16. It has long been known that some twisted and unhappy people derive a kind of satisfaction from (**calumniating, colluding**) others.

17. The phrase "We the people" in the Constitution indicates that the ultimate (**mandate, vacillation**) of our government comes from the popular will.

18. If we (**vacillate, increment**) now at adopting a tough energy policy, we may find ourselves in a desperate situation in the future.

19. How do you have the nerve to offer such a(n) (**paltry, unremitting**) sum for this magnificent "antique" car!

20. A (**paroxysm, pedantry**) of indignation flashed though the community, and the streets filled with angry people ready to protest the proposal.

21. It is easy to criticize him, but how can we overlook the fact that for 20 years he has worked (**unremittingly, charily**) to help the homeless?

22. Although Martin thinks he is an expert software developer, many of his dissatisfied clients view him as merely a (**paroxysm, tyro**).

23. The senate candidate claimed that her opponent's most recent television ad (**calumniated, vacillated**) her husband and children.

24. During our family's recent (**peregrination, acclamation**) to the New Orleans French Quarter, we attended several jazz concerts.

25. (**Paltry, Refulgent**) attendance on opening night caused a financial crisis.

Synonyms

Choose the word from this unit that is the same or most nearly the same in meaning as the **boldface** *word or expression in the phrase. Write that word on the line. Use a dictionary if necessary.*

1. large **gain** in tax revenues — increment
2. in **cahoots** with the competition — collusion
3. kept up the **constant** pressure to surrender — unremitting
4. a stunningly **luminous** smile — refulgent
5. bored us with his **hairsplitting** — pedantry
6. **seesawed** in their commitments — vacillated
7. keeps repeating the tired old **catchphrases** — shibboleths
8. labeled a mere **trifler** by the experts — dilettante
9. **wary** of flattery and favor-seekers — chary
10. painted a charming **country** scene — bucolic

CCSS Vocabulary: 5. (See pp. T14–15.)

The synonyms and antonyms here do not appear on the Definitions page.

Antonyms

*Choose the word from this unit that is most nearly opposite in meaning to the **boldface** word or expression in the phrase. Write that word on the line. Use a dictionary if necessary.*

1. a **scholar** of poetry — dilettante
2. a **colossal** amount of debt — paltry
3. reported a steady **loss** in annual sales — increment
4. felt relief that the market was able to **stabilize** — vacillate
5. prefers the **urban** lifestyle — bucolic

Completing the Sentence

From the words in this unit, choose the one that best completes each of the following sentences. Write the word in the space provided.

1. In a series of searing orations, filled with the most ___vituperative___ language, Cicero launched the full battery of political invective against the hapless Mark Antony.

2. The scene may seem ordinary to you, but I find it ___redolent___ with memories of happy summers spent in these woods.

3. As we waited through the long night for the arrival of the rescue party, we ___vacillated___ between hope and despair.

4. However long and hard the struggle, we must be ___unremitting___ in our efforts to wipe out racism in this country.

5. Since Lucy had expected no more than polite applause, she was delighted by the ___acclamation___ she received from the audience.

6. The contractor was suspected of having acted in ___collusion___ with a state official to fix the bids on certain public works contracts.

7. The painting shows a restfully ___bucolic___ scene, with some cows grazing placidly in a meadow as their shepherd dozes under a bush.

8. I thought I was unexcitable, but she is as ___imperturbable___ as the granite lions in front of the public library.

9. In my various ___peregrinations___ through that vast metropolis, I ran across many curious old buildings that the ordinary tourist never sees.

10. It is sheer ___pedantry___ to insist upon applying the rules of formal literary composition to everyday speech and writing.

CCSS Vocabulary: 4.a. (See pp. T14–15.)

11. I have learned from long experience to be extremely **chary** about offering advice when it has not been requested.

12. The Pledge of Allegiance is no mere **shibboleth** to be recited mechanically and without understanding like some advertising jingle.

13. She may have great musical talents, but she will get nowhere as long as she has the casual attitude of the **dilettante**.

14. Since Lincoln is now considered a great national hero, it is hard to believe that he was bitterly **calumniated** when he was President.

15. I had expected a decent tip from the party of six that I waited on early that evening, but all I got was a(n) **paltry** two bucks!

16. "The overwhelming victory I have won at the polls," the Governor-elect said, "has given me a clear **mandate** to carry out my program."

17. Seized by a(n) **paroxysm** of rage, he began to beat the bars of his cell with his bare hands.

18. Even the merest **tyro** in the use of firearms knows that a gun should never be pointed at another person.

19. Every time I sign a new lease on my apartment, my rent goes up, though the **increments** are not usually very large.

20. As a(n) **refulgent** summer sun sank slowly in the west, the skies were ablaze with color.

Writing: Words in Action

Answers to both prompts will vary.

1. Look back at "Security Status: It's Complicated" (pages 108–109). Suppose that you work for an organization that educates the public about the potential dangers of social networking sites. You want to write a letter to the editor that persuades parents to take steps to ensure their young children use such sites appropriately and safely. Use at least two details from the essay and three unit words in your letter.

2. Think about how the experience of communicating with somebody by phone is different from that of communicating through social networking sites. Write an essay of at least three paragraphs in which you compare and contrast telephone and computer conversations. Use examples from your reading (refer to pages 108–109), prior knowledge, and personal experience to support your points of comparison. Use three or more words from this unit.

Writing prompt #2 is modeled on that of standardized tests.

CCSS Vocabulary: 6; Writing: 2.d., 3.d. (See pp. T14–15.)

Vocabulary in Context: Informational Text for Unit 9 is available online at **vocabularyworkshop.com**.

Vocabulary in Context
Literary Text

The following excerpts are from George Eliot's novels The Mill on the Floss *and* Romola. *Some of the words you have studied in this unit appear in* **boldface** *type. Complete each statement below the excerpt by circling the letter of the correct answer.*

1. Once before, since his illness, he had had a similar **paroxysm**, in which he had beaten his horse, and the scene had left a lasting terror in Maggie's mind. The thought had risen, that some time or other he might beat her mother if she happened to speak in her feeble way at the wrong moment. (*The Mill on the Floss*)

A **paroxysm** is a(n)

a. convulsion
b. disease
c. inclination
d. hallucination

2. "They're **paltry** times, these are. Why, mum, look at the printed cottons now, an' what they was when you wore 'em, — why you wouldn't put such a thing on now, I can see." (*The Mill on the Floss*)

Paltry times are definitely NOT

a. diverse
b. memorable
c. wealthy
d. inevitable

3. The nineteenth of May had come, and by that day's sunshine there had entered into Florence the two Papal Commissaries, charged with the completion of Savonarola's trial. They entered amid the **acclamations** of the people, calling for the death of the Frate. (*Romola*)

Acclamations are

a. demands for revenge
b. angry protests
c. shouts of welcome
d. frightened cries

4. "Pardon, Messer Piero," said Tito, with his **imperturbable** good-humor; "I acted without sufficient reflection. I remembered nothing but your admirable skill in inventing pretty caprices, when a sudden desire for something of that sort prompted me to come to you." (*Romola*)

Something that is **imperturbable** is

a. undeniable and obvious
b. quiet and understated
c. witty and sarcastic
d. steady and not easily excited

5. Every day the distress became sharper: every day the murmurs became louder. And, to crown the difficulties of the government, for a month and more—in obedience to a **mandate** from Rome—Fra Girolamo had ceased to preach. *(Romola)*

A **mandate** is a

a. document
b. command
c. deliberation
d. plea

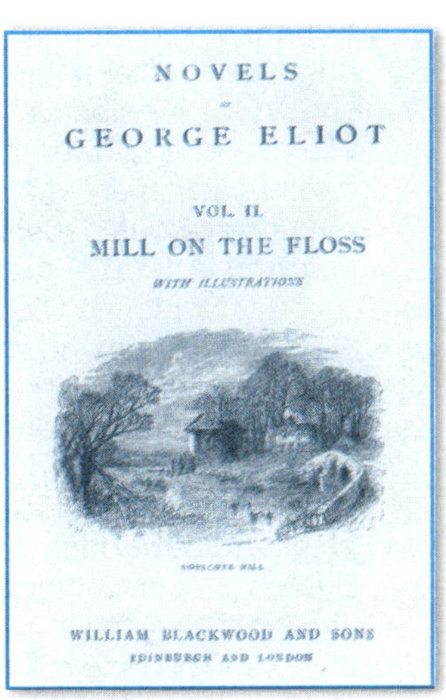

Mary Ann Evans used the pen name George Eliot when she published *The Mill on the Floss* in 1860.

Snap the code, or go to **vocabularyworkshop.com**

Vocabulary for Comprehension

*Read the following selection in which some of the words you have studied in Units 7–9 appear in **boldface** type. Then answer the questions on page 119.*

As this passage shows, the central goal of the League of Women Voters is good citizenship.

(Line)

The League of Women Voters is a citizen advocacy organization that was developed as a result of the women's suffrage movement. It was founded in 1920 by the suffragist Carrie Chapman Catt, an **unremitting** champion of women's rights and social reform. Its immediate mission was to help inform and empower the 20 million American women who were enfranchised as a result of the passage in 1920 of the Nineteenth Amendment to the U.S. Constitution.

Over the years, however, the League has advocated issues less directly related to the women's movement. It has supported programs as diverse as assistance to the **indigent** during the Great Depression, civil rights in the 1960s, and environmental conservation and campaign finance reform today. Though the League vigorously champions its causes, it sees itself as staunchly nonpartisan. In other words, the League supports programs and policies but **demurs** when asked to endorse specific parties or candidates. This stance has led critics on both the left and the right to **allege** that the League is a **coterie** of activists with a hidden agenda concealed behind a banner of nonpartisanship. The League replies that it is undeniably political but definitely not partisan.

The League also takes great pride in its grassroots style of organization. Policy decisions are not made by a few leaders in the upper **echelons** of the organization, but rather are arrived at by intense study, debate, and consensus building among the rank-and-file membership at the chapter level. This reflects the League's attitude toward the power of well-informed citizens in a democracy, who ideally will make choices that will lead to a better life for all.

CCSS Vocabulary: 4.a.; Reading (Informational Text): 2, 4, 6. (See pp. T14–15.)

1. The main purpose of the first paragraph (lines 1–14) is to
   (a.) discuss the origins of the League
   b. explain why women had to wait so long for the vote
   c. analyze the opposition to the Nineteenth Amendment
   d. highlight the career of Carrie Chapman Catt
   e. show how the League of Women Voters got its name

2. According to the passage, the League's original mission was to
   a. advise Republican candidates in the 1920 election
   (b.) inform and empower newly enfranchised women voters
   c. lobby for campaign finance reform
   d. create a grassroots organization of local chapters
   e. lobby for passage of the Nineteenth Amendment

3. The meaning of **unremitting** (line 7) is
   a. controversial
   b. incomparable
   (c.) unrelenting
   d. undefeated
   e. intolerant

4. **Indigent** (line 20) most nearly means
   (a.) penniless
   b. handicapped
   c. despondent
   d. oppressed
   e. homeless

5. **Demurs** (line 28) is best defined as
   a. debates
   (b.) objects
   c. waffles
   d. consents
   e. rethinks

6. The meaning of **allege** (line 32) is
   a. refute
   b. imply
   (c.) claim
   d. deny
   e. dispute

7. **Coterie** (line 33) most nearly means
   a. conspiracy
   b. party
   (c.) clique
   d. family
   e. gang

8. From the details the author provides in paragraph 2 (lines 15–37), you may reasonably infer that the League has at times been
   a. undemocratic
   b. partisan
   c. unsuccessful
   d. inconsistent
   (e.) controversial

9. Which of the following best identifies the comparison/contrast the writer makes in paragraph 2?
   a. Republicans vs. Democrats
   b. critics on the left vs. critics on the right
   (c.) political vs. partisan
   d. the Great Depression vs. the Civil Rights movement
   e. national issues vs. local issues

10. The author identifies all of the following as activities of the League EXCEPT
    a. assisting the indigent
    b. supporting environmental conservation
    c. informing citizens
    (d.) lobbying for tax cuts
    e. advocating campaign finance reform

11. **Echelons** (line 41) most nearly means
    a. floors
    b. classes
    c. salaries
    d. offices
    (e.) levels

12. The author's attitude toward the League may best be described as
    a. romantic
    b. skeptical
    c. reflective
    d. hostile
    (e.) admiring

CCSS Vocabulary: 4.a.; Reading (Informational Text): 2, 4, 6. (See pp. T14–15.)

Two-Word Completions

Select the pair of words that best complete the meaning of each of the following passages.

1. The ____________ rains had so ____________ the ground over which we passed that it actually squished and gurgled in protest as we trod on it, and our attack had to be postponed until the sun came out again.

   a. inordinate . . . razed
   b. ephemeral . . . embellished
   (c.) unremitting . . . saturated
   d. bestial . . . jettisoned

2. In Chaucer's *Canterbury Tales*, twenty-nine travelers from various ____________ of society set out for Canterbury on a pilgrimage to the shrine of Saint Thomas Beckett. At night the ____________ of travelers shares its stories in order to help time pass.

   a. mandates . . . collusion
   b. litanies . . . raiment
   (c.) echelons . . . coterie
   d. shibboleths . . . paucity

3. Though the official is ____________ to have been in cahoots with the swindlers, so far no substantive evidence has been brought forward to prove ____________.

   a. portended . . . acclamation
   b. demurred . . . peregrination
   (c.) alleged . . . collusion
   d. calumniated . . . badinage

4. At the June 1961 summit meetings in Vienna, President John Kennedy met with his Soviet ____________, Nikita Khrushchev, in an effort to deal with sources of friction between the two superpowers and ____________ international fears that the so-called Cold War was heating up.

   (a.) counterpart . . . allay
   b. raiment . . . mandate
   c. coterie . . . exacerbate
   d. shibboleth . . . conciliate

5. The speed with which the Kaiser issued, then ____________, then reissued orders during the crisis was indicative of his essentially weak and ____________ personality.

   a. embellished . . . pertinacious
   b. recanted . . . imperturbable
   c. demurred . . . fatuous
   (d.) countermanded . . . vacillating

6. Only a thoroughgoing ____________ would enjoy castigating other people's behavior in such unremittingly harsh and ____________ language.

   a. pedant . . . felicitous
   (b.) misanthrope . . . vituperative
   c. tyro . . . arrant
   d. dilettante . . . convivial

7. The horribly ____________ furnishings sent the shocked homeowner into a(n) ____________ of anger.

   a. macabre . . . increment
   b. refulgent . . . slough
   c. chary . . . effrontery
   (d.) garish . . . paroxysm

 CCSS Vocabulary: 4.a. (See pp. T14–15.)

Idioms

In "A Passage to Power" (pages 98–99), in a response to a question about the job of Speaker of the House of Representatives, the interviewee notes that Henry Clay, a previous Speaker, "stirred the pot" in several ways. The phrase "stir the pot" is an idiom that means "cause trouble" or "deliberately bring issues to the surface." The interviewee wants to convey that Clay's actions provoked thought about and changes in the Speaker's duties and power.

An **idiom** is a phrase with a figurative, not literal, meaning. Like other figures of speech, idioms create fresh images in the minds of readers or listeners. Sometimes you will be able to figure out an idiom's meaning from context clues. Other times you may need to consult an online or print dictionary to discover or verify an idiom's meaning.

Choosing the Right Idiom

Read each sentence. Use context clues to figure out the meaning of each idiom in ***boldface*** *print. Then write the letter of the definition for the idiom in the sentence.*

1. The aging band's concert tour across Europe this summer is likely to be their **swan song**. __g__
2. The parade organizers worried that high wind gusts might **play havoc with** the streamers tied to the flag poles. __h__
3. Noting that her father had worked two jobs to pay for her college education, Maria described him as the **salt of the earth**. __d__
4. After our golden retriever left muddy paw prints on the kitchen floor, we worked hard to get it **spick and span** again. __j__
5. Derrick's two talkative aunts hoped to arrive at the reunion early so that they would have time to **chew the fat**. __c__
6. When the **well-heeled** customer took the luxury convertible for a test drive, the salesman began dreaming of a huge commission. __b__
7. The news story about the protest included a photo of several local residents who are **up in arms** over the road expansion. __e__
8. "Although you might not like the turnip casserole at first," Karen added, "I hope it will **grow on you** after you've had several bites." __i__
9. The judge vowed not to **split hairs** when he clarifies his ruling in the tax evasion case. __a__
10. "Please **lay it on the line** when you tell me what happened," Grandma told the fidgety children as she stared at her shattered crystal vase. __f__

a. argue about small details

b. having plenty of money

c. have a long chat

d. a most worthy person

e. angry

f. be totally honest

g. final performance

h. ruin

i. become increasingly liked

j. neat and clean

CCSS Vocabulary: 5.a. (See pp. T14–15.)

Writing with Idioms

Find the meaning of each idiom. (Use an online or print dictionary if necessary.) Then write a sentence for each idiom. **Answers will vary.**

1. on the dot **Sample answer: Because the flight is oversold, we must be at the gate and ready to board by 8 pm on the dot.**
2. hit pay dirt ______
3. behind the eight ball ______
4. scratch the surface ______
5. on the same wavelength ______
6. with flying colors ______
7. pick up the tab ______
8. home free ______
9. on the table ______
10. neither here nor there ______
11. hem and haw ______
12. play fast and loose with ______

 CCSS Vocabulary: 5. (See pp. T14–15.)

Denotation and Connotation

A dictionary provides the objective meaning of a word, its **denotation.** A word's **connotation** is its subjective meaning, which includes the emotional and implied meanings associated with the word. Connotations can be *positive*, *neutral*, or *negative*.

Suppose you were writing an essay about a famous historical figure. To convey your esteem for the person's determination, you might use words like *tenacious* or *resolute*. To suggest an excessive inflexibility, you might choose words like *obstinate* or *peremptory*.

Consider these synonyms for the neutral word *chary*:

prudent *circumspect* *calculating* *diffident*

Prudent and *circumspect* have positive connotations, whereas *calculating* and *diffident* have negative connotations.

> **Think:** Successful financial advisers are prudent and circumspect in giving advice, but calculating or diffident advisers consider their own self-interest or are overly cautious.

Look at these examples of words that are similar in denotation but have different connotations.

NEUTRAL	POSITIVE	NEGATIVE
approachable	**convivial**	**boisterous**
nerve	**aplomb**	**effrontery**
meager	**streamlined**	**paltry**

A single word may have different connotations in different contexts. For example, *family* may have a neutral connotation when it identifies a category in a biology textbook but a positive connotation when it describes loving relatives in a memoir.

Shades of Meaning

Write a plus sign (+) in the box if the word has a positive connotation. Write a minus sign (–) if the word has a negative connotation. Put a zero (0) if the word is neutral.

1. calumniate –	**2.** refulgent +	**3.** shibboleth 0	**4.** vacillate –
5. portend 0	**6.** exacerbate –	**7.** bestial –	**8.** embellish +
9. fatuous –	**10.** furtive –	**11.** raiment 0	**12.** saturnine –
13. mandate 0	**14.** indigent –	**15.** felicitous +	**16.** paucity –

CCSS Vocabulary: 5.b. (See pp. T14–15.)

Expressing the Connotation

Read each sentence. Select the word in parentheses that expresses the connotation (positive, negative, or neutral) given at the beginning of the sentence.

negative **1.** The fairgrounds surrounding the roller coaster rides were (**redolent, odorous**) with the smells of the nearby food tents.

positive **2.** After Officer Ramirez (**alleged, verified**) that the vehicle had been traveling 65 mph, the driver reluctantly admitted to speeding.

neutral **3.** The arrival of Kenny and his (**coterie, mob**) of friends did not disrupt the other passengers on the plane.

negative **4.** The mayor's relentless focus on making (**unimportant, picayune**) changes to the bill's wording frustrated the council members.

negative **5.** On their course evaluations, students frequently complained about the pompous professor's (**pedantry, proficiency**) during lectures.

neutral **6.** Minutes after the storms began, the white linen tablecloth became (**saturated, discolored**) with water.

neutral **7.** The army veteran acknowledged the (**acclamation, reception**) from the audience with a nod of her head and a salute.

positive **8.** Everyone in our family likes to discuss my (**intense, inordinate**) interest in cars and motorcycles.

Challenge: Using Connotation

Choose vocabulary words from Units 7–9 to replace the highlighted words in the sentences below. Then explain how the connotation of the replacement word changes the tone of the sentence. **Answers will vary.**

badinage	**litany**	**slough**
garish	**peregrination**	**vituperative**

1. When the actress first saw her costume, she thought that the dress and coat were extremely **bright** ___garish___. **Sample response: The negative connotation of *garish* suggests that the actress might have been unhappy because the outfit was tasteless and gaudy.**

2. The hikers were surprised that the marked trail took them so close to a large **meadow** ___slough___. **Sample response: The negative connotation of *slough* reveals that the hikers' surprise at being near a muddy mire, not a grassy plain, might have been unpleasant.**

3. Upon returning home after her blind date, Anna regaled her roommates with details of the **discussion** ___badinage___ she had with her date. **Sample response: The positive connotation of *badinage* makes the talk between the two people seem less neutral and serious and more pleasant and playful.**

 CCSS Vocabulary: 5. (See pp. T14–15.)

Classical Roots

clam, claim—to cry out, shout, call

The root *clam* appears in **acclamation** (page 110). The literal meaning of acclamation is "shouting at," but it now suggests "applause" or "an overwhelmingly favorable oral vote." Some other words based on the same root are listed below.

acclaim	**clamorous**	**disclaimer**	**proclamation**
claimant	**declaim**	**irreclaimable**	**reclamation**

From the list of words above, choose the one that corresponds to each of the brief definitions below. Write the word in the blank space in the illustrative sentence below the definition. Use an online or print dictionary if necessary.

1. a denial or disavowal of responsibility or connection; a formal refusal of one's rights or claims

   The manufacturer issued a swift ____**disclaimer**____ after mediocre reviews of its new product.

2. to applaud; to indicate strong approval; noisy and enthusiastic applause

   The winning team enjoyed vigorous public ____**acclaim**____ in a ticker-tape parade.

3. to speak like an orator; to recite in public, make a public speech; to speak bitterly against

   The actor would ____**declaim**____ lines from Shakespeare in response to any comment.

4. incapable of being reformed; incapable of being rendered useful

   That region of the park is nothing more than ____**irreclaimable**____ swampland.

5. an official or formal public announcement

   The clerk posted the latest mayoral ____**proclamation**____ at the entrance to City Hall.

6. the act of bringing back or restoring to a normal or useful condition (*"to call back"*)

   Innovative irrigation techniques have resulted in the ____**reclamation**____ of much of the desert.

7. marked by loud confusion or outcry; noisily insistent (*"crying out"*)

   The protesters outside the White House made ____**clamorous**____ demands for reform.

8. a person who asserts a right or title

   After many years, the estranged son resurfaced as the last ____**claimant**____ to the estate.

CCSS Vocabulary: 4.c. (See pp. T14–15.)

UNIT 10

Note that not all of the 20 unit words are used in this passage. *Cavil*, *obtuse*, *oscillate*, *penitent*, and *peremptory* are not included in the passage.

*Read the following selection, taking note of the **boldface** words and their contexts. These words are among those you will be studying in Unit 10. As you complete the exercises in this unit, it may help to refer to the way the words are used below.*

CCSS Vocabulary: 4; Reading (Informational Text): 4, 6. (See pp. T14–15.)

What Happened to the Franklin Expedition?

<Magazine Article>

By Simon Devoucoux

The tragic story of the Franklin Expedition began promisingly enough. In 1845, Sir John Franklin and his crew of about 130 set sail with great fanfare from England to the Arctic Ocean to find the fabled Northwest Passage. Franklin, a seasoned Polar explorer, was charged with **reconnoitering** the island mazes and channels of Arctic Canada in search of a route that linked the North Atlantic to the Pacific, a transit that could save many arduous months at sea for ships traveling to the other side of the world. That was the last time Franklin and his men would ever see home, and the expedition is known as one of the most disastrous in history.

Although the expedition was **fraught** with potential dangers, the British Admiralty believed it had planned for all exigencies and addressed all **foibles** that might weaken the expedition. It commissioned two warships, the HMS *Erebus* and HMS *Terror*, both refitted for navigating treacherous ice floes. Each vessel carried provisions for three years—including 2,500 pounds of tea and 9,000 pounds of chocolate!—and each had thousands of books. The officers and crew were clearly not required to **forgo** luxury onboard.

Although the expedition was well stocked, the Royal Navy had not fully reckoned with subzero temperatures and hazardous Arctic conditions. Officers and crew were outfitted in traditional navy uniforms, skimpy outerwear, and woolen gloves—the navy looked **askance** at changes to convention in clothing. It proved impossible for them to adapt to their new environment as the indigenous

Sir John Franklin led the lost Franklin Expedition, one of the great unsolved mysteries of the nineteenth century.

In 1895, W. Thomas Smith painted how he imagined the end of the Franklin Expedition looked.

people, the Inuit, had over centuries. The Inuit, hunter-gatherers who relied on dog sleds for transportation and animal skins for warmth, had become **inured** to the formidable cold.

Before long, the two ships were irrevocably trapped in pack ice. The expedition lay in **shambles**. Franklin perished in 1847, according to notes later found by search teams, and starvation, scurvy and lead poisoning from tinned food **decimated** the crew. Under the **luminous** northern lights, more and more fell victim to disease, hypothermia, and exposure. With their ranks **attenuated**, some of the crew set out on foot to try to reach an outpost of the Hudson Bay Company, but fate was not **benign**, and the crew members died before reaching the outpost.

Three years after the doomed expedition set out, there was still no word. How could the pride of the Royal Navy disappear without a trace? The country mourned Franklin—explorers and adventurers were national heros and the attention given them by the public bordered on **obsequious**. Lady Jane Franklin campaigned vigorously for search parties to locate her husband and his ships. A reward was offered, and scores of British and American vessels set sail for the unforgiving North. What they eventually found was unsettling: a few graves, disturbing notes that made little sense, then skeletons and a trail of more than 1,000 artifacts, from sextants to silver utensils to Bibles—even some novels. But a string of facts does not add up to the truth.

Newspapers of the day referred to it as the "awful mystery," and the fate of the Franklin Expedition still intrigues us—Franklin was an experienced explorer, not a **charlatan**, and previous expeditions had been trapped in pack ice and survived, so why did his entire crew perish? **Sporadic** attempts are made today to retrace the expedition, locate the two famous shipwrecks, and uncover what really happened to Franklin and his men. But the full truth may lie submerged somewhere in the frozen depths, where it continues to **rebuff** attempts to uncover it.

Simon Devoucoux lives in Newfoundland. He is a regular contributor to Victorian Exploration Quarterly.

Snap the code, or go to **vocabularyworkshop.com**

Note the spelling, pronunciation, part(s) of speech, and definition(s) of each of the following words. Then write the word in the blank spaces in the illustrative sentence(s) following. Finally, study the lists of synonyms and antonyms.

1. askance (ə skans′)
(*adv.*) with suspicion, distrust, or disapproval

The English teacher looked **askance** at the suggestion that students read compendiums of Dickens's novels.

SYNONYMS: distrustfully, suspiciously

2. attenuate (ə ten′ yü āt)
(*v.*) to make thin or slender; to weaken or lessen in force, intensity, or value

After making sure the wound was clean, the doctor took steps to **attenuate** the victim's pain.

SYNONYMS: thin out, dilute, water down
ANTONYMS: thicken, strengthen, bolster

3. benign (bi nīn′)
(*adj.*) gentle, kind; forgiving, understanding; having a favorable or beneficial effect; not malignant

Abraham Lincoln's sensitive stepmother had a **benign** influence on the lonely boy who had lost his mother.

SYNONYMS: benevolent, salubrious, harmless
ANTONYMS: malevolent, deleterious

4. cavil (kav′ əl)
(*v.*) to find fault in a petty way, carp; (*n.*) a trivial objection or criticism

I suggest you do not **cavil** over small things but instead focus on what is important.

Despite a few **cavils** I might make, I still find her to be an excellent poet.

SYNONYM: (*v.*) nitpick

5. charlatan (shär′ lə tən)
(*n.*) one who feigns knowledge or ability; a pretender, impostor, or quack

The reporter exposed the real estate agent as a **charlatan** who routinely deceived her customers.

SYNONYM: mountebank

6. decimate (des′ ə māt)
(*v.*) to kill or destroy a large part of

Again and again, Napoleon was able to **decimate** the armies of his enemies and lead his men to further victories.

SYNONYM: devastate

CCSS Vocabulary: 4.c., 4.d. (See pp. T14–15.)

7. foible (foi′ bəl)

(*n.*) a weak point, failing, minor flaw

Backbiting is one human **foible** not likely to be eradicated.

SYNONYMS: shortcoming, quirk
ANTONYMS: forte, virtue

8. forgo (fôr gō′)

(*v.*) to do without, abstain from, give up

One of the best, if not the easiest, ways to lose weight is to **forgo** dessert.

SYNONYMS: refrain from, renounce
ANTONYMS: indulge in, partake of

9. fraught (frôt)

(*adj.*) full of or loaded with; accompanied by

Even with the most advanced equipment, expeditions to the top of Mt. Everest are still **fraught** with danger.

SYNONYM: charged with
ANTONYMS: devoid of, lacking, deficient in

10. inure (in yür′)

(*v.*) to toughen, harden; to render used to something by long subjection or exposure

The Inuit have become **inured** to the hardships of the long Arctic winters through years of experience.

SYNONYMS: accustom, acclimate

11. luminous (lü′ mə nəs)

(*adj.*) emitting or reflecting light, glowing; illuminating

Walking under that **luminous** night sky induced in me weighty thoughts not often pondered.

SYNONYMS: bright, refulgent, lustrous
ANTONYMS: dark, opaque, dim, murky

12. obsequious (əb sē′ kwē əs)

(*adj.*) marked by slavish attentiveness; excessively submissive, often for purely self-interested reasons

Jane Austen ridiculed characters who were **obsequious** to the aristocracy but condescending to their social inferiors.

SYNONYMS: fawning, servile, sycophantic, mealymouthed
ANTONYMS: assertive, bumptious, candid, frank, independent

13. obtuse (äb tüs′)

(*adj.*) blunt, not coming to a point; slow or dull in understanding; measuring between 90° and 180°; not causing a sharp impression

The lieutenant was too **obtuse** to see the danger and led his company right into the hands of the enemy.

SYNONYMS: dumb, thick, mild, dull-witted
ANTONYMS: perceptive, quick-witted

CCSS Vocabulary: 4.c. (See pp. T14–15.)

14. oscillate (äs′ ə lāt)
(*v.*) to swing back and forth with a steady rhythm; to fluctuate or waver

The terrified narrator in Poe's story "The Pit and the Pendulum" watches the dreaded instrument **oscillate** as it slowly moves toward him.

SYNONYM: vibrate

15. penitent (pen′ ə tənt)
(*adj.*) regretful for one's sins or mistakes; (*n.*) one who is sorry for wrongdoing

The thief was sincerely **penitent**.

In the Middle Ages, **penitents** often confessed their sins publicly and were publicly punished.

SYNONYMS: (*adj.*) remorseful, regretful, rueful
ANTONYM: (*adj.*) remorseless

16. peremptory (pə remp′ tə rē)
(*adj.*) having the nature of a command that leaves no opportunity for debate, denial, or refusal; offensively self-assured, dictatorial; determined, resolute

The board members resented the director's **peremptory** tone of voice.

SYNONYM: unconditional; ANTONYMS: irresolute, mild, unassuming

17. rebuff (ri bəf′)
(*v.*) to snub; to repel, drive away; (*n.*) a curt rejection, a check

The old man **rebuffed** his neighbors by refusing all offers of friendship.

Her **rebuff** of my invitation was quite rude.

SYNONYMS: (*v.*) repulse, reject; (*n.*) setback
ANTONYMS: (*v.*) accept, welcome

18. reconnoiter (rē kə noit′ ər)
(*v.*) to engage in reconnaissance; to make a preliminary inspection

Infantry officers often ask for volunteers to **reconnoiter** the terrain ahead before ordering their soldiers to advance.

SYNONYM: scout

19. shambles (sham′ bəlz)
(*n.*) a slaughterhouse; a place of mass bloodshed; a state of complete disorder and confusion, mess

The burglars made a complete **shambles** of the apartment in their search for money and jewelry.

20. sporadic (spô rad′ ik)
(*adj.*) occurring at irregular intervals, having no set plan or order

The soldiers heard **sporadic** gunfire from the other side of the river.

SYNONYMS: intermittent, spasmodic
ANTONYMS: steady, continuous, uninterrupted

CCSS Vocabulary: 4.c. (See pp. T14–15.)

Choosing the Right Word

*Select the **boldface** word that better completes each sentence. You might refer to the selection on pages 126–127 to see how most of these words are used in context.*

1. A grandfather clock works by gravity; when the pendulum (**oscillates, reconnoiters**), it moves a system of weights attached to the clock's hands.

2. At an autocrat's court, free speech is usually replaced by the (**penitent, obsequious**) twaddle of flunkies and toadies.

3. We believe that classes taught by teachers with specialized training will have a (**sporadic, benign**) effect on the troubled children.

4. Though I admire the woman's strong points, I find her (**rebuffs, foibles**) comic.

5. Over the years, her (**luminous, obtuse**) descriptions and scintillating wit have helped her students master the difficult subject she taught.

6. Since he didn't want to give me credit for having done a good job, he took refuge in endless (**foibles, cavils**) about my work.

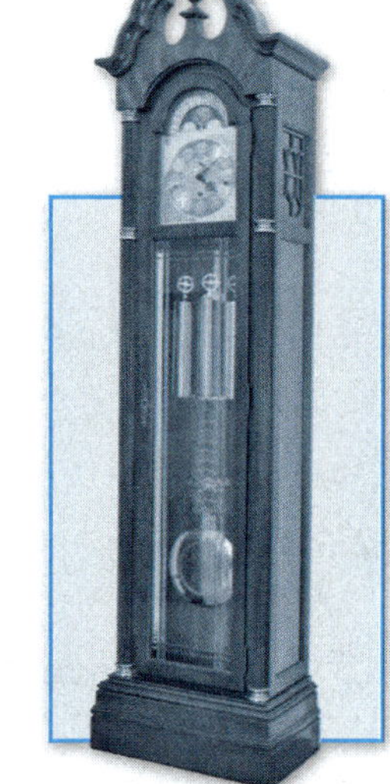

Galileo discovered that a pendulum could be used to keep time and developed the first plans for what is now known as a grandfather clock.

7. Though the small nation was always ready to settle a conflict peacefully, it was not afraid to use (**luminous, peremptory**) force when necessary.

8. We must never allow our passion for justice to be (**inured, attenuated**) to mere halfhearted goodwill.

9. I have learned that (**sporadic, peremptory**) sessions of intense "cramming" can never take the place of a regular study program.

10. Somehow or other, a bull got into the china shop and turned it into a complete (**shambles, foibles**).

11. Since he is not guided by firm principles, he (**attenuates, oscillates**) between the rival factions, looking for support from both of them.

12. During the Civil War the ranks of both armies were (**decimated, rebuffed**) as much by disease as by enemy action.

13. When I found that people I admired were looking (**askance, sporadic**) at my unconventional clothing, I resolved to remedy the situation.

14. The (**decimated, penitent**) youths agreed to work without pay until they could make restitution for the damage their carelessness had caused.

15. How could you have the heart to (**rebuff, cavil**) those people's piteous appeals for aid?

16. Even though my experiences in battle have (**inured, caviled**) me to scenes of suffering, I was horrified by the devastation wrought by the tornado.

17. Their relationship has been so (**fraught, benign**) with strife and malice that I don't see how they can ever patch things up.

18. All angles are classified as acute, right, (**obtuse, benign**), or straight, according to the number of degrees they contain.

19. Imagine the general disappointment when the so-called "miracle cure" was exposed as a fraud promoted by a (**charlatan, cavil**).

20. Bank robbers often spend a good deal of time (**reconnoitering, rebuffing**) the neighborhood where the bank they intend to rob is located.

21. Do you want to be a ballet dancer enough to (**oscillate, forgo**) all other activities?

22. Although the judge offered two minor (**shambles, cavils**) about our choreography, our dance troupe won first place in the competition.

23. The play featured the stereotypical (**obsequious, fraught**) butler who treated his employer's family with excessive and artificial politeness.

24. Was it Juan's gentle stroking of the frightened dog's neck that produced a (**benign, peremptory**) change in the animal's mood?

25. The (**penitent, obtuse**) young woman begged her mother for forgiveness.

*Choose the word from this unit that is the same or most nearly the same in meaning as the **boldface** word or expression in the phrase. Write that word on the line. Use a dictionary if necessary.*

1. **quibble** over who is at fault _____cavil_____
2. exposed him as a complete **fraud** _____charlatan_____
3. a **salutary** effect on consumer confidence _____benign_____
4. **vacillated** between two choices _____oscillated_____
5. looked **skeptically** at their proposals _____askance_____
6. feeling **sorry** about the decision _____penitent_____
7. willing to overlook its **defects** _____foibles_____
8. will **spurn** his offer of marriage _____rebuff_____
9. his **high-handed** challenge to our authority _____peremptory_____
10. embarrassed by his **stupid** questions _____obtuse_____

CCSS Vocabulary: 5. (See pp. T14–15.)

The synonyms and antonyms here do not appear on the Definitions page.

Antonyms

*Choose the word from this unit that is most nearly opposite in meaning to the **boldface** word or expression in the phrase. Write that word on the line. Use a dictionary if necessary.*

1. a **tentative** request for money ____peremptory____
2. set the fan to **stay still** ____oscillate____
3. her **acute** handling of the issue ____obtuse____
4. an entirely **unrepentant** gambler and thief ____penitent____
5. prone to **praise** unnecessarily ____cavil____

Completing the Sentence

From the words in this unit, choose the one that best completes each of the following sentences. Write the word in the space provided.

1. Although there had been some ____sporadic____ fighting earlier, the real battles of the Civil War did not begin until Bull Run in July 1861.

2. Although the moon appears to be a(n) ____luminous____ body, the fact is that it only reflects light from the sun.

3. Life on the family farm has ____inured____ me to hard physical labor and long hours of unremitting toil.

4. I was relieved to learn that the officials were ____benign____ and that I would only have to pay a small fine.

5. During imperial times, the Roman Senate was little more than a collection of ____obsequious____ yes-men, intent upon preserving their own lives by gratifying the emperor's every whim.

6. No doubt he's very sorry he got caught, but that does not mean that he's at all ____penitent____ about what he did.

7. I was totally taken aback when they ____rebuffed____ my kind offers of assistance so rudely and nastily.

8. During the fourteenth century, the Black Death suddenly swept across Europe, ____decimating____ the population and paralyzing everyday life.

9. His statements have been so uniformly ____obtuse____ that I get the impression that he is wearing a permanent pair of mental blinders.

10. Though my childhood recollections have been ____attenuated____ by the passage of time, they have not been totally effaced from my memory.

11. We look **askance** at any program that makes it harder for city dwellers to get out and enjoy the beauties of nature.

12. The general sent scouts on ahead of the army to **reconnoiter** the area for a suitable site to pitch camp.

13. Good supervisors know that they can get more cooperation from their staff by making polite requests than by issuing **peremptory** orders.

14. Any "investment counselor" who promises to double your money overnight must be regarded as a(n) **charlatan** or a crook.

15. Unless the title Special Aide to the Assistant Section Manager involves a salary increase, I would just as soon **forgo** it.

16. The man's personality was a strange mixture of strengths and weaknesses, fortes and **foibles**.

17. In a typical James Bond movie, Agent 007 has a series of adventures that are **fraught** with tongue-in-cheek peril.

18. As all kinds of wild rumors ran rampant through the besieged city, the mood of the populace **oscillated** between hope and despair.

19. The riot converted the quiet streets of that suburban community into a ghastly **shambles**.

20. Though critics **caviled** at minor faults in the new Broadway show, the general public loved it.

Writing: Words in Action

Answers to both prompts will vary.

1. Look back at "What Happened to the Franklin Expedition?" (pages 126–127). Suppose that it is 1845 and you are a member of Franklin's crew. You want to write a letter to your family members explaining the goal of the expedition and letting them know how you feel as you depart England. Use at least two details from the passage and three unit words in your explanation.

2. *"The World is a book, and those who do not travel read only a page."*
—Saint Augustine

   Do you agree with Saint Augustine's statement? What is your view on the importance of traveling? Write a brief essay in which you develop your point of view about the value of travel. Support your position with specific examples from your reading (refer to pages 126–127), studies, experiences, or observations. Write at least three paragraphs, and use three or more words from this unit.

Writing prompt #2 is modeled on that of standardized tests.

CCSS Vocabulary: 6; Writing: 2.d., 3.d. (See pp. T14–15.)

Vocabulary in Context: Informational Text for Unit 10 is available online at **vocabularyworkshop.com**.

Vocabulary in Context

Literary Text

The following excerpts are from E.M. Forster's novels Howards End *and* A Room with a View. *Some of the words you have studied in this unit appear in* ***boldface*** *type. Complete each statement below the excerpt by circling the letter of the correct answer.*

1. Only in legend does the sinner come forth **penitent**, but terrible, to conquer pure woman by his resistless power. Henry was anxious to be terrible, but had not got it in him. He was a good average Englishman, who had slipped. (*Howards End*)

A **penitent** person

a. appears to be confident **c.** shows strength
b. is sorry for wrongdoing **d.** seems worried

2. It pleased Margaret to hear her brother and sister talking. They did not get on overwell as a rule. For a few moments she listened to them, feeling elderly and **benign**. (*Howards End*)

If you feel **benign**, you feel

a. forgiving **c.** dutiful
b. invincible **d.** sentimental

3. Margaret had given instructions that no one who mentioned her name should ever be **rebuffed**. Putting the door on the chain—for Leonard's appearance demanded this—she went through to the smoking-room, which was occupied by Tibby. (*Howards End*)

Someone who is **rebuffed** is

a. interrogated **c.** snubbed
b. ignored **d.** detained

A scene from the 1985 film version of *A Room with a View*, with Julian Sands as George Emerson and Helena Bonham Carter as Lucy Honeychurch.

4. In silence the two women watched him. His last remark, they knew, was nonsense, but was he going after it or not? Would not he, the cad, the **charlatan**, attempt a more dramatic finish? No. He was apparently content. (*A Room with a View*)

A **charlatan** is a(n)

a. intellectual **c.** impostor
b. snob **d.** aristocrat

5. Mrs. Honeychurch had been civil, but **obtuse** in essentials, while as for Freddy—"He is only a boy," he reflected. "I represent all that he despises. Why should he want me for a brother-in-law?" (*A Room with a View*)

An **obtuse** person is NOT

a. optimistic **c.** decisive
b. remorseful **d.** perceptive

Snap the code, or go to **vocabularyworkshop.com**

UNIT 11

Note that not all of the 20 unit words are used in this passage. *Cabal*, *ambient*, and *rife* are not included in the passage.

*Read the following selection, taking note of the **boldface** words and their contexts. These words are among those you will be studying in Unit 11. As you complete the exercises in this unit, it may help to refer to the way the words are used below.*

CCSS Vocabulary: 4; Reading (Informational Text): 4, 6. (See pp. T14–15.)

Apollo 11 Poised for Take-Off

<Press Release>

For Immediate Release

Tomorrow, July 16, 1969, will mark the beginning of a bold new phase in humankind's **inexorable** quest to explore the universe. At approximately 9:30 a.m. EST, the Apollo 11 spacecraft will lift off from Cape Kennedy, Florida, for an eight-day, round-trip journey to the moon. The climax of this flight will come on July 20, when a manned lunar module will descend to the moon's surface. For the first time in history, humans will walk on another celestial body. The astronauts will explore the moon and gather rocks, dust, and other celestial **detritus** for analysis.

This mission represents the fulfillment of a universal dream. Throughout history, in every time and place, humans have stared at the moon and wondered. Wizards and **necromancers** of the past have claimed to have traveled to the moon, and storytellers and novelists have shared **delectable** tales of imaginary lunar adventures. In the past, these trips were, at best, mere flights of fancy. Today, in the shadow of the six-million-ton Saturn rocket poised for take-off, such imaginings pale and become **flaccid**, for America's astronauts will embark on a real adventure more gripping than any fiction.

The Apollo 11 mission is a response to a specific challenge. Eight years ago, President John F. Kennedy challenged the United States to land a man on the moon by the end of the decade. Such an achievement would require Americans to adopt a new and ambitious scientific outlook, discarding old and **moribund** attitudes. A few critics **deprecated** the President's challenge, saying the nation should focus on achievements closer to home. Others saw the task, rife with problems and danger, as too **onerous**. The program's expense also was at issue: Would the cost of a program culminating in a moon landing, estimated at some $25 billion, leave the United States **impecunious**? Despite these concerns and the **asperity** of the President's response to naysayers, the majority of Americans rose to the challenge, realizing that a lunar landing would open the door to "the last frontier." In spirit, the entire nation would be going to the moon along with its astronauts.

For its part, the National Aeronautics and Space Administration (NASA) has never considered **abrogating** its commitment to a lunar landing. By mastering the **rudiments** of manned space flight during the early Mercury and Gemini flights and by learning the lessons of recent Apollo missions, NASA scientists have developed a deep and **eclectic** set of aerospace engineering skills. These have enabled NASA to construct the most complex and sophisticated equipment on earth, and thanks to these tools the agency is **ebullient** about the prospects of tomorrow's extraordinary mission. The astronauts themselves—Neil Armstrong, Michael Collins, and Edwin "Buzz" Aldrin—are also cause for optimism. To select the three candidates, NASA **winnowed** a list of thousands of the country's best pilots and aeronautical engineers. Furthermore, these three men have undergone months of intense training for the upcoming mission, **burnishing** their considerable talents and skills. Tonight they are **sequestered** near the Florida launch site, confidently awaiting their chance to make history.

Although tomorrow's thunderous takeoff will begin a journey of more than 400,000 miles, it reminds us that even a journey of one thousand miles begins with a single step. Indeed, the Apollo 11 flight is but the beginning of a much longer voyage for humankind. The question of where our scientific explorations will take us—whether to Mars, to Venus, or to other solar systems—will not be answered for many years. Undoubtedly such destinations will be on future itineraries, but as tomorrow's launch reminds us, science's ultimate destination is limited only by mankind's knowledge, individual courage, and the forces of our expanding universe.

The Apollo 11 crew: Neil Armstrong, Michael Collins, Edwin "Buzz" Aldrin

Apollo 11 ready to take off

iWords

Snap the code, or go to
vocabularyworkshop.com

Note the spelling, pronunciation, part(s) of speech, and definition(s) of each of the following words. Then write the word in the blank spaces in the illustrative sentence(s) following. Finally, study the lists of synonyms and antonyms.

1. abrogate (ab′ rə gāt)

(*v.*) to repeal, cancel, declare null and void

Often with no legal or moral grounds, the U.S. government would **abrogate** treaties made with Native Americans.

SYNONYMS: annul, revoke
ANTONYMS: renew, ratify

2. ambient (am′ bē ənt)

(*adj.*) completely surrounding, encompassing

The new filtering system is capable of cleaning and deodorizing the **ambient** air.

3. asperity (a sper′ ə tē)

(*n.*) roughness, severity; bitterness or tartness

The **asperity** of the drama critic's statements undermined the young actor's confidence.

SYNONYMS: rigor, harshness
ANTONYMS: mildness, blandness, softness, lenience

4. burnish (bər′ nish)

(*v.*) to make smooth or glossy by rubbing, polish; (*n.*) gloss, brightness, luster

The hotel manager ordered the waiters to **burnish** all the brass candlesticks before the formal banquet.

The **burnish** on the metal frame had faded with age and neglect.

SYNONYMS: (*v.*) shine, buff
ANTONYMS: (*v.*) dull, abrade

5. cabal (kə bäl′)

(*n.*) a small group working in secret

The members of the **cabal** met at an unknown location for the purpose of fixing prices and stifling competition.

SYNONYMS: ring, gang, plot, conspiracy

6. delectable (di lek′ tə bəl)

(*adj.*) delightful, highly enjoyable; deliciously flavored, savory; (*n.*) an appealing or appetizing food or dish

The banquet ended with a truly **delectable** dessert made of peaches, raspberries, and ice cream.

The eatery attracted customers with a mouth-watering display of **delectables** in its front window.

SYNONYM: (*adj.*) scrumptious
ANTONYMS: (*adj.*) repugnant, repulsive, distasteful

CCSS Vocabulary: 4.c., 4.d. (See pp. T14–15.)

7. deprecate
(dep′ rə kāt)

(*v.*) to express mild disapproval; to belittle

The administration **deprecated** such foolish practices as the hazing of new students.

SYNONYMS: deplore, frown upon
ANTONYMS: smile on, approve

8. detritus
(di trīt′ əs)

(*n.*) loose bits and pieces of material resulting from disintegration or wearing away; fragments that result from any destruction

Pieces of people's homes, furniture, and toys could be seen in the **detritus** of the landslide.

SYNONYMS: wreckage, ruins, rubble

9. ebullient
(i bül′ yənt)

(*adj.*) overflowing with enthusiasm and excitement; boiling, bubbling

After a string of very favorable reviews, the dance company was in an **ebullient** mood for weeks.

SYNONYMS: exhilarated, elated
ANTONYMS: gloomy, morose, sullen, apathetic, blasé

10. eclectic
(e klek′ tik)

(*adj.*) drawn from different sources; (*n.*) one whose beliefs are drawn from various sources

Stanford White developed an **eclectic** style of architecture that made use of classic and modern elements.

The critics accused the composer of being a mere **eclectic** with no original style of her own.

SYNONYMS: (*adj.*) selective, synthetic, pick-and-choose
ANTONYMS: (*adj.*) uniform, monolithic

11. flaccid
(flas′ əd)

(*adj.*) limp, not firm; lacking vigor or effectiveness

Because the injured bodybuilder had not worked out for weeks, his muscles grew **flaccid**.

SYNONYMS: soft, flabby; ANTONYMS: hard, solid

12. impecunious
(im pə kyü′ nē əs)

(*adj.*) having little or no money

In my present **impecunious** state, I will not be able to pay for dinner.

SYNONYMS: impoverished, indigent
ANTONYMS: affluent, wealthy, prosperous, rich

13. inexorable
(in ek′ sər ə bəl)

(*adj.*) inflexible, beyond influence; relentless, unyielding

In the Greek tragedies, nothing could save characters like Oedipus Rex from their **inexorable** fates.

SYNONYMS: ineluctable, obdurate
ANTONYMS: avoidable, yielding, pliant

14. moribund (môr′ ə bənd)

(*adj.*) dying, on the way out

In the age of electronic communication, writing letters by hand seems to be a **moribund** custom.

SYNONYM: obsolescent; ANTONYM: thriving

15. necromancer (nek′ rə man sər)

(*n.*) one who claims to reveal or influence the future through magic, especially communication with the dead; in general, a magician or wizard

When the stock market began to tumble, some desperate investors resorted to **necromancers** for financial advice.

SYNONYMS: sorcerer, conjurer

16. onerous (än′ ər əs)

(*adj.*) burdensome; involving hardship or difficulty

Informing patients of bad news is an **onerous** duty that every doctor has to perform.

SYNONYM: weighty; ANTONYMS: light, easy, undemanding, untaxing

17. rife (rīf)

(*adj.*) common, prevalent, widespread, happening often; full, abounding; plentiful, abundant, replete

Since rumors were **rife**, the president announced that the company had been bought out by its major competitor.

ANTONYMS: devoid of, lacking

18. rudiments (rüd′ ə mənts)

(*n. pl.*) the parts of any subject or discipline that are learned first; the earliest stages of anything

At a very young age, the girl learned the **rudiments** of chess from her father, a professional player.

SYNONYMS: basics, fundamentals

19. sequester (si kwes′ tər)

(*v.*) to set apart, separate for a special purpose; to take possession of and hold in custody

The parties agreed to **sequester** the disputed funds pending a decision by the court.

SYNONYMS: segregate, isolate, closet

20. winnow (win′ ō)

(*v.*) to get rid of something unwanted, delete; to sift through to obtain what is desirable; to remove the chaff from the wheat by blowing air on it; to blow on, fan

Spelling and grammar software programs are designed to help writers **winnow** inaccuracies from their documents.

SYNONYMS: sift, strain, filter, sort

CCSS Vocabulary: 4.c. (See pp. T14–15.)

Choosing the Right Word

*Select the **boldface** word that better completes each sentence. You might refer to the selection on pages 136–137 to see how most of these words are used in context.*

Oliver Wendell Holmes, Jr., was appointed to the U.S. Supreme Court in 1902 by President Theodore Roosevelt.

1. Oliver Wendell Holmes, Jr., once observed that he did not wish to lead a(n) (**sequestered, abrogated**) life far from the conflicts of his times.
2. Though she entered this country as a(n) (**impecunious, rife**) child, she eventually made a fortune in the garment industry.
3. "The (**inexorable, moribund**) march of the years," said the aged speaker, "decrees that this is the last time I will address you."
4. The old adage that "one man's meat is another man's poison" simply means that what is considered (**delectable, onerous**) is often quite subjective.
5. The charm of this musical comedy lies in its slam-bang pacing, its sprightly music, and its generally (**onerous, ebullient**) good cheer.
6. What appeared to be an informal study group was in reality a highly organized (**detritus, cabal**) determined to overthrow the establishment.
7. Though the presidency confers great powers on the person who holds the office, it also saddles that person with (**onerous, eclectic**) responsibilities.
8. It is one thing to (**burnish, deprecate**) human follies and pretensions; it is quite another to correct them.
9. The (**moribund, burnished**) helmets and breastplates of the warriors gleamed and twinkled in the morning sunlight.
10. No one, however powerful or dominant, can (**abrogate, sequester**) the basic moral laws on which civilization rests.
11. Writing that is so full of soggy clichés, gummy sentence structure, and excessive wordiness can best be described as (**inexorable, flaccid**).
12. (**Eclectic, Ambient**) schools of art are typical of a period when there is little original inspiration or bold experimentation.
13. Since archaeologists spend a lot of time rummaging through the (**detritus, asperity**) of vanished civilizations, they bear a striking resemblance to junk collectors and ragpickers.
14. Though skeptics insist that patriotism is (**onerous, moribund**) in America, I believe that it is alive and well in the hearts of the people.
15. The investigating committee spent long hours trying to (**burnish, winnow**) fact from fiction in the witnesses' testimony.

CCSS Vocabulary: 4.d. (See pp. T14–15.)

16. As we sat in the locker room after our heartbreaking loss, the (**ambient, impecunious**) gloom was so thick you could almost cut it.

17. Any political party that is (**rife, ebullient**) with petty jealousies and backbiting can never hope to present a united front in an election.

18. (**Asperity, Necromancy**) and other forms of witchcraft were punishable by death during the Middle Ages.

19. As one veteran aptly observed, a soldier had to be hardy to cope with the (**asperities, cabals**) of life in the trenches during World War I.

20. Anyone who has the slightest acquaintance with the (**rudiments, cabals**) of economic theory understands that we cannot solve our financial problems simply by borrowing more and more money.

21. Despite our prodding, Aunt Eileen would not disclose the secret ingredient that makes her marinara sauce so (**delectable, ebullient**).

22. The film critic complained that some of the (**sequestered, inexorable**) tension in the original film has been lost in this year's milder remake.

23. The unconventional artist liked to incorporate glass shards, plastic strips, pieces of string, and assorted (**detritus, rudiments**) into his sculptures.

24. "Did you use a cotton or a velvet cloth to (**burnish, abrogate**) the antique mirror?" Bryan inquired.

25. The (**cabal, asperity**) of the stones in the patio hurt the soles of my feet.

*Choose the word from this unit that is the same or most nearly the same in meaning as the **boldface** word or expression in the phrase. Write that word on the line. Use a dictionary if necessary.*

1. cleaned up the **debris** from the parade — detritus
2. **secluded** on a remote country estate — sequestered
3. a ruthless **clique** of gangsters — cabal
4. the **inescapable** consequences of her actions — inexorable
5. a garden **filled** with weeds — rife
6. a **varied collection** of opinions — eclectic
7. the **exuberant** cheerleading squad — ebullient
8. sheltered the **penniless** immigrants — impecunious
9. rebelled against the **oppressive** taxation — onerous
10. noticed another **fading** tradition — moribund

 CCSS Vocabulary: 5. (See pp. T14–15.)

The synonyms and antonyms here do not appear on the Definitions page.

*Choose the word from this unit that is most nearly opposite in meaning to the **boldface** word or expression in the phrase. Write that word on the line. Use a dictionary if necessary.*

1. will **reaffirm** his oath to the king ______abrogate______
2. noticed her **firm** handshake ______flaccid______
3. a snack **low in** nutritional value ______rife (with)______
4. the **flourishing** downtown area ______moribund______
5. **countenanced** our peaceful protest ______deprecated______

Completing the Sentence

From the words in this unit, choose the one that best completes each of the following sentences. Write the word in the space provided.

1. I thought the job of revising the manuscript would be a relatively simple matter, but it proved to be a(n) ______onerous______ task.

2. Some superstitious Roman emperors consulted ______necromancers______ and other dabblers in black magic to find out what the future held.

3. The plot of the novel centers on a(n) ______impecunious______ adventurer who attempts to remedy his financial embarrassment by marrying into money.

4. The copper pots had been so highly ______burnished______ that I could see my face in them.

5. Though monarchies still exist in some parts of the world, they are more or less a(n) ______moribund______ form of government.

6. One of Darwin's theories suggests that nature ensures the survival of a species by slowly ______winnowing______ out the less fit members.

7. There is nothing more ______delectable______ on a hot day than to stretch out in a hammock with a good book and pitcher of icy lemonade!

8. I could tell that my boss was really "riled" by the ______asperity______ of his tone of voice when he summoned me.

9. The conversation at dinner tables all over town was ______rife______ with speculation as to the outcome of the big game.

10. All the facts and figures point to one ______inexorable______ conclusion: we are hopelessly outnumbered.

CCSS Vocabulary: 4.a. (See pp. T14–15.)

11. We will never allow anyone to curtail or ___abrogate___ the basic rights and liberties guaranteed to us in the Constitution.

12. She is a very private person who ___deprecates___ any attempt to honor publicly her great services to humanity.

13. Even before they said a word, I could tell from their ___ebullient___ expressions that our team had won.

14. Late that night, we began the heartbreaking task of sifting through the ___detritus___ of our ravaged home.

15. Unless you have mastered the ___rudiments___ of French grammar, you will find it difficult to speak the language fluently.

16. As air slowly seeped out through the tiny puncture, the inner tube became more and more ___flaccid___.

17. It was then that he began to organize the ___cabal___ that would later depose the king.

18. In order to prevent outside influences from coming into play, a jury is normally ___sequestered___ until it reaches a decision.

19. It is often difficult to hold a conversation while walking on a busy city street because of the high level of ___ambient___ traffic noise.

20. In a sense, the man is a(n) ___eclectic___ philosopher because his ideas have been influenced by many different schools of thought.

Writing: Words in Action

Answers to both prompts will vary.

1. Look back at "Apollo 11 Poised for Take-Off" (pages 136–137). If you were offered the opportunity, would you like to be a passenger on a space flight to the moon? Why or why not? In a short expository essay, explain your opinion, using at least two details from the passage and three unit words.

2. In recent years, the United States has reduced funding for its manned space exploration programs. Some people argue that the money spent on space exploration could be better used elsewhere. However, others claim that the potential benefits of space exploration justify its costs. In your opinion, how important is continued manned space exploration? Explain your position on this question in a short essay. Use specific examples from your reading (refer to pages 136–137), studies, and personal observations to support your point. Write at least three paragraphs, and use at least three words from this unit.

Writing prompt #2 is modeled on that of standardized tests.

CCSS Vocabulary: 6; Writing: 2.d., 3.d. (See pp. T14–15.)

Vocabulary in Context: Informational Text for Unit 11 is available online at **vocabularyworkshop.com**.

Vocabulary in Context

Literary Text

The following excerpts are from Anthony Trollope's novels The Eustace Diamonds *and* Barchester Towers. *Some of the words you have studied in this unit appear in* **boldface** *type. Complete each statement below the excerpt by circling the letter of the correct answer.*

1. Frank began pretty well, getting some little work in London, and perhaps nearly enough to pay the cost of his circuit out of the county in which the cathedral was situated. But he began life after that **impecunious** fashion for which the Greystocks had been noted. (*The Eustace Diamonds*)

An **impecunious** life is NOT

a. random
b. prosperous
c. lively
d. bland

Anthony Trollope was one of the most prolific Victorian novelists, writing 47 novels before his death in 1882. Above, an illustration from one of his novels

2. Having pronounced this terrible sentence, Mrs. Carbunkle stalked out of the room. "That they can **sequester** your property for your creditors, I know," she said, returning for a moment and putting her head within the door. (*The Eustace Diamonds*)

To **sequester** is to

a. auction off
b. abandon
c. take possession of
d. display

3. Now, Dr. Proudie certainly liked the lady, but, seeing that he was a bishop, it was not probable that he was going to instruct a little girl in the first **rudiments** of her catechism; so he said he'd send a teacher. (*Barchester Towers*)

Rudiments are

a. facts
b. performances
c. strict rituals
d. the earliest stages

4. Even the compliment did not soften the **asperity** of the maimed beauty. "Every woman is charming according to Lotte," she said; "I never knew an eye with so little true appreciation." (*Barchester Towers*)

Asperity is

a. admiration
b. brilliance
c. severity
d. judgment

5. Mr. Slope's only preferment has hitherto been that of reader and preacher in a London district church; and on the consecration of his friend the new bishop, he readily gave this up to undertake the **onerous** but congenial duties of domestic chaplain to his lordship. (*Barchester Towers*)

Duties that are **onerous** are

a. burdensome
b. virtuous
c. traditional
d. abundant

Snap the code, or go to **vocabularyworkshop.com**

CCSS Vocabulary: 4.c.; Reading (Literature): 4. (See pp. T14–15.)

UNIT 12

Note that not all of the 20 unit words are used in this passage. Interpolate, laconic, mendacious, requite, and tantamount are not included in the passage.

Read the following selection, taking note of the ***boldface*** *words and their contexts. These words are among those you will be studying in Unit 12. As you complete the exercises in this unit, it may help to refer to the way the words are used below.*

CCSS Vocabulary: 4; Reading (Informational Text): 4, 6. (See pp. T14–15.)

Pyramids: Monuments to Gods and Men

<Compare and Contrast Essay>

Imposing, mysterious pyramids, found in areas from Asia to the Middle East to South America, have fascinated people for millennia. Some pyramids are lauded for their **aesthetic** qualities; some, though not as beautiful, are equally intriguing. Who built these architectural wonders? Why were they built, and what is their significance? And how were they built, given the technological limitations?

The world's largest pyramids are in Egypt, in the Valley of the Kings, near Cairo, and in Teotihuacan, in proximity to Mexico City, where these massive constructions seem **omnipresent** and command the attention of all onlookers. The two pyramids were built for different reasons—as tombs for Egypt's pharaohs and as places of worship and ritual for the Teotihuacans, but **impeccable** planning went into the erecting of each.

The Great Pyramid of Giza (also known as the Great Pyramid of Khufu, or Cheops) was one of the Seven Wonders of the Ancient World. It was constructed circa 2560 B.C. and is made up of 2.3 million limestone blocks. Estimates vary, but it took perhaps 30,000 men 20 years to complete the first Great Pyramid and its remarkable complex of secret chambers and hidden passages. It was created as a tomb for Pharoah Khufu, who **espoused** a belief in the afterlife and wanted a resting place for himself, his wives, and his treasures within a structure that would thwart and **discomfit** his enemies. Nearby, as part of the Giza Necropolis, are another two pyramids and the Great

Ancient artifacts have been uncovered from the pyramids and other monuments in Giza, Egypt.

Sphinx. All have withstood the natural elements: As an old proverb says, the pyramids mock time.

Unlike Egyptian pyramids, Mesoamerican pyramids are typically step pyramids with a temple at the peak. The three magnificent pyramids of Teotihuacan—the Pyramid of the Moon, the Pyramid of the Sun and the Feathered Serpent Pyramid—are part of a massive archaeological site in the Basin of Mexico. The main street, the "Avenue of the Dead," is lined with smaller temples and residences, and excavations throughout the site have turned up fertility **fetishes** and other talismans. The largest structure, the Pyramid of the Sun, was completed by A.D. 100 and is about half as tall as the Great Pyramid of Giza. The pyramid's core was mainly volcanic ash and gravel, while a thick layer of stone and mortar made up its walls. Incredibly, the builders were able to erect these marvels without the aid of the wheel or metal tools.

The early history of Teotihuacan is enigmatic because no one is completely sure which ancient, **gregarious** society built North America's first great city. The inhabitants used the pyramids in their religious rites and sacrifices. Ignoring the **plaintive** wails of their **hapless** victims, they **importuned** the gods for favors. The city's **nadir** came about A.D. 600, when the Teotihuacans abandoned their home, but a later Indian civilization, the Aztecs, adopted the city and kept it from becoming **defunct**. They dubbed the place the "City of the Gods," or "Place Where Men Become Gods."

Over time, explorers and treasure hunters have done lasting and **irreparable** damage to the world's pyramids, including those in Egypt and Teotihuacan. In many cases, authorities have made inferior, **perfunctory** repairs or allowed the damaged pyramids to **languish** and fall into disrepair, but now both sites are protected as national treasures by their governments. Thousands of tourists visit the pyramids in the Valley of the Kings and Teotihuacan every year.

iWords™

Snap the code, or go to **vocabularyworkshop.com**

Ceramics such as this seated figure were found at Teotihuacan in Mexico.

Note the spelling, pronunciation, part(s) of speech, and definition(s) of each of the following words. Then write the word in the blank spaces in the illustrative sentence(s) following. Finally, study the lists of synonyms and antonyms.

1. aesthetic
(es thet′ ik)

(*adj.*) pertaining to beauty; sensitive or responsive to beauty

Since the structure had no practical purpose, keeping it in place could only be justified on ____**aesthetic**____ grounds.

SYNONYM: artistic

2. defunct
(di fəŋkt′)

(*adj.*) no longer in existence or functioning, dead

I could find no forwarding address or phone number for the ____**defunct**____ organization.

SYNONYMS: extinct, nonexistent
ANTONYM: alive

3. discomfit
(dis kəm′ fit)

(*v.*) to frustrate, thwart, or defeat; to confuse, perplex, or embarrass

The general tried to ____**discomfit**____ his enemies by repeatedly beginning an advance and then pulling back.

SYNONYMS: nonplus, foil

4. espouse
(es paüz′)

(*v.*) to take up and support; to become attached to, adopt; to marry

To appeal to the large number of dissatisfied voters, the candidate ____**espoused**____ a strong program of reform.

SYNONYMS: embrace, wed
ANTONYMS: repudiate, disavow, renounce

5. fetish
(fet′ ish)

(*n.*) an object believed to have magical powers; an object of unreasoning devotion or reverence

The rabbit's foot, once a very popular ____**fetish**____, seems to have lost its hold on the public imagination.

SYNONYMS: charm, obsession

6. gregarious
(grə gār′ ē əs)

(*adj.*) living together in a herd or group; sociable, seeking the company of others

I would expect the recreation director of a cruise ship to be a ____**gregarious**____ person.

SYNONYMS: outgoing, extroverted
ANTONYMS: aloof, introverted, reclusive

CCSS Vocabulary: 4.c., 4.d. (See pp. T14–15.)

7. hapless (hap′ lis)

(*adj.*) marked by a persistent absence of good luck

Once again, my younger brother has become the **hapless** victim of a silly practical joke.

SYNONYMS: unlucky, ill-starred, unfortunate
ANTONYMS: lucky, charmed, fortunate

8. impeccable (im pek′ ə bəl)

(*adj.*) faultless, beyond criticism or blame

We always consulted my grandmother about what to wear because she had **impeccable** taste in clothing.

SYNONYMS: flawless, spotless, immaculate
ANTONYMS: grimy, soiled, spotted

9. importune (im pôr tyün′)

(*v.*) to trouble with demands; to beg for insistently

My bankrupt uncle **importuned** my father for a loan.

SYNONYMS: implore, dun, tax

10. interpolate (in tər′ pə lāt)

(*v.*) to insert between other parts or things; to present as an addition or correction

At the director's request, the screenwriter **interpolated** some new lines into the script.

SYNONYMS: interpose, introduce

11. irreparable (i rep′ ər ə bəl)

(*adj.*) incapable of being repaired or rectified

The husband believed that the surgeon did **irreparable** harm to his wife and sued the doctor and the hospital.

SYNONYM: irremediable
ANTONYMS: remediable, fixable, reversible

12. laconic (lə kän′ ik)

(*adj.*) concise, using few words

The senator issued a **laconic** statement declaring her innocence after the accusations of fraud were made public.

SYNONYMS: succinct, pithy, compact
ANTONYMS: garrulous, prolix, loquacious

13. languish (laŋ′ gwish)

(*v.*) to become weak, feeble, or dull; to droop; to be depressed or dispirited; to suffer neglect

Without the constitutional guarantee of a speedy trial, the accused could **languish** in jail for years.

SYNONYMS: flag, fade, pine

CCSS Vocabulary: 4.c. (See pp. T14–15.)

14. mendacious (men dā 'shəs)

(*adj.*) given to lying or deception; untrue

The deputy gave a **mendacious** account of his employer's actions on the day of the alleged crime.

SYNONYMS: untruthful, false

ANTONYM: veracious

15. nadir (nā' dər)

(*n.*) the lowest point

At the **nadir** of his popularity, the prime minister decided to resign his office and call for new elections.

SYNONYMS: rock bottom

ANTONYMS: pinnacle, zenith

16. omnipresent (äm ni pre' zənt)

(*adj.*) present in all places at all times

They believed in an **omnipresent** deity that existed in all things.

SYNONYMS: ubiquitous, ever-present

17. perfunctory (per fəŋk' tə rē)

(*adj.*) done in a superficial or halfhearted manner; without interest or enthusiasm

The police made a **perfunctory** search for the missing handbag, but they really did not expect to find it.

SYNONYMS: slapdash, shallow

ANTONYMS: thorough, assiduous, diligent, meticulous

18. plaintive (plān' tiv)

(*adj.*) expressive of sorrow or woe, melancholy

The recently widowed man spoke of his loneliness in a **plaintive** tone of voice.

SYNONYMS: sad, lugubrious

ANTONYMS: cheerful, blithe, joyous, merry

19. requite (ri kwīt')

(*v.*) to make suitable repayment, as for a kindness, service, or favor; to make retaliation, as for an injury or wrong; to reciprocate

We made sure to **requite** the neighbors for looking after our house while we were away.

SYNONYMS: reimburse, avenge

20. tantamount (tan' tə maůnt)

(*adj.*) equivalent, having the same meaning, value, or effect

The armed invasion of their territory was **tantamount** to a declaration of war.

SYNONYM: indistinguishable from

CCSS Vocabulary: 4.c. (See pp. T14–15.)

Choosing the Right Word

*Select the **boldface** word that better completes each sentence. You might refer to the selection on pages 146–147 to see how most of these words are used in context.*

1. One of the best-known figures of American folklore is the lean, tough, (**laconic, hapless**) cowboy.
2. I hope to (**espouse, requite**) my parents for all the care they have shown me.
3. Although fate has decreed that he make his living as a stockbroker, his main interests and talents are definitely (**irreparable, aesthetic**).
4. Though I left the house feeling "as fit as a fiddle," my spirits began to (**requite, languish**) after only five minutes in that withering heat.

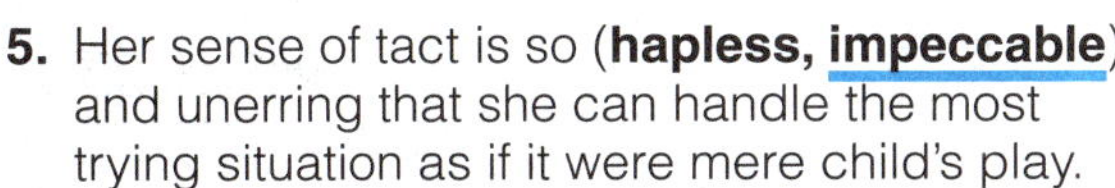

5. Her sense of tact is so (**hapless, impeccable**) and unerring that she can handle the most trying situation as if it were mere child's play.

The popularity of cowboy music grew after the recording of the first cowboy song in 1925.

6. The sternness of my boss's expression so (**discomfited, languished**) me that at first I had difficulty responding to the question.
7. Many scholars believe that Beaumont or Fletcher (**interpolated, requited**) a scene or two into the present text of Shakespeare's *Macbeth*.
8. One of the comforting things about reaching the (**fetish, nadir**) of one's career is that the only place to go from there is up.
9. Perhaps we should be overjoyed that the great man condescended to give us a(n) (**aesthetic, perfunctory**) nod as we passed by.
10. Though few of us today stand on ceremony to quite the extent that our ancestors did, common courtesy is by no means (**plaintive, defunct**).
11. Prehistoric peoples banded together into tribes, not only for protection, but also to satisfy their (**gregarious, mendacious**) instincts.
12. She sang a (**laconic, plaintive**) little ditty about a man who yearns wistfully for the girl he left behind many years before.
13. A diplomat must always proceed on the assumption that no rupture between nations, no matter how serious, is (**irreparable, perfunctory**).
14. The (**omnipresent, gregarious**) threat of a nuclear holocaust that characterized the Cold War era changed many people's attitudes toward war in profound ways.
15. The legal adage "Silence implies consent" means that not objecting to an action that concerns you is (**perfunctory, tantamount**) to approving it.

16. In our desire to improve the quality of life in America, we should not be too quick to (**importune, espouse**) an idea simply because it is new.

17. When the scandal broke, the man found himself the (**hapless, impeccable**) victim of other people's misdeeds.

18. It is one thing to be concerned about discipline; it is quite another to make a (**perfunctory, fetish**) of it.

19. I don't know which is more painful—to have to ask someone for a favor or to have some unfortunate (**importune, discomfit**) one for help.

20. Fortunately, our lawyer was able to produce documents that disproved the (**mendacious, omnipresent**) assertions of our former partner.

21. Faced with a tight deadline, the exhausted editor gave the young reporter's article a hurried and (**perfunctory, gregarious**) edit.

22. In the *Poetics* and the *Metaphysics*, Greek philosopher Aristotle discusses the purpose of art and identifies important (**omnipresent, aesthetic**) principles.

23. After the death of his wife of seven decades, a grieving Mr. Johnson (**languished, espoused**) in their quiet apartment.

24. "Despite taking an oath to tell the truth, Laurie offered clearly (**tantamount, mendacious**) testimony," complained the frustrated defense attorney.

25. The whiny toddler (**importuned, requited**) his mother for a snack.

*Choose the word from this unit that is the same or most nearly the same in meaning as the **boldface** word or expression in the phrase. Write that word on the line. Use a dictionary if necessary.*

1. **recompensed** them for their hospitality — requited
2. tried to **interject** a different opinion — interpolate
3. **entreated** the governor for a pardon — importuned
4. cautioned me against the **dishonest** salesperson — mendacious
5. **disconcerted** the conservative audience — discomfited
6. kept repeating that **doleful** melody — plaintive
7. **wilt** under the hot sun — languish
8. listened to a **terse** summary — laconic
9. no more than a **cursory** note of apology — perfunctory
10. **equal** to betraying a friend — tantamount

CCSS Vocabulary: 5. (See pp. T14–15.)

Antonyms

*Choose the word from this unit that is most nearly opposite in meaning to the **boldface** word or expression in the phrase. Write that word on the line. Use a dictionary if necessary.*

1. **spurn** her desire for friendship ______requite______
2. gave a **verbose** tribute to his partner ______laconic______
3. **unlike** a fair deal ______tantamount (to)______
4. prone to **delete** unimportant text ______interpolate______
5. a **truthful** account of the events ______mendacious______

Completing the Sentence

From the words in this unit, choose the one that best completes each of the following sentences. Write the word in the space provided.

1. I was greatly relieved to learn that the accident I had with my car last week didn't do any ______irreparable______ damage to the motor.

2. Every general seems to have one defeat that marks the ______nadir______ of his military fortunes—for example, Lee at Gettysburg or Grant at Cold Harbor.

3. One wall of the museum was filled with charms and ______fetishes______ designed to ward off everything from a hangnail to the evil eye.

4. They claim to have made a thorough search of the premises, but I suspect that their efforts were no more than ______perfunctory______.

5. Last night, Central High's Shooting Stars captured the basketball championship by ______discomfiting______ the South High Slammers, 61 to 44.

6. When you get more experience on the job, you will learn that a "request" from your employer is ______tantamount______ to an order.

7. No matter where candidates for high political office go these days, the ______omnipresent______ eye of the TV camera seems focused on them.

8. "Don't you think it's a little foolish to pursue the young lady when your warm feelings for her are clearly not ______requited______?" I asked.

9. Since extroverts are ______gregarious______ by nature, they usually prefer not to live alone.

10. Responding to the melancholy note in the song of the nightingale, Keats wrote of its "______plaintive______ anthem."

11. To say that he is **mendacious** does not even begin to convey just how alienated he is from any regard for the truth.

12. Never once has the least whiff of a scandal or impropriety tainted the man's **impeccable** reputation as an upstanding member of this agency.

13. I thought our state legislators would consider the proposal at the earliest opportunity, but they let it **languish** in committee for months.

14. From a(n) **aesthetic** point of view, the painting didn't appeal to me, but I kept it because it was a memento of my childhood.

15. Suddenly I was surrounded by a mob of street urchins loudly **importuning** me for a handout.

16. It's easy enough to back a popular program, but it takes real courage to **espouse** a cause that most people oppose.

17. I felt a little foolish when the librarian told me that I was asking for the current issue of a magazine that had long been **defunct**.

18. The **hapless** creature had somehow gotten its foot caught in the grate and could not extricate it without help.

19. As his irrepressible flow of reminiscences continued without a letup, I tried in vain to **interpolate** a few observations of my own.

20. When asked what terms he would offer the Confederate army, General Grant made the **laconic** reply, "Unconditional surrender!"

Writing: Words in Action

Answers to both prompts will vary.

1. Look back at "Pyramids: Monuments to Gods and Men" (pages 146–147). Suppose that you are helping to raise funds to repair the pyramids in Egypt or Teotihuacan. You want to persuade contributors to make a donation by convincing them that the pyramids have historical and cultural significance, not only to Egypt or Mexico but also to the world. Write a persuasive business letter, using at least two details from the passage and three unit words.

2. *"Those who cannot remember the past are condemned to repeat it."*
—George Santayana

   Do you agree with poet and philosopher George Santayana's statement about remembering the past? How important is it for high school students to study world history, to learn, for example, about the ancient civilizations of Egypt and Teotihuacan? In a brief expository essay, explain your opinion with specific examples from your studies, observations and experiences, or current events. Write at least three paragraphs, and use three or more words from this unit.

Writing prompt #2 is modeled on that of standardized tests.

CCSS Vocabulary: 6; Writing: 2.d., 3.d. (See pp. T14–15.)

Vocabulary in Context: Informational Text for Unit 12 is available online at **vocabularyworkshop.com**.

Vocabulary in Context

Literary Text

The following excerpts are from James Fenimore Cooper's novels The Last of the Mohicans *and* The Pioneers. *Some of the words you have studied in this unit appear in* **boldface** *type. Complete each statement below the excerpt by circling the letter of the correct answer.*

1. "Why die at all!" said Cora, advancing from the place where natural horror had, until this moment, held her riveted to the rock; "the path is open on every side; fly, then, to the woods, and call on God for succor. Go, brave men, we owe you too much already; let us no longer involve you in our **hapless** fortunes!" (*The Last of the Mohicans*)

Something that is **hapless** is NOT

a. relevant **c.** predictable
b. impressive **d.** lucky

Wood engraving from an 1872 edition of *The Last of the Mohicans*

2. Heyward gathered from the manners of the different speakers, that the father and son **espoused** one side of a disputed question, while the white man maintained the other. (*The Last of the Mohicans*)

If something is **espoused**, it is

a. investigated **c.** supported
b. rejected **d.** debated

3. "His time has come," said the **laconic** scout, thrusting the long barrel of his rifle through the leaves, and taking his deliberate and fatal aim. But, instead of pulling the trigger he lowered the muzzle again, and indulged himself in a fit of his peculiar mirth. (*The Last of the Mohicans*)

Someone who is **laconic**

a. uses few words **c.** shows no fear
b. acts impulsively **d.** appears fatigued

4. "Nay, Natty," rejoined the traveller, with undisturbed good-humor, "it is for the honor that I contend. A few dollars will pay for the venison, but what will **requite** me for the lost honor of a buck's tail in my cap?" (*The Pioneers*)

To **requite** is to

a. annoy slightly **c.** produce shame
b. repay suitably **d.** offer revenge

5. Once, just as her eyes had opened, apparently in the last stage of drowsiness, the roaring winds brought with them a long and **plaintive** howl, that seemed too wild for a dog, and yet resembled the cries of that faithful animal, when night awakens his vigilance, and gives sweetness and solemnity to its charms. (*The Pioneers*)

Something that is **plaintive** is

a. melancholy **c.** fierce
b. shrill **d.** jubilant

Snap the code, or go to **vocabularyworkshop.com**

Vocabulary for Comprehension

*Read the following selection in which some of the words you have studied in Units 10–12 appear in **boldface** type. Then answer the questions on page 157.*

This passage focuses on the brief but remarkable era of silent films.

(Line)

It may be tempting for modern viewers to **deprecate** silent films. After all, they are technically primitive compared with today's movies. Much of the acting is exaggerated and overwrought, and the plots are often melodramatic or sentimental. Also, there is no dialogue except for some **laconic** titles that appear on the screen from time to time. Yet in their day, audiences flocked to see these movies, marveling at the **luminous** images on the flickering screen. To these enthusiastic new moviegoers, there was nothing as exciting as moving pictures!

Two men, Louis Lumiere and Thomas Alva Edison, one French and one American, are usually credited with the invention of the motion picture camera. In 1895 Louis Lumiere invented what he called the *cinematographe*. This compact, versatile instrument was **tantamount** to a camera, film-processing unit, and projector all in one. Because Edison's camera was bulkier and less portable than Lumiere's, the Europeans took an early lead in the development of motion pictures. The Americans soon caught up, however, and Hollywood eventually became the capital of a vastly profitable international film industry that began in the 1910s with the production of silent movies.

Many contemporary viewers have overlooked the masterpieces of the silent era because they find the adjustments they must make to watch these films **onerous**. Without knowing it, however, they are depriving themselves of some unparalleled pleasures. These include the brilliant physical comedy of Buster Keaton, the visual expressiveness of Charlie Chaplin, and the landmark editing, camera work, and set designs of the great pioneer filmmakers D.W. Griffith, Sergei Eisenstein, F.R. Murnau, and Fritz Lang.

CCSS Vocabulary: 4.a.; Reading (Informational Text): 2, 4, 6. (See pp. T14–15.)

1. In the first paragraph (lines 1–17), the writer's main focus is on
   a. discussing camera types
   b. introducing some of the writer's favorite silent films
   (c.) contrasting the drawbacks of silent films with the excitement they inspired in audiences of the day
   d. describing landmark camera work
   e. comparing Keaton and Chaplin

2. The meaning of **deprecate** (line 2) is
   (a.) belittle
   b. ignore
   c. overpraise
   d. underestimate
   e. misunderstand

3. In paragraph 1, the author mentions all of the following as drawbacks of silent films EXCEPT
   a. melodramatic plots
   b. overwrought acting
   c. laconic captions
   (d.) unattractive set designs
   e. primitive technical achievements

4. **Laconic** (line 9) most nearly means
   a. brilliant
   b. obscure
   (c.) succinct
   d. humorous
   e. redundant

5. **Luminous** (line 13) is best defined as
   a. timeless
   b. blurred
   (c.) bright
   d. lifelike
   e. shocking

6. From the details given in paragraph 2 (lines 18–37), one may reasonably infer that the Americans caught up with the Europeans because
   a. the leading actors were American
   (b.) refinements made film equipment less bulky and more portable
   c. the Americans made more films
   d. Hollywood was appealing
   e. Lumiere's equipment often broke

7. **Tantamount** (line 25) most nearly means
   a. similar
   b. supplementary
   c. opposed
   d. compared
   (e.) equivalent

8. In paragraph 2, it may be inferred that the author believes that the *cinematographe* was
   a. expensive
   b. worthless
   (c.) useful
   d. disappointing
   e. beautiful

9. According to the passage, the international film industry began in
   a. the 1930s
   b. the 1920s
   (c.) the 1910s
   d. the 1890s
   e. the 1880s

10. In paragraph 3 (lines 38–53), the writer most likely includes so many examples in order to
    a. explain the cost of silent movies
    b. trace the ways in which silent film stars influenced one another
    (c.) persuade the reader of the claims made for silent films in the passage
    d. display a high level of expertise
    e. prove that directors were more skilled than actors

11. **Onerous** (line 42) most nearly means
    a. annoying
    b. costly
    c. silly
    (d.) burdensome
    e. easy

12. The writer's attitude toward silent films might best be described as
    (a.) enthusiastic
    b. skeptical
    c. respectful
    d. neutral
    e. dismissive

CCSS Vocabulary: 4.a.; Reading (Informational Text): 2, 4, 6. (See pp. T14–15.)

Two-Word Completions

Select the pair of words that best complete the meaning of each of the following passages.

1. In *Of Human Bondage,* W. Somerset Maugham's main character Philip Carey is ________________ by external adversity as well as his own self-consciousness because he was so ________________ as to have been born with a club foot.

a. rebuffed . . . sporadic
b. requited . . . benign
c. decimated . . . laconic
(d.) discomfited . . . hapless

2. Though the man appeared to be the most ________________ pauper on the face of the earth, he had actually ________________ large sums of money in various hiding places in the hovel he called home.

a. flaccid . . . burnished
(b.) impecunious . . . sequestered
c. ambient . . . interpolated
d. benign . . . decimated

3. As soon as I heard its ________________ cries for help, I knew that the ________________ animal had once again got its paw caught in the grillwork on the front porch.

a. obsequious . . . moribund
b. laconic . . . impeccable
c. onerous . . . defunct
(d.) plaintive . . . hapless

4. Although many of the pioneers found it difficult at first to cope with the ________________ of frontier life, they were a hardy race who quickly became ________________ such rough-and-tumble living.

a. rudiments . . . importuned by
(b.) asperities . . . inured to
c. detritus . . . decimated by
d. shambles . . . discomfited by

5. Though Seneca embraced the tenets of Stoicism in their entirety, Cicero ________________ not just one school of Greek philosophy but, like a true ________________, chose what he thought best from each.

a. discomfited . . . penitent
b. abrogated . . . aesthetic
(c.) espoused . . . eclectic
d. deprecated . . . foible

6. The "truth-in-advertising" laws that many states have passed were designed to stop crooks and ________________ from making ________________ claims about the products they offer to the unsuspecting public.

(a.) charlatans . . . mendacious
b. necromancers . . . sporadic
c. fetishes . . . laconic
d. cabals . . . eclectic

7. The dietician looked ________________ at the sugary cereal and suggested that we ________________ it and try whole-wheat toast and fruit instead.

a. ambient . . . attenuate
(b.) askance . . . forgo
c. tantamount . . . cavil
d. obtuse . . . winnow

 CCSS Vocabulary: 4.a. (See pp. T14–15.)

In the passage about the mystery of the Franklin Expedition (see page 127), the author notes that "a string of facts does not add up to the truth." This saying is a proverb. The author means that the pieces of evidence that were found on Franklin's vessels (the facts) do not provide a full explanation of what happened to Franklin and his crew (the truth).

A **proverb** is a traditional and brief saying that expresses advice or a widely recognized truth about life in a memorable way. Proverbs may owe their appeal to a play on words (*Don't bite off more than you can chew*), an unusual metaphor (*A clear conscience is a soft pillow*), effective parallel structure (*Justice delayed is justice denied*), or even rhyme (*A friend in need is a friend indeed*).

Choosing the Right Proverb

Read each sentence. Use context clues to figure out the meaning of each proverb in ***boldface*** *print. Then write the letter of the definition for the proverb in the sentence.*

1. When my friend broke up with her boyfriend, I reminded her that **there are other fish in the sea**. __h__
2. Be sure that you have completed each line of the application. Remember, **for want of a nail, the kingdom was lost**. __f__
3. "Don't get discouraged because you didn't make the team," the coach said to the athlete. "**When one door closes, another one opens**." __a__
4. "**Don't bite the hand that feeds you**," Grandpa said when I complained about Dad's work hours. __g__
5. There is no use asking Troy to pay rent since he's been living here free. After all, **give a man an inch and he'll take a mile**. __c__
6. It means little that we lost the game by only one touchdown because **a miss is as good as a mile**. __j__
7. Mr. Chang advised, "You should pay your credit card bills now, since **out of debt, out of danger**." __e__
8. "I have no desire for a promotion," Sally said. "**The highest branch is not the safest roost**." __i__
9. **Pride goes before a fall**, which may be why the singer who predicted she would win the talent competition now has laryngitis. __b__
10. If we want the senator to vote against the bill, we need to publicize our complaints because **the squeaky wheel gets the grease**. __d__

a. Failure is often followed by a new opportunity.

b. Overconfidence can lead to trouble.

c. People are inclined to take advantage of others' generosity.

d. Those who make the most fuss get what they want.

e. Nobody who owes money is secure.

f. Do not neglect small details.

g. Be kind to those on whom you depend.

h. Other people and other opportunities are available.

i. Those with the most power are often the most uneasy.

j. If you fail, the margin of failure doesn't matter.

CCSS Vocabulary: 5.a. (See pp. T14–15.)

Writing with Proverbs

Find the meaning of each proverb. (Use an online or print dictionary if necessary.) Then write a sentence for each proverb. **Answers will vary.**

1. Life is no bed of roses. **Sample answer: I know that life is no bed of roses when you train for a marathon, but I'm surprised how much my feet hurt.**
2. Strike while the iron is hot.
3. Dig the well before you are thirsty.
4. As you sow, so shall you reap.
5. Always put your best foot forward.
6. A bad workman quarrels with his tools.
7. You can lead a horse to water, but you can't make him drink.
8. Fools rush in where angels fear to tread.
9. Might makes right.
10. One good turn deserves another.
11. What's good for the goose is good for the gander.
12. The eye is bigger than the belly.

 CCSS Vocabulary: 5. (See pp. T14–15.)

Denotation and Connotation

To speak or write with precision, you need to know both the denotation and the connotation of the words you use. The **denotation** is the literal dictionary meaning of a word. A word's **connotation** is the emotional implications and associations that a word can have. Connotations may be *positive*, *negative*, or *neutral*.

Consider these synonyms for the word *obsequious*:

amenable *complaisant* *servile* *sycophantic*

Amenable and *complaisant* refer to positive behaviors marked by respect and a disposition to please. *Servile* and *sycophantic* refer to negative behaviors, characterized by fawning and excessive submissiveness.

Think: A cooperative worker is amenable and complaisant when working with others, but a self-serving employee is servile or sycophantic.

Look at these examples of words that are similar in denotation but have different connotations.

NEUTRAL	POSITIVE	NEGATIVE
emotional	**sentimental**	**plaintive**
attribute	**virtue**	**foible**
inactive	**relaxed**	**flaccid**

Writers and speakers need to analyze nuances in the meaning of words with similar denotations. They should choose the word that best conveys the exact meaning and tone they intend. Selecting a word with positive connotations in a situation that calls for a negative or neutral term (or vice versa) can distract or confuse the audience.

Shades of Meaning

Write a plus sign (+) in the box if the word has a positive connotation. Write a minus sign (–) if the word has a negative connotation. Put a zero (0) if the word is neutral.

1. attenuate [0]	**2.** delectable [+]	**3.** ambient [0]	**4.** rife [0]
5. discomfit [–]	**6.** interpolate [0]	**7.** moribund [–]	**8.** impecunious [–]
9. gregarious [+]	**10.** abrogate [0]	**11.** irreparable [–]	**12.** languish [–]
13. sequester [0]	**14.** impeccable [+]	**15.** onerous [–]	**16.** reconnoiter [0]

Expressing the Connotation

Read each sentence. Select the word in parentheses that expresses the connotation (positive, negative, or neutral) given at the beginning of the sentence.

neutral **1.** The timid student tried to make sense of the (**cavil, observation**) the teacher wrote in the margins of the essay.

positive **2.** The desert scene was beautiful, with the sand and palm trees bathed in (**luminous, glaring**) moonlight.

negative **3.** After watching Roger bumble about in the kitchen, I realized he was not a skilled chef, but rather a(n) (**amateur, charlatan**).

neutral **4.** Ruth's (**response, rebuff**) to the stranger's offer to take her photograph in front of the White House surprised our entire family.

negative **5.** The high winds and torrential rains (**decimated, transformed**) the newly planted rose gardens.

neutral **6.** After a difficult loss, the team captain (**deprecated, delineated**) the effort shown by his teammates.

positive **7.** The (**ebullient, agitated**) crowd jammed the streets outside the football stadium after the Scouts' surprising victory in overtime.

negative **8.** The lifeguards looked (**skeptically, askance**) at the antics of the children who were chasing the birds along the beach.

Challenge: Using Connotation

Choose vocabulary words from Units 10–12 to replace the highlighted words in the sentences below. Then explain how the connotation of the replacement word changes the tone of the sentence. Answers will vary.

tantamount	**fraught**	**mendacious**
perfunctory	**penitent**	**benign**

1. After taking a **swift** perfunctory glance at the appointment book, the receptionist advised the client to call back later. Sample response: The negative connotation of *perfunctory* suggests that the receptionist's check of the appointment book was not simply quick, but also superficial and careless.

2. The pediatrician reassured the parents that letting little Marie suck her thumb frequently would have a **harmless** benign influence on the baby's development. Sample response: The positive connotation of benign means that Marie's thumb sucking could be beneficial, not merely innocuous.

3. Mrs. Garcia suspected that the mechanic's detailed explanation of the problem with her car's engine was **questionable** mendacious. Sample response: The negative connotation of *mendacious* suggests that Mrs. Garcia's concerns were more serious because the mechanic may have lied.

 CCSS Vocabulary: 5. (See pp. T14–15.)

Classical Roots

rog—to ask, beg, call

The root *rog* appears in **abrogate** (page 138), meaning "to cancel, to abolish by authoritative action." Some other words based on the same root are listed below.

abrogation	**derogation**	**interrogative**	**supererogatory**
arrogance	**interrogation**	**prorogue**	**surrogate**

From the list of words above, choose the one that corresponds to each of the brief definitions below. Write the word in the blank space in the illustrative sentence below the definition. Use an online or print dictionary if necessary.

1. a substitute, deputy; a judge in charge of the probate of wills, administration of estates, and appointment of guardians

   While my parents were on vacation, my aunt served as a ___**surrogate**___ guardian.

2. performed or observed beyond the degree required; demanded, or expected; unnecessary; superfluous

   "We could do with fewer ___**supererogatory**___ remarks," the teacher observed.

3. a cancellation; the act of repealing or annulling (*"calling off"*)

   Unfavorable evidence has emerged, forcing the ___**abrogation**___ of the agreement between the two parties.

4. exaggerated self-importance, haughty pride

   The king was corrupted by power and, over time, exchanged his humility for ___**arrogance**___.

5. an act or expression that detracts from reputation, value, power, etc. (*"to call down"*)

   The aid workers deeply resented any ___**derogation**___ of their motives.

6. asking a question; having the form or character of a question; a word or sentence that asks a question

   In Spanish class, we are learning how to phrase ___**interrogative**___ sentences.

7. to discontinue a session of a legislative body; to defer, postpone

   The prime minister was determined to ___**prorogue**___ the legislative assembly until all members were present.

8. an act of formal or systematic questioning

   The detective asked question after question during the ___**interrogation**___ of the prime suspect.

CCSS Vocabulary: 4.c. (See pp. T14–15.)

Note that not all of the 20 unit words are used in this passage. *Desiccated* and *ghoulish* are not included in the passage.

*Read the following selection, taking note of the **boldface** words and their contexts. These words are among those you will be studying in Unit 13. As you complete the exercises in this unit, it may help to refer to the way the words are used below.*

CCSS Vocabulary: 4; Reading (Informational Text): 4, 6. (See pp. T14–15.)

More Than Just a Pretty Face

<Profile>

One of many Hollywood stars who **mesmerized** moviegoers of the 1940s was Hedy Lamarr. But it was not only Lamarr's striking looks and dramatic talent that **engendered** admiration in audiences. As fans learned about the actress's life story, many became more interested in Lamarr herself than in the characters she portrayed in her work onscreen.

Born in 1914 in Vienna, Austria, Hedwig Kiesler was the only child of Jewish parents who encouraged their daughter to study ballet and piano. Hedy began her acting career as a teenager, appearing in a number of German films. In 1933, she played a lovesick young wife in a Czech film called *Ecstasy*, a suggestive film derided by **captious** critics as an **affront** to moral decency. Despite the **opprobrium** levied against the film, *Ecstasy* undeniably raised the young actress's profile.

Not long after the film's release, Hedy married Fritz Mandl, an arms manufacturer some thirteen years her senior. They were an **incongruous** couple, and Mandl proved a jealous and tyrannical husband. He forbade his wife from pursuing her acting career, and ordered her to accompany him to business meetings. Though frustrated with the relationship, Hedy enjoyed discussions of Mandl's business affairs and became acquainted with weapons systems technology. Soon, dismayed to learn that her husband was a Nazi sympathizer, Hedy fled Austria, escaping both her husband and the Nazis.

An undated portrait of Hedy Lamarr

Various rumors about the **machinations** of her escape would later surface. According to one story, the actress used sleeping pills to drug her maid, who had instructions from Mr. Mandl to see that his wife did not leave the house. Then Hedy put on the maid's uniform and fled through the servants' entrance.

However she escaped, it wasn't long before Hedy arrived in Hollywood and adopted her stage name, Hedy Lamarr. Soon she was starring in motion pictures; she appeared in 18 films during her heyday in the 1940s. Her biggest box-office success was *Samson and Delilah*, the highest-grossing movie of 1949.

While fans at the time recognized Lamarr as an **ethereal** beauty, few were **cognizant** of the celebrity's off-screen pursuits as an inventor. In 1940, in collaboration with her Hollywood neighbor, composer George Antheil, Lamarr developed a "Secret Communication System" designed to make the radio signals used to control missiles harder to detect or jam. With World War II underway, the duo received a patent for the design in 1942. Though their device was never produced, the underlying concept of "frequency hopping" proposed by Lamarr was implemented in a similar form by the United States military in later years, and eventually became an essential feature of wireless communication systems.

In a less **abstruse** contribution to the war effort, Lamarr, with other leading Hollywood actresses, toured major cities to promote the sale of war bonds to help fund the war. Lamarr visited 16 cities in ten days, selling a **putative** $25 million in war bonds in all. Sales received a boost from the unsurprising **efficacy** of Lamarr's offer to kiss any man who purchased $25,000 worth of war bonds—an offer that reportedly raised $7 million in one night.

Lamarr's career declined from 1950, as she gradually fell out of favor with audiences and was no longer considered a bankable **cynosure** in Hollywood. Over time, rumors of less than **decorous** behavior pursued her, including accusations of shoplifting. Lamarr seldom assented to interviews, and after dismissing the rumors as **canards**, she maintained her characteristic silence. Some fans admired Lamarr for not **deigning** to behave in a **contrite** manner, but the rumors proved hard to shake.

Still waters run deep, and there is little doubt that behind the **facade** of silence, Lamarr remained the intelligent and complex person she had always been behind the gloss of Hollywood celebrity. The Electronic Frontier Foundation recognized her talents when it gave Lamarr the Pioneer Award in 1997 for her invention. Lamarr died in 2000.

Snap the code, or go to **vocabularyworkshop.com**

Lamarr gives the V-for-Victory sign while selling war bonds in 1942.

Note the spelling, pronunciation, part(s) of speech, and definition(s) of each of the following words. Then write the word in the blank spaces in the illustrative sentence(s) following. Finally, study the lists of synonyms and antonyms.

1. abstruse (ab strüs′)

(*adj.*) extremely difficult to understand

The physicist tried to explain her **abstruse** research in the field of quantum mechanics.

SYNONYMS: arcane, recondite, occult
ANTONYMS: simple, straightforward

2. affront (ə frənt′)

(*n.*) an open or intentional insult; a slight; (*v.*) to insult to one's face; to face in defiance, confront

The student felt that being referred to by number rather than by name was an **affront** to her dignity.

In the nineteenth century, Irish immigrants to the United States were **affronted** by signs reading: No Irish Need Apply.

SYNONYMS: (*n.*) offense; (*v.*) offend
ANTONYMS: (*n., v.*) compliment, praise

3. canard (kə närd′)

(*n.*) a false rumor, fabricated story

The tabloid journalist was responsible for spreading the **canard** about the candidate's mental health.

SYNONYM: hoax

4. captious (kap′ shəs)

(*adj.*) excessively ready to find fault; given to petty criticism; intended to trap, confuse, or show up

She is an invariably **captious** critic.

SYNONYMS: faultfinding, carping
ANTONYM: uncritical

5. cognizant (käg′ ni zənt)

(*adj.*) aware, knowledgeable, informed; having jurisdiction

Police officers must make sure that crime suspects are made **cognizant** of their rights before they are questioned.

SYNONYM: acquainted
ANTONYMS: unaware, unconscious, oblivious

6. contrite (kən trīt′)

(*adj.*) regretful for some misdeed or sin; plagued by a sense of guilt; thoroughly penitent

The convicted felon had the look of someone who was truly **contrite** and ready to pay for his crimes.

SYNONYMS: remorseful, rueful
ANTONYMS: unapologetic, impenitent

CCSS Vocabulary: 4.c., 4.d. (See pp. T14–15.)

7. cynosure (sī′ nə shür)

(*n.*) the center of attraction, attention, or interest; something that serves to guide or direct

For over a century, the Statue of Liberty has been the **cynosure** for millions of immigrants entering New York Harbor.

SYNONYM: focus

8. decorous (dek′ ər əs)

(*adj.*) well behaved, dignified, socially proper

On formal occasions, participants are expected to behave in a **decorous** manner.

SYNONYMS: seemly, becoming, tasteful
ANTONYMS: unbecoming, improper, tasteless

9. deign (dān)

(*v.*) to think it appropriate or suitable to one's dignity to do something; to condescend

The enlisted men were surprised that the four-star general **deigned** to speak to them in the camp.

SYNONYM: deem

10. desiccated (des′ ə kā tid)

(*adj., part.*) thoroughly dried out; divested of spirit or vitality; arid and uninteresting

The cornfield was **desiccated** by the scorching sun after the long, hot summer without rain.

SYNONYMS: dehydrated, shriveled
ANTONYMS: sodden, waterlogged, drenched

11. efficacy (ef′ ə kə sē)

(*n.*) the power to produce a desired result

The pharmaceutical company has done extensive research to prove the **efficacy** of the new drug.

SYNONYMS: effectiveness, potency, reliability
ANTONYM: impotence

12. engender (in jen′ dər)

(*v.*) to bring into existence, give rise to, produce; to come into existence, assume form

The university has made an appealing video in order to **engender** student interest in studying abroad.

SYNONYMS: generate, cause, form; ANTONYMS: stop, deter

13. ethereal (i thēr′ ē əl)

(*adj.*) light, airy, delicate; highly refined; suggesting what is heavenly (rather than earthbound)

The Renaissance painter Fra Angelico captured the **ethereal** beauty of angels in his frescoes.

SYNONYMS: heavenly, celestial, gossamer
ANTONYMS: infernal, hellish, thick, heavy

CCSS Vocabulary: 4.c. (See pp. T14–15.)

14. facade (fə säd′)

(*n.*) the front or face of a building; a surface appearance (as opposed to what may lie behind)

After years of neglect, the sooty ___**facade**___ of the structure is finally getting a much needed cleaning.

SYNONYMS: exterior, surface, mask
ANTONYM: interior

15. ghoulish (gül′ ish)

(*adj.*) revolting in an unnatural or morbid way; suggestive of someone who robs graves or otherwise preys on the dead

The ___**ghoulish**___ practice of grave robbing is motivated by the desire to find and sell valuables.

SYNONYMS: barbarous, monstrous

16. incongruous (in kän′ grü əs)

(*adj.*) not in keeping, unsuitable, incompatible

Abraham Lincoln, the backwoods lawyer, and Mary Todd, the socialite, seemed an ___**incongruous**___ couple.

SYNONYM: discordant
ANTONYMS: compatible, harmonious, consistent

17. machination (mak ə nā′ shən)

(*n.*) a crafty, scheming, or underhanded action designed to accomplish some (usually evil) end

Shakespeare's Othello was the victim not only of Iago's evil ___**machinations**___ but also of his own jealous nature.

SYNONYMS: plot, maneuver

18. mesmerize (mez′ mə rīz)

(*v.*) to hypnotize, entrance; to fascinate, enthrall, bewitch

The magician was able to ___**mesmerize**___ the audience with his fast-moving hands and distracting chatter.

19. opprobrium (ə prō′ brē əm)

(*n.*) disgrace arising from shameful conduct; contempt, reproach

Despite the passage of centuries, ___**opprobrium**___ is still attached to the name of the traitor Benedict Arnold.

SYNONYMS: infamy, dishonor, odium
ANTONYMS: acclaim, honor, glory, renown

20. putative (pyü′ tə tiv)

(*adj.*) generally regarded as such; reputed; hypothesized, inferred

Ancient Celtic rituals and ceremonies are the ___**putative**___ origins of some of our modern Halloween customs.

SYNONYMS: supposed, presumed
ANTONYMS: corroborated, confirmed

CCSS Vocabulary: 4.c. (See pp. T14–15.)

Choosing the Right Word

*Select the **boldface** word that better completes each sentence. You might refer to the selection on pages 164–165 to see how most of these words are used in context.*

1. Workers dismantled and cleaned parts of the Parthenon's exterior (**affront, facade**) during recent restoration work on the temple.

2. The audience was so quiet after the curtain fell that I couldn't tell whether they were bored or (**deigned, mesmerized**) by her artistry.

3. Philologists believe that many Western languages can be traced back to a (**putative, decorous**) parent tongue known as Indo-European.

4. A government that fails to create reform (**engenders, deigns**) the social unrest that makes violent revolution inevitable.

Built in the fifth century BC, the Parthenon in Athens endures as a lasting symbol of the glory of ancient Greece.

5. In my youthful folly, I inadvertently (**affronted, engendered**) the very people whose aid I was attempting to enlist.

6. The President must always be on his toes because a careless answer to a (**contrite, captious**) question could land him in political hot water.

7. It wasn't at all hard to recognize signs of extreme uneasiness beneath her (**canard, facade**) of buoyant optimism.

8. His unmistakable interest in the gruesome details of the tragedy revealed that he possessed the sensibilities of a (**canard, ghoul**).

9. Her quiet speech, subdued clothes, and (**decorous, desiccated**) manner made it hard to believe that she was a famous rock star.

10. "Do we have sufficient evidence at hand," I asked, "to judge the (**efficacy, cognizance**) of the new method of teaching reading?"

11. It has been said that humor is essentially the yoking of (**incongruous, ethereal**) elements within a familiar or recognizable framework.

12. For any actor, it is a unique thrill to know that when you are alone on stage, you are the (**facade, cynosure**) of hundreds of pairs of eyes.

13. If you had listened to my warnings in the first place, there would be no need for you to feel (**contrite, desiccated**) now.

14. I resent your nasty question about whether or not I will "(**deign, affront**) to speak to ordinary students" after I'm elected class president.

15. He acts like someone whose vital juices have long since dried up, leaving only a drab and (**desiccated, contrite**) shell behind.

CCSS Vocabulary: 4.d. (See pp. T14–15.)

16. The (**efficacy, opprobrium**) of history forever attaches itself to the name of Lee Harvey Oswald, the assassin of President Kennedy.

17. The book describes in great detail the odious (**machinations, facades**) involved in Adolf Hitler's rise to power in Germany.

18. The candidate's "shocking revelation" about his opponent was later shown to be nothing more than a malicious (**canard, cynosure**).

19. The play is so peopled with spirits and other incorporeal beings that it has the (**ethereal, captious**) quality of a dream.

20. He tried to conceal his lack of scholarship and intellectual depth by using unnecessarily (**efficacious, abstruse**) language.

21. Like many people who are completely wrapped up in themselves, she simply isn't (**cognizant, decorous**) of the larger world around her.

22. The daring feats of the acrobats on the high wire completely (**engendered, mesmerized**) everyone in the crowd.

23. The 1938 radio broadcast by Orson Welles that described a Martian invasion is on many lists of the greatest (**canards, efficacies**) of the twentieth century.

24. Sitting in the back of the cathedral, I strained to hear the lovely, (**ethereal, desiccated**) voices of the children wafting down from the choir loft.

25. Guests at the formal reception exhibited (**putative, decorous**) behavior.

Choose the word from this unit that is the same or most nearly the same in meaning as the ***boldface*** *word or expression in the phrase. Write that word on the line. Use a dictionary if necessary.*

1. a **fiendish** interest in death ghoulish
2. the **parched** desert landscape desiccated
3. **esoteric** concepts developed by experts abstruse
4. **stooped** to give a few interviews deigned
5. **conscious** of our mutual responsibilities cognizant
6. disliked for his **nit-picking** tendencies captious
7. foiled the **schemes** of the villain machinations
8. **begets** mistrust by covering up mistakes engenders
9. brought **shame** on the whole family opprobrium
10. the **jarring** reunion of longtime rivals incongruous

CCSS Vocabulary: 5. (See pp. T14–15.)

The synonyms and antonyms here do not appear on the Definitions page.

*Choose the word from this unit that is most nearly opposite in meaning to the **boldface** word or expression in the phrase. Write that word on the line. Use a dictionary if necessary.*

1. the **unrepentant** ringleaders of the riot — contrite
2. looked over the **soggy** farmland — desiccated
3. the **unseemly** appearance of the judge — decorous
4. the **known** whereabouts of the fugitive — putative
5. the **angelic** statue — ghoulish

Completing the Sentence

From the words in this unit, choose the one that best completes each of the following sentences. Write the word in the space provided.

1. There is little evidence that supports the idea that poverty tends to ___engender___ poor language skills.
2. The only surefire way to establish the ___efficacy___ of a new drug in treating a disease is to test it "in the field."
3. His fantastic stories about his academic, athletic, financial, and romantic achievements are a(n) ___affront___ to common sense.
4. Except for a balcony built during the Truman administration, the ___facade___ of the White House has remained virtually unchanged since it was constructed.
5. No one knows for sure who really wrote the scene, but Shakespeare is generally regarded as its ___putative___ author.
6. Some historians question whether Benedict Arnold really deserves all the ___opprobrium___ he has been accorded as America's arch-traitor.
7. At the risk of appearing a trifle ___captious___, I would like to raise a few small objections to the wording of this proposal.
8. Some teachers are able to present the most ___abstruse___ subjects in terms that are clear to all students.
9. I didn't really believe that he was sorry for what he had done until I saw the ___contrite___ expression on his face.
10. The cherubic faces and ___ethereal___ voices of the choristers almost moved me to tears.

CCSS Vocabulary: 4.a. (See pp. T14–15.)

11. Only a thoroughly naive and gullible person would actually believe every preposterous ___canard___ that circulates in this school.

12. What could be more ___incongruous___ than the 6-foot, 7-inch center on the basketball team dolled up in baby clothes for the class play!

13. The longer I study this country's history, the more ___cognizant___ I become of my rich heritage of freedom.

14. The child's conduct during the ceremony may not have been appropriately ___decorous___, but it wasn't horrendous either.

15. After the battle, camp followers began the ___ghoulish___ process of stripping the dead of whatever valuables they possessed.

16. The ___machinations___ of the unscrupulous wheeler-dealers involved in that unsavory scandal boggle the imagination.

17. The pages of the old book were so ___desiccated___ that they began to crumble as soon as we touched them.

18. To be the ___cynosure___ of all eyes could be the joyous fulfillment of a dream or the unhappy realization of a nightmare.

19. For more than five minutes she stared at the telegram containing the bad news, as if she were ___mesmerized___.

20. Am I supposed to feel honored simply because that arrogant lout sometimes ___deigns___ to nod vaguely in my direction?

Writing: Words in Action

Answers to both prompts will vary.

1. Look back at "More Than Just a Pretty Face" (pages 164–165). Suppose you have been hired by a publishing company to promote an upcoming biography of Hedy Lamarr. Write a press release to interest people in Lamarr's life and persuade them to buy the book. Use at least two details from the essay and three unit words.

2. Today it seems that cordless and wireless phones are a commonplace—if not a necessity—in the daily lives of many Americans. Think about the positive and negative consequences that these devices have had on modern life. Write an expository essay of at least three paragraphs in which you analyze the pros and cons of cell phones. Support your ideas with specific details and examples from personal experience or observations, as well as information you have gained from your own reading or media viewing. Use three or more words from this unit in your essay.

Writing prompt #2 is modeled on that of standardized tests.

CCSS Vocabulary: 6; Writing: 2.d., 3.d. (See pp. T14–15.)

Vocabulary in Context: Informational Text for Unit 13 is available online at **vocabularyworkshop.com**.

Vocabulary in Context
Literary Text

The following excerpts are from Jane Austen's novels Emma, Sense and Sensibility, *and* Pride and Prejudice. *Some of the words you have studied in this unit appear in* **boldface** *type. Complete each statement below the excerpt by circling the letter of the correct answer.*

1. The consciousness of having done amiss, had exposed her to a thousand inquietudes, and made her **captious** and irritable to a degree that must have been—that had been—hard for him to bear. (*Emma*)

A person who is **captious**

a. appears passive
b. finds fault readily
c. acts impetuously
d. refuses to speak

2. Was it new for anything in this world to be unequal, inconsistent, **incongruous**—or for chance and circumstance (as second causes) to direct the human fate? (*Emma*)

Something **incongruous** is

a. inflexible
b. misunderstood
c. unsuitable
d. unpredictable

3. But I had no inclination for the law, even in this less **abstruse** study of it, which my family approved. (*Sense and Sensibility*)

Something that is **abstruse** is NOT

a. precise
b. expensive
c. serious
d. simple

A scene from the 2005 film version of *Pride and Prejudice*, with Brenda Blethyn, Talulah Riley, Jena Malone, and Keira Knightley

4. "Could he expect that her friends would not step forward? Could he expect to be noticed again by the regiment, after such an **affront** to Colonel Forster? His temptation is not adequate to the risk!" (*Pride and Prejudice*)

An **affront** is a(n)

a. embarrassment
b. act of generosity
c. lie
d. insult

5. "And so ended his affection," said Elizabeth impatiently. "There has been many a one, I fancy, overcome in the same way. I wonder who first discovered the **efficacy** of poetry in driving away love!" (*Pride and Prejudice*)

Poetry's **efficacy** is its

a. mixture of rhythm and rhyme
b. layers of meaning
c. power to produce a desired result
d. capacity to stir emotions

Snap the code, or go to **vocabularyworkshop.com**

UNIT 14

Note that not all of the 20 unit words are used in this passage. *Behemoth*, *blandishment*, *euphemism*, *moratorium*, and *pariah* are not included in the passage.

*Read the following selection, taking note of the **boldface** words and their contexts. These words are among those you will be studying in Unit 14. As you complete the exercises in this unit, it may help to refer to the way the words are used below.*

CCSS Vocabulary: 4; Reading (Informational Text): 4, 6. (See pp. T14–15.)

Artificial Intelligence and Social Robots

<Technical Essay>

Robots are machines programmed to interact with their surroundings. They can be stationary or mobile. They can be stand-alone systems or "insects" in a fleet. Some robots perform household chores or provide entertainment, but the most common are industrial robots **consigned** to assembly lines and service robots used for repetitive tasks such as milking cows. Some critics complain that the use of industrial and service robots can foster unemployment. Proponents claim the use of robots frees human workers from tedious physical labor that many are **loath** to do, enabling people to do more satisfying work.

The term "robot" appeared for the first time in a 1920 fantasy play by Karel Capek, and comes from a Czech word meaning "forced labor." In Capek's **visionary** tale, robots develop self-awareness, tire of servitude, and stage a **coup** that destroys the human race.

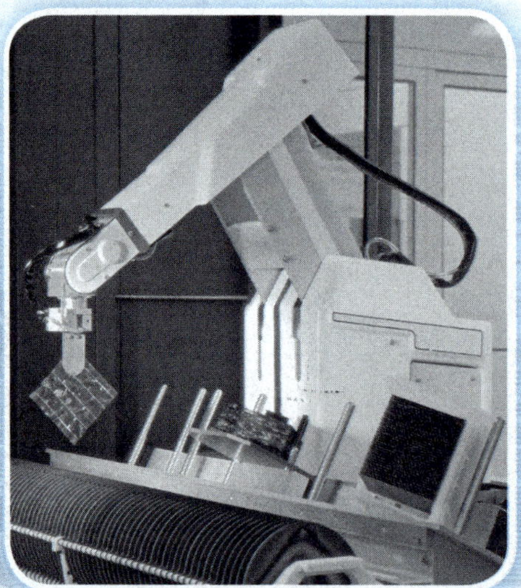

A robot completes repetitive tasks at a solar cell manufacturer.

Of course, most scientists would be skeptical and **gainsay** claims about the **imminent** threat of robots rebelling against humanity. However, the notion that robots might learn to think for themselves can no longer be treated as an impossibility.

Robotics developed with **febrile** intensity in the 1990s, following advances in the field of artificial intelligence. The breakthroughs improved computer systems' capacity to perform tasks involving perception, speech recognition, decision-making, translation, and related skills. Early attempts to design intelligent robots focused on simple interactions with the environment, like getting a machine to learn to navigate down a hallway. With time, scientists began to produce robots that perceive subtle features of the world around them, even distinguishing **cacophonous** laughter from harmonious singing. Recent efforts have focused on robots that cooperate with humans by using realistic social behaviors. These "social robots" engage in interactive behaviors and respond to human actions. Some even interpret emotions normally **manifest** only to humans and make appropriate responses, including facial expressions.

In order to make interaction with social robots feel natural, many are designed to look like humans, animals, or cartoon-like characters. One Korean-made robot, modeled after famed scientist Albert

The robot Alex Hubo was made to look like Albert Einstein.

Einstein, has a rubber face shaped to resemble the **wizened** old physicist in his later years. Designers took great pains to make the face lifelike, down to **minutiae** like a bushy mustache, fuzzy eyebrows, and gleaming eyes. Beneath its familiar appearance, the robot contains sophisticated artificial intelligence software, 32 motors to guide facial movements, and two cameras housed in its eyes. The Einstein robot has learned to mimic a range of facial expressions, from a **beatific** smile to a wide-eyed look of surprise.

Researchers are exploring a variety of potential uses for social robots. Autism patients whose **innate** ability to interpret emotions is impaired might benefit from interaction with social robots. Emotionally responsive robots could provide companionship for the elderly and help them operate digital devices. Law-enforcement robots could help police by detecting concealed weapons and bombs. They could even take measurements of heart rate, respiration, and body temperature to recognize the **chicanery** of a lying suspect.

Some researchers and entrepreneurs claim that social robots will soon provide a **nostrum** for a range of socioeconomic ills. It is more likely that decades of research will be required before social robots have a deep impact on human life and work. However long it takes, it is clear that the die is cast. Intelligent social robots are destined to become increasingly integrated into human society.

iWords™

Snap the code, or go to **vocabularyworkshop.com**

Georgia Tech University developed this social robot named Simon.

Definitions

Note the spelling, pronunciation, part(s) of speech, and definition(s) of each of the following words. Then write the word in the blank spaces in the illustrative sentence(s) following. Finally, study the lists of synonyms and antonyms.

1. beatific (bē ə tif′ ik)
(*adj.*) blissful; rendering or making blessed

During the awards ceremony, the gold medal winner had a positively ___beatific___ expression on her face.

SYNONYMS: rapturous, ecstatic
ANTONYMS: disconsolate, dejected, doleful

2. behemoth (bi hē′ məth)
(*n.*) a creature of enormous size, power, or appearance

The Loch Ness monster is a famous ___behemoth___.

SYNONYMS: whale, elephant, colossus
ANTONYMS: dwarf, pygmy, midget

3. blandishment (blan′ dish mənt)
(*n.*, *often pl.*) anything designed to flatter or coax; sweet talk, apple-polishing

The king was often influenced by subtle ___blandishments___.

SYNONYMS: allurement, cajolery
ANTONYM: intimidation

4. cacophonous (kə käf′ ə nəs)
(*adj.*) harsh-sounding, raucous, discordant, dissonant

The scene opened with ___cacophonous___ laughter coming from three witches gathered around a steaming cauldron.

ANTONYMS: harmonious, melodious, mellifluous

5. chicanery (shi kā′ nə rē)
(*n.*) trickery, deceptive practices or tactics, double-dealing

The accountants used legal ___chicanery___ to cover up the company's shaky financial position.

ANTONYM: fair dealing

6. consign (kən sīn′)
(*v.*) to give over to another's care, charge, or control; to entrust, deliver; to set apart for a special use

The ship's captain ___consigned___ many duties to her trusted first mate.

SYNONYMS: remit, convey

7. coup (kü)
(*n.*) a highly successful stroke, masterstroke, tour de force, act, plan, or stratagem; a sudden takeover of power or leadership

The surprise ___coup___ by high-ranking military officers toppled the weak government in a matter of hours.

ANTONYMS: blunder, faux pas, gaffe

CCSS Vocabulary: 4.c., 4.d. (See pp. T14–15.)

8. euphemism (yü′ fə miz əm)

(*n.*) a mild or inoffensive expression used in place of a harsh or unpleasant one; a substitute

Common **euphemisms** for *die* include the expressions *pass away* and *go to the other side.*

9. febrile (feb′ ril)

(*adj.*) feverish; pertaining to or marked by fever; frenetic

The journalist wrote with **febrile** intensity.

ANTONYM: leisurely

10. gainsay (gān′ sā)

(*v.*) to deny, contradict, controvert; to dispute, oppose

Some wished to **gainsay** the conclusions of the United States Supreme Court in the matter of the 2000 presidential election.

ANTONYMS: confirm, corroborate, support, admit

11. imminent (im′ ə nənt)

(*adj.*) about to happen, threatening

An **imminent** hurricane forced the islanders back to the mainland.

SYNONYM: looming
ANTONYMS: distant, remote, faraway

12. innate (i nāt′)

(*adj.*) natural, inborn, inherent; built-in

Musical excellence often comes from **innate** ability.

SYNONYM: congenital
ANTONYMS: learned, acquired, extrinsic, accidental

13. loath (lōth)

(*adj.*) unwilling, reluctant, disinclined

My hard-working grandfather was **loath** to retire.

SYNONYMS: averse, indisposed
ANTONYMS: eager, inclined

14. manifest (man′ ə fest)

(*adj.*) clear, evident to the eyes or mind; (*v.*) to show plainly, exhibit, evince; (*n.*) a list of cargo and/or passengers

It was **manifest** to many nineteenth-century Americans that the nation was destined to extend to the Pacific Ocean.

When the man began to **manifest** signs of hearing loss, he went to a specialist.

The passenger **manifest** helps investigators find out who is on board a plane.

SYNONYMS: (*adj.*) apparent; (*v.*) reveal, disclose
ANTONYMS: (*adj.*) unrevealed, hidden; (*v.*) hide, conceal

CCSS Vocabulary: 4.c. (See pp. T14–15.)

15. minutiae (mə nü′ shē ə)

(*pl. n.*) small or trivial details, trifling matters

Because the researcher was too concerned with **minutiae**, she was unlikely to make an original discovery.

SYNONYM: trifles
ANTONYM: essentials

16. moratorium (môr ə tōr′ ē əm)

(*n.*) a suspension of activity; an official waiting period; an authorized period of delay

The conference was held to try to negotiate a **moratorium** on arms sales to both sides of the conflict.

SYNONYMS: postponement, stoppage
ANTONYM: escalation

17. nostrum (näs′ trəm)

(*n.*) an alleged cure-all; a remedy or scheme of questionable effectiveness

The federal Food and Drug Administration was created in part to keep unsavory characters from peddling **nostrums** to the public.

SYNONYM: elixir

18. pariah (par ī′ ə)

(*n.*) one who is rejected by a social group or organization

In most of the world today, those who are suffering from the disease of leprosy are no longer treated as **pariahs**.

SYNONYMS: untouchable, persona non grata

19. visionary (vizh′ ə ner ē)

(*adj.*) not practical, lacking in realism; having the nature of a fantasy or dream; (*n.*) one given to far-fetched ideas; a dreamer or seer characterized by vision or foresight

Ideas that once were considered **visionary** often become widely accepted over time.

The Reverend Martin Luther King, Jr., was a **visionary** whose dreams inspired the American civil rights movement.

SYNONYMS: (*adj.*) utopian, idealistic, impractical
ANTONYM: (*adj.*) practical

20. wizened (wiz′ ənd)

(*adj., part.*) dry, shrunken, and wrinkled (often as the result of aging)

The **wizened** old woman walked with the aid of a cane.

SYNONYMS: withered, shriveled
ANTONYMS: bloated, distended

CCSS Vocabulary: 4.c. (See pp. T14–15.)

Choosing the Right Word

Select the ***boldface*** *word that better completes each sentence. You might refer to the selection on pages 174–175 to see how most of these words are used in context.*

In the sixteenth century, Copernicus concluded that the planets revolve around the sun.

1. Many scientists view Nicolaus Copernicus as a (**visionary, nostrum**), not simply a talented mathematician and the founder of modern astronomy.

2. The (**wizened, febrile**) tempo of the symphony's opening movement gives way to a placid and stately largo in the next.

3. "How much of a chance do you suppose a 98-pound weakling like me actually stands against that 320-pound (**coup, behemoth**)?" I asked incredulously.

4. (**Imminent, Loath**) disaster stared us in the face when we were thrown for a loss and then fumbled the ball on our own five-yard line.

5. It didn't make me any happier to learn that my firing was being referred to (**euphemistically, cacophonously**) as a "termination."

6. The (**cacophony, moratorium**) that suddenly greeted my ears made me suspect that a fox had somehow gotten into the henhouse.

7. No one who knows the facts would venture to (**gainsay, consign**) your claim to have done your utmost to improve this community.

8. Only when we tried to implement the plan did its (**innate, imminent**) defects become clear to us.

9. Although I play a fair game of chess, I'm not capable of the brilliant (**coups, manifests**) that mark a true master of the game.

10. Someone who "can't see the forest for the trees" is usually too concerned with (**minutiae, nostrums**) to be aware of the overall picture.

11. When he took his first bite of Mother's famous coconut custard pie, a look of (**visionary, beatific**) joy spread over his face.

12. Accidents at nuclear power plants have prompted some people to agitate for a (**moratorium, nostrum**) on the construction of such facilities.

13. After he killed Alexander Hamilton in a duel, Aaron Burr found himself no longer a respected statesman, but a social and political (**coup, pariah**).

14. Although I am (**febrile, loath**) to boast, I must acknowledge my superior qualities as a student, athlete, financier, and all-round social luminary.

15. "The evidence that we will present in this trial," the prosecutor told the jury, "will make the defendant's guilt abundantly (**beatific, manifest**)."

CCSS Vocabulary: 4.d. (See pp. T14–15.)

16. After it had been left to rot in the sun for a few days, the plump little apple began to take on the (**visionary, wizened**) appearance of a prune.

17. It is a rare leader indeed who can tell the public unpleasant truths without evasions or (**pariahs, blandishments**).

18. The solution to our problems is to be found in long-term programs of social planning, not in easy (**pariahs, nostrums**).

19. The plan is certainly ingenious, but it strikes me as far too (**visionary, imminent**) to serve as the basis for practical legislation.

20. "As soon as we received the order," I said, "we crated the equipment and (**gainsaid, consigned**) it to the buyer in Atlanta."

21. The kind of financial (**minutiae, chicanery**) involved in bringing off that deal may not have been illegal, but it was certainly unethical.

22. I discovered my grandfather's name on the (**moratorium, manifest**) of a ship that carried immigrants from Italy to Boston in 1919.

23. In September 1973, President Salvador Allende of Chile was ousted in a (**coup, blandishment**) organized by the military.

24. "Does anybody dare to (**manifest, gainsay**) my decision to paint the house orange?" Uncle Max inquired with a twinkle in his eye.

25. After touching the baby's (**febrile, imminent**) cheek, Harry called the doctor.

Synonyms

*Choose the word from this unit that is the same or most nearly the same in meaning as the **boldface** word or expression in the phrase. Write that word on the line. Use a dictionary if necessary.*

1. open to the **enticement** of lobbyists — blandishments
2. a **replacement** for the word *ugly* — euphemism
3. prepared for the **delay** — moratorium
4. considered an **outcast** by her neighbors — pariah
5. when **mammoths** roamed the Earth — behemoths
6. warned of an **impending** investigation — imminent
7. **transcendent** vision of another world — beatific
8. fascinated by the **trivia** of celebrity gossip — minutiae
9. **transferred** to an underground facility — consigned
10. an **intrinsic** capacity for learning — innate

CCSS Vocabulary: 5. (See pp. T14–15.)

Antonyms

*Choose the word from this unit that is most nearly opposite in meaning to the **boldface** word or expression in the phrase. Write that word on the line. Use a dictionary if necessary.*

1. demanded an immediate **acceleration** ____moratorium____
2. a **realistic** blueprint for change ____visionary____
3. **threats** from one's enemies ____blandishments____
4. was **willing** to make a compromise ____loath____
5. looked like a **miniature** ____behemoth____

Completing the Sentence

From the words in this unit, choose the one that best completes each of the following sentences. Write the word in the space provided.

1. If you spend all your time on ____minutiae____, you won't have any left for really important matters.
2. Suddenly I was overcome by such a feeling of ____beatific____ peace that I began to wonder whether I was still on earth.
3. Before you dismiss him as just another impractical ____visionary____, think of how many great inventors were once regarded as mere "cranks."
4. Though her body had become bent and ____wizened____ with age, her mind was as alert and active as ever.
5. Some Civil War generals weren't professional soldiers and got their jobs through pulling strings and other forms of political ____chicanery____.
6. Some people enjoy the type of atonal music written by such composers as Arnold Schoenberg; others find it ____cacophonous____.
7. Only a fool would have succumbed to the cloying ____blandishments____ of that smooth-talking rascal!
8. However much I may dispute your views, I will never ____gainsay____ your right to hold them.
9. When it became clear just how shamelessly he had treated his brother, he became a virtual ____pariah____ in his own family.
10. On the first play, our diminutive quarterback was "sacked" by a veritable ____behemoth____ of a linebacker, ominously nicknamed "Bone Crusher."

CCSS Vocabulary: 4.a. (See pp. T14–15.)

11. Since I was brought up in a sleepy country town, I found it very hard to adjust to the **febrile** pace of big-city life.

12. We were all surprised that someone with the reputation of a frivolous playboy could **manifest** such courage and determination.

13. No matter what **euphemism** you use to describe his conduct, you can't disguise the fact he betrayed his best friend.

14. Just when it seemed that defeat was inevitable, she pulled off a dazzling **coup** that totally discomfited her opponent.

15. You may be, as you say, "**loath** to leave such a fascinating book," but I'm telling you right now to take out the garbage!

16. In a touching ceremony, the soldiers **consigned** the body of their fallen leader to the grave and his memory to their hearts.

17. Though the ability to paint is probably a(n) **innate** gift, it can certainly be improved by training and practice.

18. When the swollen river threatened to overflow its banks, a devastating flood seemed **imminent**.

19. One way to bring relief to small farmers who cannot meet their mortgage payments is to declare a temporary **moratorium** on foreclosures.

20. The nation's economic ills call for a variety of remedies; they cannot be cured by any single, miraculous **nostrum**.

Writing: Words in Action

Answers to both prompts will vary.

1. Look back at "Artificial Intelligence and Social Robots" (pages 174–175). Imagine you work for a company that designs and manufactures social robots. Your task is to write an editorial that first educates the public about the nature of social robots and then explains the ways in which their use will improve the lives of many people. Use at least two details from the essay and three unit words.

2. Today, some analysts argue that the growing use of robots and other forms of automation will have a negative long-term impact on unemployment. Others claim that the use of robots will free more workers from menial and repetitive jobs and will result in an increase in satisfying jobs for highly skilled technicians and other specialists. In a brief essay, explain your viewpoint on this issue. Support your ideas with specific examples from your studies, the reading (pages 174–175), or personal observations and experience. Write at least three paragraphs, and use three or more words from this unit.

Writing prompt #2 is modeled on that of standardized tests.

CCSS Vocabulary: 6; Writing: 2.d., 3.d. (See pp. T14–15.)

Vocabulary in Context: Informational Text for Unit 14 is available online at **vocabularyworkshop.com**.

Vocabulary in Context

Literary Text

The following excerpts are from F. Scott Fitzgerald's novel The Beautiful and Damned. *Some of the words you have studied in this unit appear in* **boldface** *type. Complete each statement below the excerpt by circling the letter of the correct answer.*

1. After his decision a gradual improvement was **manifest.** He had taken at least a step in the direction to which hope pointed, and he realized that the less he brooded upon her the better he would be able to give the desired impression when they met.

If an improvement is **manifest**, it is

a. evident
b. anticipated
c. fleeting
d. astonishing

In the four novels and many short stories he wrote before his death in 1940, F. Scott Fitzgerald depicted the optimism and the excesses of the Jazz Age.

2. It had seemed at the time that they were always having company—she had indulged in an unspoken conviction that each guest was ever afterward slightly indebted to her. They owed her a sort of moral ten dollars apiece, and should she ever be in need she might, so to speak, borrow from them this **visionary** currency.

Something that is **visionary** is NOT

a. worthless
b. common
c. forgettable
d. practical

3. The argument faded off, but reoccurred to Anthony several times thereafter. It was disturbing to find this old belief, evidently assimilated from her mother, inserting itself again under its immemorial disguise as an **innate** idea.

An idea that is **innate** is

a. novel
b. inborn
c. hackneyed
d. indisputable

4. It seemed a tragedy to want nothing—and yet he wanted something, something. He knew in flashes what it was—some path of hope to lead him toward what he thought was an **imminent** and ominous old age.

Something that is **imminent** is

a. extremely destructive
b. lacking in energy
c. full of sadness
d. about to happen

5. Just before the engagement was announced Anthony had gone up to Tarrytown to see his grandfather, who, a little more **wizened** and grizzly as time played its ultimate chuckling tricks, greeted the news with profound cynicism.

A **wizened** person is

a. shrunken and wrinkled
b. solemn and serious
c. drowsy and forgetful
d. outspoken and loud

Snap the code, or go to **vocabularyworkshop.com**

CCSS Vocabulary: 4.c.; Reading (Literature): 4. (See pp. T14–15.)

UNIT 15

Note that not all of the 20 unit words are used in this passage. *Dissidence*, *obeisance*, *presage*, and *seraphic* are not included in the passage.

Read the following selection, taking note of the ***boldface*** *words and their contexts. These words are among those you will be studying in Unit 15. As you complete the exercises in this unit, it may help to refer to the way the words are used below.*

CCSS Vocabulary: 4; Reading (Informational Text): 4, 6. (See pp. T14–15.)

Private Life in the Public Eye

<Humorous Essay>

There are many reasons to keep a private diary. Jotting down your thoughts helps you sort out **nascent** feelings. Sketching plans helps you make way toward your goals. Whatever your reasons, keeping a diary is a perfect way to exercise your **inviolable** right to take yourself too seriously. The only problem is, it's hard to keep your private scribblings safe from prying eyes. To keep a diary is to run the risk that your secret thoughts might be discovered by some snooping relative or friend, even **promulgated** round the world, like the evening news or the latest scandal on the Internet.

One of history's great examples of private thoughts gone public is a diary penned in the seventeenth century by Samuel Pepys (1633–1703). Pepys was an ambitious man who climbed the ranks of English society by skillful work and diligent networking, eventually becoming a member of Parliament, a Fellow of the Royal Society, and Secretary for the Admiralty. On account of his public achievements, we should consider him a leading man of his day. But the diary he left to his **progeny**, having slipped into the records of history, provides another **aperture** through which to view the man.

Visscher's view of London, 1616

In the pages of his private thoughts, Pepys, for all his hard work, high culture, and dignified connections, seems a man of **restive** habits and **mutable** character. He wrestles with his vices in his diary, time and again falling short of moral **rectitude** and raking over the ashes of his chief **iniquities**: his **epicurean** love of wine, his addiction to the theater, and his lust for women other than his wife.

To the historian, Pepys's diary provides an insider's glimpse of the English Restoration: meetings with the king and other men of high office, eyewitness accounts of the Great Fire and the Great Plague of London, and views on the politics of war and peace. But the casual reader—who might not care a **pittance** for international affairs of the seventeenth century—is more apt to enjoy the diary's personal anecdotes. Mr. Pepys rolls over one night in his sleep accidentally to smash his wife in the nose with his elbow. Another evening, he's threatening to fling her poor dog out the window. For months on end he's racked with jealousy, afraid his wife might have an eye for other men, though he doesn't let the sentiment interfere with his own thoughts on comely women. He criticizes the king's skill at tennis, reports on the monarch's drinking habits and mistresses, and complains about the flatterers who praise their ruler far more than he deserves.

For all the notable accomplishments of his public life, Samuel Pepys is most commonly remembered as a funny fellow who kept a diary and who could not **subsist** without wine, plays, or the other **amenities** of his times. His honesty and enthusiasm for the details of his life might be worth a **panegyric**, but for some of his flaws the man deserves to be **pilloried**. We would know nothing of his shortcomings if it weren't for the **improvident** decision, or perhaps the odd pride, that led Pepys to leave his diary behind. On the other hand, if it weren't for that diary, most of us would not know the man at all. This very public legacy is a reminder to anyone who aspires to be a "private" diarist. Be careful what you commit to print!

King Charles II was the subject of many of Pepys's diary entries.

Definitions

Note the spelling, pronunciation, part(s) of speech, and definition(s) of each of the following words. Then write the word in the blank spaces in the illustrative sentence(s) following. Finally, study the lists of synonyms and antonyms.

1. amenity (ə men′ ə tē)

(*n.*) that which is pleasant or agreeable; (*pl.*) attractive features, customs, etc.

When I backpack, there are certain basic **amenities**, such as hot meals and a dry tent, that I will not go without.

ANTONYMS: unpleasantness, disagreeableness

2. aperture (ap′ ər chər)

(*n.*) an opening, gap, hole; orifice

After the earthquake, rain and cold came through the **aperture** in the wall of the damaged house.

ANTONYMS: closure, blockage, occlusion

3. dissidence (dis′ ə dəns)

(*n.*) a difference of opinion; discontent

When the commanding officer announced that all leave was cancelled, there was widespread **dissidence** in the ranks.

SYNONYMS: disagreement, disaffection
ANTONYMS: harmony, concord

4. epicurean (ep ə kyü′ rē ən)

(*adj.*) devoted to the pursuit of pleasure; fond of good food, comfort, and ease; with discriminating tastes; (*n.*) a person with discriminating tastes

The chef took an **epicurean** delight in presenting the most delicious dishes to his demanding clientele.

Even the most fervent **epicurean** should not expect fine dining in a poor, war-torn country.

SYNONYMS: (*adj.*) sybaritic, discriminating
ANTONYMS: (*adj.*) ascetic, self-denying, abstemious

5. improvident (im präv′ ə dənt)

(*adj.*) not thrifty; failing to plan ahead

Some people are so **improvident** that despite high incomes they struggle to make ends meet.

SYNONYMS: prodigal, spendthrift, extravagant
ANTONYMS: frugal, economical, cautious

6. iniquity (i nik′ wə tē)

(*n.*) wickedness, sin; a grossly immoral act

English Puritans looked upon the court that surrounded King Charles I as a den of **iniquity**.

SYNONYMS: evil, crime
ANTONYMS: probity, rectitude, uprightness

CCSS Vocabulary: 4.c., 4.d. (See pp. T14–15.)

7. inviolable
(in vī′ ə lə bəl)

(*adj.*) sacred; of such a character that it must not be broken, injured, or profaned

Safeguarding the retirement income of millions of Americans is an ___**inviolable**___ trust of the federal government.

SYNONYM: unassailable
ANTONYMS: vulnerable, assailable

8. mutable
(myü′ tə bəl)

(*adj.*) open to or capable of change, fickle

Most people would agree that one's principles and moral values should not be as ___**mutable**___ as fashion.

SYNONYMS: changeable, variable
ANTONYMS: changeless, steadfast, constant

9. nascent
(nā′ sənt)

(*adj.*) just beginning to exist or develop; having just come into existence

Recent public opinion polls registered ___**nascent**___ opposition to the proposed tax increase.

SYNONYMS: incipient, embryonic
ANTONYMS: dying, moribund, senescent

10. obeisance
(ō bē′ səns)

(*n.*) a deep bow or other body movement indicating respect or submission; deference, homage

Upon entering the throne room, each courtier made a respectful ___**obeisance**___ before the king and queen.

SYNONYM: honor
ANTONYMS: disrespect, irreverence

11. panegyric
(pan ə ji′ rik)

(*n.*) formal or elaborate praise; a tribute

The speaker delivered a ___**panegyric**___ in honor of the award-winning author.

SYNONYMS: tribute, encomium, testimonial
ANTONYMS: tirade, philippic

12. pillory
(pil′ ə rē)

(*n.*) a device for publicly punishing offenders; a means for exposing one to public contempt or ridicule; (*v.*) to expose to public contempt or ridicule

The ___**pillory**___ was placed in the center of town so that everyone could view the outlaws and their shame.

The candidate tried to ___**pillory**___ her political opponent by suggesting that he had ties to organized crime.

ANTONYMS: (*v.*) extol, laud, acclaim

13. pittance (pit′ əns)

(*n.*) a woefully meager allowance, wage, or portion

In comparison to the overwhelming need for food and medicine, the shipment was a mere ___**pittance**___.

SYNONYM: trifle; ANTONYM: fortune

14. presage (pres′ ij)

(*v.*) to foreshadow or point to a future event; to predict; (*n.*) a warning or indication of the future

The skirmishes at the border ___**presaged**___ a war.

The fall in stock prices and retail sales may be a ___**presage**___ of hard economic times to come.

SYNONYMS: (*v.*) augur, foretell

15. progeny (präj′ ə nē)

(*n.*) descendants, offspring, children, followers, disciples

The Bill of Rights guarantees certain civil rights and protections to us and our ___**progeny**___.

SYNONYMS: issue, posterity; ANTONYMS: forebears, antecedents

16. promulgate (präm′ əl gāt)

(*v.*) to proclaim or issue officially; to make known far and wide

The School Board ___**promulgated**___ a new approach to education that emphasized phonics.

SYNONYM: announce
ANTONYMS: withdraw, retract, abrogate, nullify

17. rectitude (rek′ tə tüd)

(*n.*) uprightness, righteousness; correctness

The mayor is a person of unquestionable ___**rectitude**___.

SYNONYMS: probity, integrity
ANTONYMS: iniquity, heinousness

18. restive (res′ tiv)

(*adj.*) restless, hard to manage, balky

The ___**restive**___ horse had not been taken out of the stable for five days.

SYNONYMS: uneasy, recalcitrant
ANTONYMS: serene, unruffled, docile

19. seraphic (sə raf′ ik)

(*adj.*) angelic, heavenly, celestial

The artist painted the children with ___**seraphic**___ smiles to suggest their innocence.

SYNONYM: cherubic; ANTONYMS: devilish

20. subsist (səb sist′)

(*v.*) to have existence; to remain alive, manage to make a living or maintain life; to persist or continue

Peasants in nineteenth-century Ireland were able to ___**subsist**___ almost exclusively on potatoes.

SYNONYMS: last, sustain

CCSS Vocabulary: 4.c. (See pp. T14–15.)

Choosing the Right Word

*Select the **boldface** word that better completes each sentence. You might refer to the selection on pages 184–185 to see how most of these words are used in context.*

1. Petty criminals in medieval England were often placed in stocks or (**progeny, pillories**) and subjected to public humiliation.

2. There was a loophole in the law, and through this (**aperture, obeisance**) the defendant escaped the legal consequences of his crime.

3. Religious (**obeisance, dissidence**) was one of the motives that led many people to found colonies in North America.

An offender sentenced to the stocks had his feet, head, or hands locked in a heavy wooden frame.

4. The novel centers on a(n) (**improvident, seraphic**) young man who squanders his inheritance and dies in the poorhouse.

5. Like so many others of his generation, he paid unquestioning (**iniquity, obeisance**) to the accepted symbols of material success.

6. The cost of living has risen so sharply that a salary that was adequate a decade ago is now no more than a mere (**panegyric, pittance**).

7. "Angelica" is indeed an apt name for one whose (**mutable, seraphic**) beauty is complemented by such sweetness of temper and gentleness of spirit.

8. Recently, the principal (**promulgated, presaged**) a new dress code that abolished some of the unnecessary strictness of the old rules.

9. Specific customs vary widely in different lands, but the basic (**apertures, amenities**) of civilized living are much the same everywhere.

10. Writers often regard their works as their (**dissidence, progeny**) in much the same way as other people regard their pets as family members.

11. The new "gourmet" deli features delicacies that are bound to delight even the most exacting of (**epicurean, nascent**) palates.

12. No matter how well defended, no boundary is (**inviolable, restive**) unless the people on either side of it respect each other.

13. Instead of being so concerned with the (**iniquities, apertures**) of others, they would do well to concentrate on correcting their own shortcomings.

14. I realize the official made a serious mistake, but that is no reason to (**pillory, subsist**) him so unmercifully in the press.

15. The resounding victory we scored at the polls is an eloquent tribute to the (**rectitude, dissidence**) of her approach as campaign manager.

CCSS Vocabulary: 4.d. (See pp. T14–15.)

16. We would like to believe that the intensifying fear of ecological catastrophe (**subsists, presages**) an era of environmental harmony in the near future.

17. Instead of mouthing empty (**panegyrics, apertures**) to the Bill of Rights, let's strive to make this great document a reality in our lives.

18. One cannot expect a(n) (**epicurean, nascent**) democracy to go through its early years without experiencing serious growing pains.

19. The study of government shows us that many political institutions thought to be unchanging are in fact highly (**inviolable, mutable**).

20. As the speaker's remarks became more inflammatory, the crowd grew more sullen and (**nascent, restive**).

21. Liberty (**subsists, presages**) only as long as people have the intelligence to know their rights and the courage to defend them.

22. I hope that Jessie's obvious nervousness during the dress rehearsal does not (**presage, promulgate**) a poor performance in the play tonight.

23. The visitors lowered their voices and made (**obeisance, iniquity**) to the distinguished gentleman who was beckoning them toward the castle entrance.

24. Grandma sighed, "Kim's taste in clothes is so (**promulgated, mutable**) that nobody even tries to guess what she'll wear from week to week."

25. (**Pittances, Amenities**) at the luxury spa include massages and steam baths.

Synonyms

*Choose the word from this unit that is the same or most nearly the same in meaning as the **boldface** word or expression in the phrase. Write that word on the line. Use a dictionary if necessary.*

1. the angry **dissent** of protestors — dissidence
2. tried to **survive** in a desert — subsist
3. dark clouds that **portend** rain — presage
4. a **saintly** figure dressed in white — seraphic
5. the **sacrosanct** principle of equality — inviolable
6. a **hedonistic** display of luxury — epicurean
7. paid **respect** to those who came before her — obeisance
8. repaid a mere **modicum** of what is owed — pittance
9. showed a **budding** interest in politics — nascent
10. **fidgety** after the caffeine — restive

CCSS Vocabulary: 5. (See pp. T14–15.)

The synonyms and antonyms here do not appear on the Definitions page.

Antonyms

Choose the word from this unit that is most nearly opposite in meaning to the ***boldface*** *word or expression in the phrase. Write that word on the line. Use a dictionary if necessary.*

1. widespread political **agreement** — dissidence
2. always treats those in authority with **disregard** — obeisance
3. a puppy with an **impish** demeanor — seraphic
4. a **thrifty** manager — improvident
5. insulted the king's **ancestors** — progeny

Completing the Sentence

From the words in this unit, choose the one that best completes each of the following sentences. Write the word in the space provided.

1. After a few days in which everything went my way, I suddenly learned just how **mutable** Lady Luck can be.
2. We are sure that their vow is **inviolable** because their sense of moral obligation will prevent them from ever breaking it.
3. "I'm afraid that the child's **seraphic** countenance belies the mischief in his heart," I observed sadly.
4. Though I'm by no means **improvident** with my money, I don't hoard it either.
5. The **aperture** on most cameras can be adjusted to admit more or less light, as required.
6. Our financial situations are so different that what she considers a mere **pittance** seems a fortune to me.
7. The biography is a pretty evenhanded appraisal of the man's strengths and weaknesses, not just another **panegyric** to a great hero.
8. Nutritionists say that most of us could **subsist** on a great deal less food than we actually consume.
9. Conscientious parents will do everything they can to foster and develop the **nascent** intellectual curiosity of a small child.
10. The President has **promulgated** a policy that commits the nation to curbing pollution.

CCSS Vocabulary: 4.a. (See pp. T14–15.)

11. The wranglers suspected that there were wolves or mountain lions nearby when the herd suddenly grew nervous and ____**restive**____.

12. For many ancient peoples, the appearance of a comet was a fearful omen that ____**presaged**____ great social upheaval.

13. The liberties that we have inherited from our forefathers are a sacred trust that we must pass on undiminished to our ____**progeny**____.

14. Am I to be ____**pilloried**____ before the entire student body because I made a few minor mistakes as a member of the Student Council?

15. The Bible tells us that visitors to the court of Solomon, the great Hebrew king, willingly paid him ____**obeisance**____.

16. Imagine someone with my ____**epicurean**____ tastes having to live for a week on that watery mush!

17. It was the ____**amenity**____ of its natural setting on those rolling hills that led the architect to dub the estate "Mount Pleasant."

18. Authoritarian governments often resort to violence and coercion in their efforts to repress political ____**dissidence**____.

19. He inveighs against the sins of society with all the stridency of an Old Testament prophet castigating the ____**iniquities**____ of the unworthy.

20. I see no reason to question the ____**rectitude**____ of her dealings with us since I know her to be "as honest as the day is long."

Writing: Words in Action

Answers to both prompts will vary.

1. Look back at "Private Life in the Public Eye" (pages 184–185). Think about how the experience of keeping a diary is different from the experience of composing an autobiography. Write a brief essay in which you compare and contrast those two genres and explain which kind of writing you would prefer to do. Use examples from your experience and prior knowledge to support your ideas. Include at least two details from the essay and three unit words.

2. *"What is a diary as a rule? A document useful to the person who keeps it. Dull to the contemporary who reads it and invaluable to the student, centuries afterwards, who treasures it." —attributed to Dame Ellen Terry*

   What do you think about Terry's statement? Do you agree with her views about diaries? In what ways might a diary be useful to the person who keeps it? In a brief essay, support your opinion with specific examples from the reading (refer to pages 184–185), your studies, or personal experiences. Write at least three paragraphs, and use three or more words from this unit.

Writing prompt #2 is modeled on that of standardized tests.

CCSS Vocabulary: 6; Writing: 2.d., 3.d. (See pp. T14–15.)

Vocabulary in Context: Informational Text for Unit 15 is available online at **vocabularyworkshop.com**.

Vocabulary in Context

Literary Text

The following excerpts are from Edith Wharton's novels The Custom of the Country *and* The House of Mirth. *Some of the words you have studied in this unit appear in* ***boldface*** *type. Complete each statement below the excerpt by circling the letter of the correct answer.*

1. She felt no compunction in continuing to accept an undiminished allowance: it was the hereditary habit of the parent animal to despoil himself for his **progeny**. (*The Custom of the Country*)

Progeny are

a. principles
b. happiness
c. descendants
d. ambitions

2. Paul, after Mrs. Heeny's departure, had grown fretful and **restive**, and Undine had found it more and more difficult to fit his small exacting personality into her cramped rooms and crowded life. (*The Custom of the Country*)

Someone who is **restive** is NOT

a. optimistic
b. docile
c. servile
d. healthy

Edith Wharton wrote about New York high society in many of her novels and stories.

3. She wanted, passionately and persistently, two things which she believed should **subsist** together in any well-ordered life: amusement and respectability; and despite her surface-sophistication her notion of amusement was hardly less innocent than when she had hung on the plumber's fence with Indiana Frusk. (*The Custom of the Country*)

To **subsist** is to

a. labor
b. exist
c. correlate
d. aspire

4. "Hallo, Selden, going too? You're an **Epicurean** like myself, I see: you don't want to see all those goddesses gobbling terrapin. Gad, what a show of good-looking women; but not one of 'em could touch that little cousin of mine." (*The House of Mirth*)

An **epicurean**

a. is extremely talkative
b. fears being alone
c. likes to take risks
d. has refined tastes

5. Everything in her surroundings ministered to feelings of ease and **amenity**. The windows stood open to the sparkling freshness of the September morning... (*The House of Mirth*)

An **amenity** is something that is

a. pleasant
b. energetic
c. poignant
d. hopeful

Snap the code, or go to **vocabularyworkshop.com**

Vocabulary for Comprehension

*Read the following selection in which some of the words you have studied in Units 13–15 appear in **boldface** type. Then answer the questions on page 195.*

This passage focuses on one of the most famous American novelists of the twentieth century, F. Scott Fitzgerald.

(Line)

Few writers have been as identified with an age as F. Scott Fitzgerald (1896–1940). Not only is his best fiction set in the 1920s, but he helped define that era as the Jazz Age, an **epicurean** decade of fevered pleasure-seeking, **improvident** spending, and gaudy excess.

Born in St. Paul, Minnesota, Francis Scott Key Fitzgerald (named after his famous ancestor) was a restless young man full of romantic dreams. In 1917 he left Princeton University, before receiving his degree, to train as an Army officer, but he never made it overseas. While stationed at Camp Sheridan near Montgomery, Alabama, Fitzgerald fell for a local southern beauty, Zelda Sayre. By dint of sheer charm and persistence, Fitzgerald got Zelda to agree to marry him, but she was too **cognizant** of his poverty to succumb permanently to his **blandishments**. When the novel he was writing was rejected for a second time, she broke off the engagement.

Scott, however, was not deterred. He went back to St. Paul and rewrote the novel again. Upon its third submission to the Scribners publishing house, the manuscript was accepted. It was published in 1920 as *This Side of Paradise* and became an instant success. Scott and Zelda were married within a week. Like the characters in Fitzgerald's Jazz Age novels, the couple spent the next decade shuttling between New York and Europe, living the high life and spending lavishly. Behind the frothy **facade**, however, lay a darker reality that Fitzgerald depicted in his most famous novel, *The Great Gatsby* (1925). In *Gatsby*, Fitzgerald examines the moral decadence **engendered** by the American dream of wealth and success. When Fitzgerald died of a heart attack at the age of 44 (Zelda died in a fire only a few years later), his works that chronicled such a discrete period of American history seemed on their way to obscurity. In the 1950s, however, critics revived such classics as *Gatsby* and *Tender Is the Night* (1934), securing a place for him in the canon of American writers.

CCSS Vocabulary: 4.a.; Reading (Informational Text): 2, 4, 6. (See pp. T14–15.)

1. According to the author, which era did Fitzgerald help to define?
   a. the Information Age
   b. the Civil Rights era
   c. the Great Depression
   d. the Jazz Age
   e. the Age of Discovery

2. The meaning of **epicurean** (line 6) is
   a. idyllic
   b. uneventful
   c. hedonistic
   d. impoverished
   e. turbulent

3. **Improvident** (line 8) most nearly means
   a. frugal
   b. extravagant
   c. prudent
   d. intermittent
   e. impressive

4. In paragraph 2 (lines 10–28), it may be inferred that when Scott was courting Zelda, her values were
   a. patriotic
   b. idealistic
   c. romantic
   d. literary
   e. materialistic

5. **Cognizant** (line 24) is best defined as
   a. aware
   b. proud
   c. oblivious
   d. ashamed
   e. scornful

6. The meaning of **blandishments** (line 25) is
   a. apologies
   b. enticements
   c. fantasies
   d. threats
   e. tantrums

7. You can infer that an important factor in Scott and Zelda's marriage was
   a. his repeated pleas to her
   b. Scott's promise to leave New York
   c. the couple's admiring European friends
   d. the instant success of *This Side of Paradise*
   e. the intervention of Zelda's parents

8. According to the author, the main focus in the novel *The Great Gatsby* is on which of the following?
   a. the corruption of American politics
   b. the pitfalls of romance
   c. the moral decadence flowing from the American dream
   d. the complex rhythms of jazz
   e. aspects of European society

9. **Facade** (line 44) most nearly means
   a. lifestyle
   b. costume
   c. mask
   d. attitude
   e. celebration

10. **Engendered** (line 49) most nearly means
    a. deterred
    b. generated
    c. enraged
    d. offended
    e. baffled

11. The primary purpose of the passage is to
    a. survey the highlights of Fitzgerald's life and literary career
    b. analyze contrasts between Fitzgerald's early novels and his later works
    c. support the claim that *The Great Gatsby* is Fitzgerald's masterpiece
    d. show how the Fitzgeralds epitomized the Jazz Age lifestyle
    e. emphasize the irony in Fitzgerald's handling of the theme of illusion versus reality

12. For the most part, what organizational scheme does the author use in the passage?
    a. comparison and contrast
    b. order of impression
    c. order of importance
    d. spatial order
    e. chronological order

CCSS Vocabulary: 4.a.; Reading (Informational Text): 2, 4, 6. (See pp. T14–15.)

Two-Word Completions

Select the pair of words that best complete the meaning of each of the following passages.

1. As soon as the famous movie star walked into my shop, she became the ____________ of all eyes. Customers stopped what they were doing to stare at her as if ____________ by the spell of her celebrity.
   a. aperture . . . engendered
   b. cynosure . . . mesmerized
   c. moratorium . . . subsisted
   d. pillory . . . promulgated

2. Disgruntled army officers and other ____________ elements in the society engineered the bloody ____________ that toppled the duly elected government a few months after it had taken office.
   a. contrite . . . nostrum
   b. restive . . . moratorium
   c. visionary . . . pittance
   d. dissident . . . coup

3. Once the news broke, the public heaped so much ____________ on the head of the hapless city official that he soon found himself a veritable political ____________, even in his own party.
   a. euphemism . . . canard
   b. dissidence . . . amenity
   c. opprobrium . . . pariah
   d. efficacy . . . ghoul

4. Behind the courtier's outward ____________ of decorous sloth there lurked the ____________ imagination of an inveterate opportunist, eager to capitalize on any windfall that came his way.
   a. aperture . . . incongruous
   b. facade . . . febrile
   c. cynosure . . . nascent
   d. chicanery . . . improvident

5. The characters in Jane Austen novels display ____________ manners, obeying the ____________ of social conventions that range from how many consecutive waltzes a couple may dance to the type of tea that should be served to guests.
   a. abstruse . . . canards
   b. ethereal . . .pariahs
   c. decorous . . . minutiae
   d. beatific . . . manifests

6. Any official who is genuinely concerned about the ____________ of his or her behavior while in public office will think twice before engaging in the kinds of political ____________ and backroom shenanigans that sometimes go on when a juicy government contract is up for grabs.
   a. rectitude . . . chicanery
   b. imminence . . . blandishments
   c. progeny . . . machinations
   d. iniquity . . . cognizance

7. At the demonstration in front of company headquarters, the protestor who ____________ to address the media described the layoffs as a hurtful ____________ to employee loyalty.
   a. consigned . . . behemoth
   b. deigned . . . affront
   c. gainsaid . . . panegyric
   d. manifested . . . obeisance

 CCSS Vocabulary: 4.a. (See pp. T14–15.)

In the essay about writer Samuel Pepys and his diary (see pages 184–185), the author describes Pepys as "raking over the ashes" his major vices and sins. This saying is an idiom. The author means that in some diary entries Pepys returns to discuss and reflect on unpleasant events from his past.

An **idiom** is an expression that cannot be translated literally. The meaning of an idiom is not suggested by the meaning of its separate words. You learn idioms in the same way that you learn many new words—by hearing or reading them in context. If you cannot understand an idiom from context clues, you may need to use an online or print dictionary to determine or confirm its meaning.

Choosing the Right Idiom

Read each sentence. Use context clues to figure out the meaning of each idiom in ***boldface*** *print. Then write the letter of the definition for the idiom in the sentence.*

1. Did you actually enjoy that movie, or did you just **jump on the bandwagon** because it received three Academy Awards? ___j___
2. The police are **barking up the wrong tree** if they think Joey broke the windows; he has an airtight alibi for the entire evening. ___f___
3. The campaign manager wants Jones to remain **above the fray** when it comes to launching personal attacks on the other candidates. ___d___
4. When the video game was released, the developer must have made money **hand over fist**. ___a___
5. "I want to speak to the manager now," Melissa demanded, "so that I can get answers to all my questions **in one fell swoop**." ___h___
6. The employees applauded their boss for keeping them **in the loop** about possible changes to the holiday delivery schedule ___e___
7. After two months of tense negotiations, union leaders decided to **throw in the towel** and urged their members to go on strike. ___i___
8. "Because you are so **quick on the draw**," Mickey said to his best friend, "we have an excellent chance to win the obstacle race." ___b___
9. The high school senior won a full scholarship to the college of his choice, so he is **sitting pretty** for the next several years. ___g___
10. Sadly, because the investment scheme was nothing but **smoke and mirrors**, hundreds of people lost their entire savings. ___c___

a. rapidly and continuously

b. able to react quickly

c. trickery and deception

d. not involved in the argument or unpleasantness

e. having knowledge of something

f. believing the wrong explanation for something

g. in a good situation

h. all at once

i. admit failure or defeat

j. support something because it is popular

CCSS Vocabulary: 5.a. (See pp. T14–15.)

WORD STUDY

Writing with Idioms

Find the meaning of each idiom. (Use an online or print dictionary if necessary.) Then write a sentence for each idiom. **Answers will vary.**

1. no great shakes **Sample answer: My sister is a skilled songwriter, but she lost the talent contest because she is no great shakes at singing.**

2. bar none

3. off the cuff

4. my cup of tea

5. stand your ground

6. cut the mustard

7. running on empty

8. for a song

9. take the plunge

10. toe the line

11. out of left field

12. have egg on your face

 CCSS Vocabulary: 5. (See pp. T14–15.)

Denotation and Connotation

The **denotation** of a word is its dictionary meaning or meanings. Beyond its denotations, many words may also have connotations. **Connotations** are the ideas and emotional associations that words carry apart from their denotative meanings

Denotations are objective, but connotations are subjective; they can vary from person to person. A word's connotation(s) may be *neutral*, *positive*, or *negative*.

Consider these synonyms for the neutral word *abstruse*:

abstract *profound* *cryptic* *unintelligible*

Abstract and *profound* have neutral or positive connotations, suggesting something is difficult to understand because of its conceptual complexity or the depth and thoughtfulness of its ideas. *Cryptic* and *unintelligible*, however, suggest a difficulty in understanding based on an unfortunate obscurity or a jumbled and incoherent explanation.

Think: The research of a learned and well-respected professor can be described as abstract or profound, while the work of a lesser scholar is deemed cryptic or unintelligible.

Look at these examples of words with similar denotations but different connotations.

NEUTRAL	POSITIVE	NEGATIVE
critical	**discerning**	**captious**
portion	**allowance**	**pittance**
discriminating	**epicurean**	**self-indulgent**

Distinguishing among sometimes subtle shades of meaning will help you say exactly what you mean, prevent misunderstandings, and create the tone or mood you intend.

Shades of Meaning

Write a plus sign (+) in the box if the word has a positive connotation. Write a minus sign (–) if the word has a negative connotation. Put a zero (0) if the word is neutral.

1. canard –	**2.** desiccated –	**3.** opprobrium –	**4.** putative 0
5. engender 0	**6.** innate 0	**7.** pillory –	**8.** seraphic +
9. nostrum –	**10.** facade 0	**11.** amenity +	**12.** cacophonous –
13. efficacy +	**14.** ghoulish –	**15.** nascent 0	**16.** pariah –

CCSS Vocabulary: 5.b. (See pp. T14–15.)

Expressing the Connotation

Read each sentence. Select the word in parentheses that expresses the connotation (positive, negative, or neutral) given at the beginning of the sentence.

positive **1.** The host and hostess were pleased with the (**decorous, staid**) behavior of all the party guests.

neutral **2.** Were you as surprised by the (**machinations, maneuvers**) of the play's protagonist as I was?

negative **3.** We couldn't believe Mike spent most of the long ride discussing the (**minutiae, features**) of his new saxophone.

negative **4.** The tenant (**consigned, abandoned**) the furniture in his apartment when he moved out.

positive **5.** The interview committee seemed impressed by the final job candidate's (**rectitude, disposition**).

positive **6.** Upon seeing Dr. Slack enter the lobby, we hastily made an (**obeisance, acknowledgment**) to him.

negative **7.** My neighbor decided for whom she would vote weeks ago, but I've learned that her political decisions are (**mutable, unstable**).

positive **8.** In the foreground of the oil painting stands an elegantly dressed elderly woman with a (**beatific, supernatural**) expression on her face.

Challenge: Using Connotation

Choose vocabulary words from Units 13–15 to replace the highlighted words in the sentences below. Then explain how the connotation of the replacement word changes the tone of the sentence. Answers will vary.

cognizant	**chicanery**	**apertures**
affronted	**deigned**	**ethereal**

1. When she first saw her costume, the actress immediately noticed how light and **flimsy** ethereal it seemed.
Sample response: The favorable connotation of *ethereal* suggests that the actress found the costume's delicacy to be a positive attribute, not a flaw.

2. The antique shop owner uses subtle **tactics** chicanery to get customers to pay top prices for his merchandise.
Sample response: The use of the word *chicanery* portrays the shop owner in a more negative light; his selling methods involve trickery or deception.

3. The young man ahead of me in line at the airport was obviously **affected** affronted by another passenger's remark about his hair.
Sample response: The negative connotation of *affronted* suggests that the remark was offensive and that the young man felt he had been insulted.

 CCSS Vocabulary: 5. (See pp. T14–15.)

Classical Roots

vid, vis—to look, see

This root appears in **visionary** (page 178), which means "lacking in practicality" or, as a noun, "a dreamer or seer." Some other words based on this same root are listed below.

advisement	**providence**	**proviso**	**visitation**
envisage	**provident**	**visage**	**vista**

From the list of words above, choose the one that corresponds to each of the brief definitions below. Write the word in the blank space in the illustrative sentence below the definition. Use an online or print dictionary if necessary.

1. a careful consideration (*"act of seeing to"*)

The committee has agreed to take your most recent request under ____advisement____.

2. a distinct view or prospect through an opening; an extensive mental view

As we rounded the bend, we suddenly beheld the most breathtaking ____vista____ of our trip.

3. to picture to oneself (*"see into"*); conceive of, especially as a future possibility

It is hard to ____envisage____ a modern America made up entirely of small farmers.

4. a face, countenance, appearance, look, aspect (*"that which is seen"*)

The links of chains he carried, which signified his sins, gave Jacob Marley a frightening ____visage____.

5. a conditional stipulation; an article or clause in a contract that introduces a condition (*"that which is foreseen"*)

They agreed to sign the deal, with the ____proviso____ that we serve as witnesses.

6. providing for future needs or contingencies; thrifty, economical

It is our agency's mission to explore the most ____provident____ use of our natural resources.

7. a visit for the purpose of making an official inspection; an act of visiting; a severe punishment or affliction

Health specialists are meeting to discuss the possibility of a new ____visitation____ of tuberculosis.

8. divine guidance or care; a manifestation of such guidance

Despite hard times, or perhaps especially during hard times, people of faith put their trust in ____providence____.

CCSS Vocabulary: 4.c. (See pp. T14–15.)

FINAL MASTERY TEST

Synonyms

Select the two words or expressions that are most nearly the same in meaning.

1.	**a.** countermand	**b.** repudiate	**c.** exonerate	**d.** embellish
2.	**a.** renovate	**b.** raze	**c.** pillory	**d.** demolish
3.	**a.** debris	**b.** frenzy	**c.** flotsam	**d.** cabal
4.	**a.** unwonted	**b.** paltry	**c.** insignificant	**d.** beneficial
5.	**a.** eulogy	**b.** juggernaut	**c.** critique	**d.** tribute
6.	**a.** object	**b.** volunteer	**c.** demur	**d.** jettison
7.	**a.** suppliant	**b.** fiat	**c.** decree	**d.** consent
8.	**a.** wretched	**b.** nefarious	**c.** fearless	**d.** abject
9.	**a.** amplify	**b.** verify	**c.** substantiate	**d.** recant
10.	**a.** sophistry	**b.** desire	**c.** gall	**d.** effrontery
11.	**a.** picayune	**b.** plenary	**c.** trifling	**d.** irrelevant
12.	**a.** overcome	**b.** foreshadow	**c.** portend	**d.** eschew
13.	**a.** echelon	**b.** mandate	**c.** objection	**d.** authorization
14.	**a.** deign	**b.** stoop	**c.** exhume	**d.** attempt
15.	**a.** deprecate	**b.** decimate	**c.** deplore	**d.** approve

Antonyms

Select the two words that are most nearly opposite in meaning.

16.	**a.** delineate	**b.** arrogate	**c.** renounce	**d.** remain
17.	**a.** intellectual	**b.** moot	**c.** indisputable	**d.** disturbed
18.	**a.** feckless	**b.** disagreeable	**c.** seraphic	**d.** effective
19.	**a.** youthful	**b.** obsequious	**c.** moribund	**d.** thriving
20.	**a.** loquacious	**b.** frenetic	**c.** calm	**d.** vituperative
21.	**a.** flatter	**b.** embezzle	**c.** hallow	**d.** calumniate
22.	**a.** restive	**b.** banal	**c.** original	**d.** militant
23.	**a.** coherent	**b.** glorious	**c.** wizened	**d.** muddled
24.	**a.** decry	**b.** presage	**c.** commend	**d.** apportion
25.	**a.** consecrate	**b.** antagonize	**c.** conciliate	**d.** forgo

Analogies

Select the item that best completes the comparison.

26. avid is to **indifference** as
- **a.** germane is to appropriateness
- **(b.)** taciturn is to prolixity
- **c.** halcyon is to serenity
- **d.** substantive is to eloquence

27. brackish is to **drink** as
- **a.** visible is to see
- **b.** incendiary is to burn
- **(c.)** indigestible is to eat
- **d.** piquant is to whet

28. mule is to **intransigent** as
- **a.** monkey is to verdant
- **b.** fly is to acquisitive
- **c.** horse is to devious
- **(d.)** bat is to myopic

29. maelstrom is to **sea** as
- **a.** foliage is to desert
- **(b.)** quicksand is to swamp
- **c.** hurricane is to shower
- **d.** skyscraper is to forest

30. acuity is to **see** as
- **a.** perspicacity is to argue
- **b.** equity is to report
- **(c.)** sensitivity is to feel
- **d.** concord is to disturb

31. depraved is to **corruption** as
- **a.** moot is to originality
- **b.** frenetic is to leisure
- **c.** mordant is to obscurity
- **(d.)** overweening is to excess

32. derelict is to **conscientiousness** as
- **a.** consummate is to perfection
- **b.** intermittent is to continuity
- **c.** pecuniary is to money
- **(d.)** ubiquitous is to prevalence

33. saturnine is to **gloom** as
- **a.** fatuous is to intelligence
- **b.** macabre is to gaiety
- **c.** refulgent is to darkness
- **(d.)** lackadaisical is to indolence

Two-Word Completions

Select the best word pair from among the choices given.

34. I don't mean to ____________ the point by telling you again, but if you don't exercise, your muscles will ____________.
- **a.** loath . . . languish
- **b.** inure . . . mesmerize
- **(c.)** belabor . . . atrophy
- **d.** requite . . . saturate

35. His artistic choices are so strange and ____________ that he runs the risk of being labeled a ____________ and not being taken seriously.
- **a.** rife . . . canard
- **b.** pejorative . . . tyro
- **c.** abstruse . . . progeny
- **(d.)** eclectic . . . dilettante

36. It simply seems ____________ to ____________ someone for not throwing away a gum wrapper properly; wouldn't a warning be more appropriate?
- **(a.)** inane . . . incarcerate
- **b.** furtive . . . vacillate
- **c.** aesthetic . . . discomfit
- **d.** ebullient . . . congeal

37. The ____________ office-holder has a decided advantage over her opponent, who has never held office and is a political ____________.
- **(a.)** incumbent . . . neophyte
- **b.** cognizant . . . utopia
- **c.** visionary . . . effigy
- **d.** felicitous . . . penitent

Supplying Words in Context

To complete each sentence, select the best word from among the choices given. Not all words in the word bank will be used. You may modify the word form as necessary.

allay	**murky**	**paucity**	**counterpart**
eschew	**undulate**	**raiment**	**pusillanimous**
pedantry	**nuance**	**accost**	**unremitting**
bucolic	**travesty**	**illusory**	**tenable**

38. The teacher sought to ____allay____ our concerns about the upcoming test.

39. The verdant and ____bucolic____ setting was soothing in its tranquility.

40. The ocean water was so ____murky____ that we couldn't see our feet.

41. The subtle ____nuance____ of this story will be lost on a reader who is less than attentive.

42. Our good fortune proved ____illusory____, and we were soon back in deep difficulty.

43. In order to lose weight, I will ____eschew____ fats and sweets and eat more fruits and vegetables.

carping	**echelon**	**emulate**	**coterie**
invidious	**dissemble**	**stratagem**	**glean**
jocular	**enervate**	**gambit**	**mundane**
garish	**litany**	**nettle**	**distraught**

44. The constant ____carping____ of the children was beginning to drive the baby-sitter to her wits' end!

45. The pop singer's ____coterie____ of admirers flattered her constantly and kept her shielded from criticism.

46. Would he ____dissemble____, or would he tell the truth?

47. Lucius didn't need to say a word: I could ____glean____ from the look on his face that he wasn't happy.

48. The ____garish____ outfit stuck out in such a staid, somber setting.

49. The man was understandably ____distraught____ when given the horrific news.

*Select the word or expression that best completes the meaning of the sentence or answers the question, with particular reference to the meaning of the word in **boldface** type.*

50. An **agnostic** will likely say
a. "I believe."
b. "I don't know."
c. "I'm running late."
d. "My socks are always missing."

51. Typical **amenities** of urban life might include
a. air pollution and litter
b. pedestrians on the street
c. bridges and cars
d. museums and concerts

52. Which advice would be most suitable for a person who is **recumbent**?
a. "Keep your eye on the ball."
b. "Rise and shine!"
c. "Turn left at the first light."
d. "Grin and bear it."

53. A **figment** usually develops in
a. a factory
b. an orchard
c. the human mind
d. the wild blue yonder

54. If you **temporize** when a decision is called for, you are
a. acting decisively
b. stalling for time
c. misjudging the situation
d. losing your temper

55. The **motif** of a play refers to its
a. financial backing
b. adaptation for television
c. basic theme
d. cast of characters

56. The wisest course of action when confronted by a **juggernaut** is to
a. get out of its way
b. take its picture
c. stand your ground
d. make up your mind

57. **Histrionic** behavior is best suited to
a. the stage
b. the laboratory
c. the classroom
d. the museum

58. **Primordial** times occurred
a. in Ancient Greece
b. first
c. as a result of negligence
d. during World War II

59. To **allege** that someone is guilty of a crime means that
a. the person is clearly guilty
b. the charge remains to be proved
c. the charge is malicious
d. an indictment will be handed down

60. In a **convivial** atmosphere, people may be expected to
a. suffer from boredom
b. enjoy themselves
c. go into shock
d. show off their erudition

61. You would be well advised not to give **credence** to
a. your friends
b. your creditors
c. a reliable witness
d. a habitual liar

Choosing the Right Meaning

Read each sentence carefully. Then select the item that best completes the statement below the sentence.

62. The audience's **acclamation** was demonstrated by its repeated standing ovations.

The word **acclamation** most nearly means

a. approval **b.** opprobrium **c.** asperity **d.** victory

63. I was able to guarantee his **collusion** by demonstrating that his participation would be to his benefit.

The word **collusion** most nearly means

a. connivance **b.** detritus **c.** chicanery **d.** foible

64. The knights had retreated into their **bastion**, where they hoped to regroup and repel the invaders' attack.

The word **bastion** most nearly means

a. aperture **b.** facade **c.** fortress **d.** significance

65. I would be extremely **chary** of taking up jogging again until the knee injury is completely healed.

The word **chary** most nearly means

a. benign **b.** fecund **c.** bestial **d.** wary

66. It was fun to watch the two puppies **cavort** in the field, dashing round and round the bushes and trees.

The word **cavort** most nearly means

a. grouse **b.** regret **c.** gambol **d.** rebuff

67. I appreciated the **celerity** with which the electricians responded to the power outage from the storm.

The best definition for the word **celerity** is

a. propriety **b.** promptness **c.** propinquity **d.** verbiage

68. The critic's review turned into a **diatribe** against contemporary music in general.

The word **diatribe** most nearly means

a. badinage **b.** surveillance **c.** tirade **d.** accusation

69. Although the man did not plan the crime, his participation in the robbery attempt was evidence of his **complicity**.

The word **complicity** most nearly means

a. animadversion **b.** collusion **c.** exigency **d.** idiosyncrasy

70. With books and clothes strewn everywhere, the bedroom was in a state of **disarray**.

The word **disarray** is best defined as

a. largesse **b.** paroxysm **c.** disorganization **d.** reconnaissance

WORD LIST

The following is a list of all the words taught in the Units of this book. The number after each entry indicates the page on which the word is defined.

INDEX